HONOR BOUND

RYAN P. BROWN

HONOR BOUND

How a Cultural Ideal Has Shaped
the American Psyche

OXFORD
UNIVERSITY PRESS

OXFORD
UNIVERSITY PRESS

Oxford University Press is a department of the University of Oxford. It furthers
the University's objective of excellence in research, scholarship, and education
by publishing worldwide. Oxford is a registered trade mark of Oxford University
Press in the UK and certain other countries.

Published in the United States of America by Oxford University Press
198 Madison Avenue, New York, NY 10016, United States of America.

Library of Congress Cataloging-in-Publication Data
Names: Brown, Ryan P.
Title: Honor bound : how a cultural ideal has shaped the american psyche /
Ryan P. Brown.
Description: New York : Oxford University Press, 2016. |
Includes bibliographical references.
Identifiers: LCCN 2015033718 | ISBN 9780199399864
Subjects: LCSH: Honor—Psychological aspects.
Classification: LCC BJ1533.H8 B76 2016 | DDC 302/.1—dc23
LC record available at http://lccn.loc.gov/2015033718

1 3 5 7 9 8 6 4 2
Printed by Sheridan, USA

FOR CATHERINE, NATHAN, AND LUKE, WHO
INSPIRE ME TO BE A MAN OF TRUE HONOR.

Contents

Preface ix
Introduction xi

ONE Genesis 1

TWO A Penchant for Violence 19

THREE Boys to Men, and the Women
Who Love Them 43

FOUR Lay Down Your Burdens 61

FIVE Reckless Abandon 79

SIX Lineage 95

SEVEN The Honor Circle 113

EIGHT A Most Honorable Place 141

NINE Embracing Honor 163

APPENDIX A Scales Measuring Endorsement
of Honor Ideology 191

APPENDIX B Analyses of Penalties in Football for Personal
Fouls and Unsportsmanlike Conduct 195

References 199
Index 203

Preface

I love what I get to do for a living. There are very few things in the world more interesting than people, so learning that I could get paid to study people as a social scientist was a wonderful discovery that I made many years ago. That realization was followed by many more, including those described in this book on the cultural patterns known as the *honor syndrome*.

During the process of discovery in my honor odyssey, I have been aided and inspired by many people. First and foremost, researchers such as Richard Nisbett, Dov Cohen, and Joseph Vandello have captured my attention and fired my imagination, so I tip my hat to them with the deference they deserve. There are many other researchers besides these three whose work I discuss in this book or whose work has helped inspire my own (such as Susan Cross, Ayesha Uskul, Allan Dafoe, PJ Henry, and others), but no one has done more to elucidate some of the core elements of honor cultures than Nisbett, Cohen, and Vandello—at least within the field of social psychology.

Second, I could not have conducted any of my own research on the honor syndrome without the hard work and perseverance of many excellent graduate students, undergraduate research assistants, and fellow faculty members. Collaboration certainly makes science better, but it also makes it more fun, and the fun is often what keeps you going. For helping to make my own studies both better and more enjoyable, my sincere thanks go out to Lindsey Osterman, Collin Barnes, Michael Tamborski, Miki Imura, Kevin

Green, Kiersten Baughman, Mauricio Carvallo, Lara Mayeux, Jennifer Barnes, Laura Thurman, Kevin Dodd, Chris Nguyen, and a host of undergraduate research assistants who have worked with me or my graduate students over the years on the studies I discuss in this book.

Third, I wish to extend special thanks to Stan Wakefield, who introduced me to the editorial team at Oxford University Press (OUP). Throughout this project, Abby Gross and her team at OUP have been a source of great encouragement as well as constructive editorial feedback. Likewise, Hunter and Kathy Miller were so gracious to open their lakefront home to me as I began writing this book. I am grateful for their generosity as hosts, and I am not sure I would have ever managed to begin the process of writing without the seclusion of this quiet retreat.

Last, I want to thank the love of my life, Catherine, and my sons, Nathan and Luke, who have had to put up with me not only as I wrote this book, but also as I continue to talk about the ideology of honor and why I think it is so important. I know you all get tired of hearing me proclaim, "Hey! You know, there's a study on that ... !" Thank you for your patience and endurance, and for making my life so blessed.

Introduction

Have you ever read something that changed your life? Almost 20 years ago, I did. It was a report on a set of studies conducted by a group of social scientists at the University of Michigan. The team was led by Richard Nisbett and Dov Cohen, and the topic of study was something they called "the culture of honor"—a phrase that social scientists use to describe a society that organizes social life around the maintenance and defense of reputation. In an honor culture, *reputation is everything*, so people go to great lengths to defend their reputations and those of their family and community against threats and insults. Indeed, as Southern historian Bertram Wyatt-Brown has noted, "Honor is reputation" (p. 14). Consequently, people who live in honor cultures are allowed or even *expected* to respond aggressively whenever they feel their honor is threatened. Furthermore, people in an honor culture seem to have their "social radars" specially attuned to detecting such honor-related insults, which can make them seem a little hypersensitive at times. "What did you just call me?" is the type of question that people in an honor culture recognize as a prelude to potential violence.

The gist of Nisbett and Cohen's studies was that college guys who had grown up in the U.S. South were more likely to respond to an insult with aggression compared to college guys who had grown up in the North. The reason for this difference, the researchers argued, was the South (and, to a lesser extent, the West) has long been influenced by the ideology of honor. Social scientists would say these regions exhibit the characteristics of an honor culture, for reasons I discuss in Chapter 1.[1] Nisbett and Cohen's research struck me as clever and creative. This was the first time I had ever seen researchers calling people insulting names in a psychology study and then measuring things such as their cortisol level (which indicates stress), or how they played a game of "chicken" with a linebacker walking down the hall. I loved it.

For about the next decade or so, I talked about this set of studies when I taught social psychology to undergraduates at The University of Texas, then later at Amherst College and The University of Oklahoma. It was fun to discuss and explain, and my students always seemed to get a kick out of hearing about this work.

It wasn't until 2007 that this work started changing the course of my own career as a researcher. At that time, I was conducting studies on forgiveness and revenge with several graduate students, including Lindsey Osterman and Collin Barnes. Lindsey was trying to run an experiment on revenge after an insult. No one was signing up for the study, however, so to keep her research assistants busy and off the streets, she decided to have them scour the Internet to find cases of school shootings.

After a few weeks of searching, she had an initial list of more than 70 shootings, and at that point she told me what she was up to. I was intrigued. We talked about the project and decided to investigate whether time of year and location make any difference in the likelihood of a school shooting occurring. I then told her all about the research by Nisbett and Cohen on the culture of honor, and she was as fascinated by it as I was. Eventually, we went on to uncover more than 100 school shootings that had occurred in the United States between 1988 and 2008. Time of year, we found, did matter. Two of the most dangerous months of the year are December and May, which probably won't surprise anyone (these are the months when students take stressful final exams and learn whether they have passed their classes). However, one additional month that seems to have nothing to do with grades or exams also stood out as

---

1. For similar arguments about honor cultures around the world, see Peristiany (1966).

being *particularly* dangerous (read Chapter 2 if you want to know what this month is and why we think that it's so dangerous).

A predictor of school violence that was even more powerful than time of year was *location*. It turns out that some regions of the United States are much more likely to experience school violence than others, and these areas are exactly those that researchers such as Nisbett and Cohen noted have been influenced the most by the ideology of honor.

When we discovered this link and published our findings, we were hooked. We began to investigate more ways that the honor syndrome might influence people's lives, including mental health and suicide (in part for personal reasons, which I discuss in Chapter 4), risk-taking and bravery, domestic violence and sexual objectification, reactions to terrorism, presidential decisions to go to war, and how parents name their babies, just to cite a few examples. The more we looked, the more we found, and the evidence came not only from regional differences in "high-level" statistics (such as state-by-state comparisons of crime data), but also from more nuanced findings in the laboratory with people who embraced or rejected the ideology of honor. This embracing or rejecting, incidentally, can occur consciously or *unconsciously*, as we eventually discovered, but even people who rejected the ideology of honor can be profoundly affected by it.

That process of discovery thoroughly transformed the nature of my research, and I am truly grateful for the change. Studying the social dynamics of honor has been the most engrossing, consuming adventure of my life as a social scientist. It has helped me understand my family and friends, and it has even helped me understand myself. Sharing that understanding with others—those who, like me, have grown up in an honor culture, as well as those who have not but who might be affected by it through other people—is what this book is all about.

In writing this book, I have one mission and two claims. My mission is simple: to convince you that the honor syndrome (broad, cultural acceptance of the ideology typical of honor cultures) is alive and well in the United States, particularly in the southern and western regions of the country. To be clear, honor ideology exists everywhere, not just in the South, and certainly not just in the United States. I strongly suspect, in fact, that most human cultures throughout most of our history have been, fundamentally, honor cultures. It is only in modern times that some societies have transitioned into what some social scientists refer to as "dignity cultures," which assert that human worth is intrinsic and need not be won (and, thus, cannot readily be lost [see Chapter 9]). All human beings care about their reputation, so people in honor cultures are not unique in this respect. However, honor cultures put this common human interest in reputation management on cultural steroids, and they also funnel the particular reputational concerns and goals that people have, which they then seek to maintain and defend. This effort to defend one's reputation, one's honor, is the primary force that makes honor cultures so often *not honorable*. That might seem paradoxical, because the term *honor culture* sounds like it ought to be a really good thing. Who, after all, would want to live in a "dishonor culture"? But it turns out that our choice is not between something as simple as honor and dishonor, as we shall see. Furthermore, we must be careful not to assume what the word *honor* means to different people. Honor does not just mean "virtue" or "goodness," although some people might use the word in these ways. If we want to understand what an honor culture is all about, we have to understand this word's other, often hidden, meanings.

My first claim in this book is that, by understanding the dynamics of honor ideology in the United States, we can better understand America as a nation. Honor ideology is like beach sand; it just gets everywhere. As a consequence, the ideology of honor affects so many aspects of our lives together, from how we interact with competitors, strangers, and family members, to who we find attractive, to our mental health, to how we vote, to how and when we choose to die. Simply put, culture matters, and this dimension of culture is no exception to that rule. Aspects of culture that have such great breadth and power to organize social life are sometimes known as *cultural syndromes*, drawing from the image of an intricate set of interrelated signs and symptoms associated with a medical condition. In keeping with that imagery, I refer throughout this book to *the honor syndrome* as a broad network of social values, beliefs, and motivational priorities that can dominate the psychological lives of individuals or whole societies.

My second claim is that for Americans, and for Westerners more broadly, understanding the cultural dynamics of honor in the United States can provide a basis for a better understanding of more extreme honor cultures across the globe. In an era of nuclear ambitions and terrorist threats from nations in the Middle East, as well as from countries such as North Korea and Russia, where the rhetoric of honor drives not only public discourse, but also foreign policy, understanding honor cultures around the world is a moral imperative.

HONOR BOUND

Chapter One

Genesis

He crept along through the trees and underbrush, careful to avoid being seen from the road, sensitive to the direction of the wind. Although he knew no human could catch his scent, even the Creek Indians who prowled these parts, there were other dangers beyond the human kind to worry about—in particular, black bears. His mother had sent him out that morning, handing him his rifle, coonskin cap, and a small sack of food in case he failed to bag any game before the sun had risen too high in the summer sky. By noon, any quarry worth pursuing would have retreated to the comfort and cool of the shade, and he was not terribly interested in bringing home a tote of squirrels.

But he wasn't just on the lookout for food that day. He was also scanning the area for any sign of two- or four-legged dangers that might pose a threat to that dear lady who kissed his forehead as he left their humble home that morning. Yes, he would gladly give his life for his mother, not to mention his two sisters. After his father died in an Indian raid the previous winter, soon after the birth of his younger sister, the lad was the sole man of the house. The safety and well-being of the family was now on his shoulders. It was a heavy burden, especially for a boy of only six years, but he knew he was up to the challenge. He *had* to be.

"Stay out of the street!" his mother called to him through an open window. "And watch out for cars!" How had she seen him? He needed to work on his camouflage skills. And what had she meant by "cars" anyway? Cars wouldn't be invented for a long, long time (he wasn't sure exactly how long). Sheesh! Moms just don't understand. That's why it was up to him. He squinted in the morning sun, ever vigilant, ever ready.

I was that boy, and I was imitating my new hero, Davy Crockett. I had learned his story from the made-for-TV miniseries on *The Wonderful World of Disney* several months before and, ever since, I was a Crockett fanatic. I not only had the coonskin hat that Crockett sported, I also had the imitation deer-skin, cotton-poly hunting shirt with the fringe down the length of the arm that moved with the wind (a helpful aid to discern which way it was blowing; just raise your arm to the sun and watch the fringe). Like many young boys growing up after the Disney show had pre-miered 20 years earlier, I wanted to be just like Crockett: brave and true, a simple but cunning man. A hero.

I was almost heartbroken to learn, many years later, that the image I had cherished of this frontier hero was more fantasy than fact. Crockett was, as the Disney ballad claimed, born in the back-woods of eastern Tennessee, although at the time of his birth in 1786, that portion of the state was actually part of North Carolina. His father, John, was a complicated and troubled man; today, he would probably be jailed for child abuse. What kind of man pawns off his 12-year-old daughter to work as a servant in another family's house just to help pay off his debts and still calls himself a father? And when that daughter turns up pregnant, apparently with the virile assistance of her employer, how could her father then turn her away in shame? Such was the character of David Crockett's father, and although David himself did not exhibit *all* his father's many failings, he was destined to repeat many of them.

Like his father, Crockett was a terrible businessman, and yet (also like his father) he frequently started new ventures he was certain would bring him great fortune. One never attains greatness without taking some risks! Although Crockett's temper was less volatile than his father's, he perpetuated the family tradition of amassing an enormous amount of debt throughout the course of his storied life, and toward the end, he complemented this weakness with a repeat of his father's serious drinking habit. Even after he finally sold his autobiography, putting into print the tall tales that had already made him famous, he still failed to crawl out from under the massive debt he had accrued from his impetuous, entrepreneurial projects.

Hoping to start fresh in Texas, he left Tennessee behind (along with his many creditors, his second wife, and eight children), perhaps thinking he might one day send for his family when he had established himself. Or perhaps not. In any case, his reputation preceded him. So, when he arrived, the Texans were sure he had come to aid them in their freedom fight against Santa Anna's forces. Eager to please those who might one day vote him back into Congress (he had lost his Congressional seat in part from spending too much time promoting his autobiography and too little time actually doing his job), Crockett soon found himself surrounded by a Mexican army at the Alamo. It is ironic that his fantastical embellishments of his prowess as a warrior led to his demise at the Alamo, which then cemented his legend as an American icon: "King of the Wild Frontier" (Disney's title) and "Lion of the West" (biographer Michael Wallis's title).[1]

In October of 1825, 11 years before Crockett died at the Alamo, Randolph ("Randall") McCoy squawked into life in the foothills of the Appalachian Mountains in Pike County, Kentucky, 130 miles due north of Crockett's birthplace. Randall McCoy was 1 of 13 children born to Daniel and Margaret McCoy. At the age of 24, he married Sarah ("Sally"), who was his first cousin on his father's side, and began to inbreed a little army of his own. In all, Randall and Sally McCoy had 16 children, many of whom would eventually die in the feud between the McCoys and the Hatfields, which, like the story of Davy Crockett, became the stuff of legend.

As with all legends, separating fact from fiction can be difficult, and many fictional accounts of these feuding families have been told over the years, starting while the feud was still burning up the border between Kentucky and West Virginia. Before the start of the Civil War, the Hatfields and McCoys appear to have had more or less amicable relations, even intermarrying on occasion. But on one fateful autumn day in 1878, all that changed. Randall stopped

---

1. See the fabulous biography of Davy Crockett by Wallis (2011).

by the farm of Floyd Hatfield, cousin of Hatfield patriarch "Devil Anse" (Anderson), apparently just to chat.

According to Randall, he saw in Floyd's pig pen one of his own hogs, which he claimed to be able to identify by a marking he had put on the animal's ear (a common practice among hog farmers). Randall immediately accused Floyd of stealing his hog, and he went straight away to file a complaint with the local justice of the peace, Deacon Anderson Hatfield. Floyd, of course, denied the charge, so the complaint went to trial. The jury, made up of six Hatfields and six McCoys, did not find sufficient evidence to support the charge and acquitted Floyd in a vote of seven to five. Both the McCoy juror (Selkirk) who voted for acquittal and the witness who supported Floyd Hatfield's claim of innocence, Bill Stanton (also a McCoy kinsman), were considered traitors by Randall's clan. For the McCoys, betrayal was considered an unpardonable sin.

In another time and another place, that trial would have been the end of the affair—but not there, and not among these folks. The McCoys felt cheated—not just Randall, but virtually all of the McCoy clan bore the stain of this perceived mistreatment—just as the Hatfields felt unfairly maligned. Hog thievery was considered to be as malicious a charge as cattle rustling out West. And, like the western frontier, people in this Appalachian community put little stock in the rule of law (a lack of faith that was partly rational, partly ideological). "Justice" was not merely a matter of truth or objectivity. Justice was about getting what you believed was due to you, regardless of whether that claim was supported by any legal authorities. Thus, a feud was born that claimed the lives of so many members of the Hatfield and McCoy families over the course of more than a decade. Although the bloodlust of Devil Anse Hatfield would eventually abate in his twilight years, Randall would die a bitter and broken man, never allowing the sun to set on his hatred for the Hatfields. He is reported to have frequently wandered the town of Pikeville in a drunken stupor toward the end of his life, cursing the Hatfield name.[2]

What do Davy Crockett and Randall McCoy have in common? One is known as a hero, the other as something of a villain. Both

---

2. For a well-researched account of these events, see Rice (1982).

died tragically—one at the hands of Santa Anna's army, the other from burns received after falling into a fire at his nephew's home (while he was most likely inebriated). Although Crockett's untimely death at the relatively young age of 49 remains a celebrated part of American history a century and a half later, McCoy's death as an old man of 88 went almost unnoticed, even by his contemporaries. Other than both being white males from the United States, what do these men have in common?

The answer to this question is the very subject of this book. What I hope to make clear in these pages is that what bound these two very different men together was a cultural heritage birthed in the Lowlands of southern Scotland, from which both men's ancestors had immigrated several generations before them. This cultural heritage—my own heritage, I might add—is called by social scientists a *culture of honor*, and it was brought to the American colonies by hundreds of thousands of immigrants from Scotland, many of them after a temporary stay in Northern Ireland. The social–psychological vestiges of this cultural syndrome can still be seen in America today, as well as in other nations around the world, although the conditions that created the syndrome might have long passed from memory. But I'm getting a little ahead of the story, for to understand this cultural code of honor, one must know something about the people who brought it here: the Scotch-Irish.

"The Problem with Scotland Is That It's Full of Scots"

So said King Edward the Long Shanks of England. Or, at least, that's what he said in the 1995 film, *Braveheart*, and it's one of my favorite lines from the movie. The protagonist of the film is William Wallace, the national hero of Scotland. Wallace is the ultimate in populist savior figures—even in his death at the hands of King Edward, after helping to lead the Lowland Scots to victory time and again against the superior forces of England.

Of the many historical inaccuracies of *Braveheart*, one is extremely mundane—so much so that it's easy to overlook. Specifically, there are too many trees in the film. Now, you're probably thinking to yourself, how would anyone know how many trees there were in southern Scotland during the 13th century? The answer is simple, actually. By the time William Wallace rode to war against his English oppressors, *there weren't any trees left* in southern Scotland. Not many, anyway.

Centuries of warfare had stripped this part of Scotland of virtually all of its few natural resources. For hundreds of years, the Scots had resisted attempts by their southern neighbors to establish English rule in Scotland. There were invasion attempts by sea, but most such attempts were by land. For simple geographic reasons, this meant that armies from England had to march up through the southern Scottish Lowlands, and they were most likely to do so through the eastern regions that had the only soil worth farming. Scottish armies from the north would then march back down through this same region, pushing the English combatants back to their own territory when they could, and often counter-invading northern England in retribution or with the belief that the northern border country actually belonged to them. It was, in a sense, a massive, long-running pissing match between the Scots and the English, and the border regions between them bore the brunt of it.

Imagine this cycle repeating itself over hundreds of years. The result, as you might expect, was that this southern region was practically a barren wasteland. The trees were among the many casualties of this cycle, because armies from both sides cut them down on their way in or out to make spears or to build wagons, or just out of spite. There's nothing better to an army of invaders than a bit of wanton destruction, after all. Except perhaps s'mores. And you need firewood to make those.

To make matters worse, when the region enjoyed brief periods of peace with England, it still labored under an outdated feudal system in which landowners rented meager plots of farmland to Scottish peasants. Equally outdated agricultural methods meant that the Scots didn't know how to cultivate their lands to maximize crop yield. They hardly understood the meaning of damming to control drainage, or crop rotation, or fertilization. If they had, it is not clear at all that it would have made much of a difference. When you don't own the land you work, there are few incentives to think about developing irrigation systems or making any kind of long-term improvements to the land. Your landlord might decide to kick you out at any time, after all, and who would tell him he couldn't? There was no king from whom a poor peasant could seek redress for such wrongs. Not a real king, anyway—one with real power backed by an organized central government.

Using the phrase "periods of peace" in this part of Scotland is also something of a joke, because life here was almost never truly peaceful, even when there was no official war going on. Raiding was a way of life for the Scots, and the wild men of the Highlands were a constant threat to the Lowland Scots. The Highland clans were even less civilized than the Lowlanders, who had largely abandoned the clan system for feudalism beginning around the 12th century. Farming in the unforgiving mountains of the Highlands was even less productive than it was in much of the Lowlands, so cattle, sheep, pigs, and goats were the primary commodities of northern Scotland at this time. Without the rule of law to inhibit them, the Highland clans preyed constantly on the meager resources of the Lowlanders, "reiving" (or "rustling") the meager herds from the south whenever they could.

Human beings, it turns out, do not thrive in lawless, uncertain, unstable environments. We thrive when we live within social systems that are orderly and predictable, where rules are understood and followed as social contracts, and where people feel safe. This is what "the rule of law" means, and it seems to be fairly fundamental to healthy societies. As such, humans appear to be acutely sensitive to cues of lawlessness in their surroundings. When people encounter these cues, they enter into a downward spiral that social scientists sometimes refer to as the *broken window effect*.

The gist of the broken window effect is that when people encounter signs of lawlessness, such as broken windows in a building, these signs communicate that rules aren't taken seriously, and this belief encourages people to break the rules themselves. A group of Dutch researchers recently examined this effect in the city of Groningen (Keizer et al., 2008). Across a series of studies in and around Groningen, the researchers created situations of either order or disorder to determine how environmental cues influence people's behavior. In one study, they put up a sign in a parking garage telling shoppers: PLEASE RETURN YOUR SHOPPING CARTS. For shoppers in the disorder condition, the researchers then placed a bunch of shopping carts in random spots around the parking lot. In addition, for shoppers in both the order and disorder conditions, the researchers placed a flyer under people's windshield wiper, ostensibly from a local sporting goods store, wishing them a happy holiday.

Now, personally, I hate it when people put flyers under my windshield wiper. I feel like it's a case of unsolicited trash that has now become my responsibility, simply because it is touching my car. It somehow feels unfair that I now have to do something with this piece of paper, especially when I already have my hands full, and that was exactly what the researchers hoped the shoppers in their study would feel. But what would shoppers then *do* with this flyer? Would they throw the flyer on the ground, insisting that it wasn't *their* trash or *their* responsibility, or would they behave in a more prosocial manner by taking the flyer to the trashcan? Of course, no such receptacle was in sight, so shoppers quickly realized they would have to go back inside the store to throw away the flyer if they chose this route. Happy holiday indeed! I must admit that I kind of hate this study. I feel like I have been a participant in it more than once.

What the researchers found was consistent with the broken window effect. Specifically, shoppers in the order condition (seemingly in an environment full of people who followed the rules about shopping carts) littered with the rogue flyer 30% of the time. Although this rate of littering might not sound encouraging, it was substantially better than the littering rate in the disorder condition—a whopping 58%. Seeing that people in their environment ignored written rules about shopping carts and appeared to be getting away with it encouraged shoppers to do the same with unwritten rules about littering.

The researchers next examined an even more extreme behavior: stealing. They first made a large, white envelope with a clear window, through which could be seen a €5 note. They then placed this envelope carefully so that it hung partly inside and partly outside the opening of a public mailbox, so that passersby could easily see the money available for the taking. Once again, the researchers created order and disorder conditions, this time representing disorder in two different ways. For the order condition, passersby saw the mailbox clean and neat, with the large, money-filled envelope sticking out of its mail slot. For the disorder conditions, the researchers used the same setup but added either graffiti to the mailbox or dropped a bunch of trash around it. Both of these disorder conditions demonstrated that people in that environment generally ignored social rules. As in their previous experiment, cues of disorder, such as broken windows, increased people's likelihood of behaving in antisocial ways—this time by stealing the money they saw peaking from the lip of the mailbox. Although "only" 13% of passersby stole the money in the order condition, 27% did so in the graffiti condition, as did 25% in the litter condition. Signs of lawlessness breed more lawlessness (with the simple lawlessness cues in these studies essentially *doubling* the rates of lawless behaviors).[3]

Let's return to the Lowland Scots in the 17th century (and for many centuries before that). As we've seen, they had almost no natural resources and no stable institutional systems in place to help them develop what little they did have. The idea of a lasting peace was little more than a mist on the marshes. War and the threat of war were all the Lowland Scots knew. English armies and bandits from the south, and Highland "reivers" from the north, made security a fantasy. There hadn't been a strong enough king in Scotland to bring stability and security and to enforce the rule of law since the reign of Robert the Bruce during the early 14th century—only barons and landlords, themselves a mostly illiterate and brutish horde of hooligans. In such an environment, what did people do to protect themselves? About the only thing they could do under the circumstances was to develop, over time, a culture of honor.[4]

Broken windows → Crime

---

3. It's probably worth noting that modern policing strategies seem to take this broken window effect seriously. Cleaning up evidence of relatively minor offenses and misdemeanors was an important piece of the strategy that New York City Mayor Rudy Giuliani used to combat crime there during the 1990s, and experimental research has provided strong evidence of the value of such a "minimalist" approach for reducing serious crimes, including robberies and assaults. In one recent study, for instance, police efforts to reduce signs of social disorder (such as cleaning up vacant lots, improving street lighting, razing abandoned buildings) reduced robberies during the following six months by 42%, and reduced assaults by 34% (Braga & Bond, 2008). For a 10,000-foot view of the rule of law over time and its potential impact on lethal violence, see Eisner (2001).

4. Eminent historian James Leyburn (1962) once described the Lowland Scots this way: "Poverty-stricken, generally lawless, still lingering in the Middle Ages in the seventeenth century (and even into the eighteenth), with agricultural methods hardly better than primitive . . . " (p. xv).

If raiders stole a man's cattle, his only source of redress was to appeal to his feudal lord, who typically issued a call to arms among his tenants to strike back at the thieves, retrieving the stolen cattle and whatever other spoils they could take away. Sometimes, of course, barons and landlords initiated the call to arms themselves, often to settle a dispute of their own making. Thus, one wrong was answered with another, leading to a constant state of feuding, raiding, and retribution. Loyalty to one's landlord and fellow tenants existed alongside loyalty to one's kin in the border country of southern Scotland, so one man's dishonor became another's rather easily within this social system.

Living in this kind of environment, one of the best forms of protection you could have was a reputation for strength, toughness, and pugnacity. If people far and wide know you as someone who should not be trifled with, thieves and raiders might steer clear of your herd and home in their pursuit of mischief. And how does one develop such a reputation? By fighting, of course—by exhibitions of strength and a quick temper, public displays of excess, boisterousness, resilience, and pride. Lots and lots of pride.

Pride, after all, is the internal storehouse of one's worth, one's status. To speak ill of a man (by, for instance, claiming he stole your hog) is to wound his pride and to threaten his reputation, and thus his social standing, and that cannot be tolerated in an honor culture. Without his reputation, a Lowland Scot was naked in a land of thistles and thorns. His reputation was almost all that stood between him and those who would take what little else he had in the world. And thus we find the heart of the honor syndrome—defense of one's name, one's reputation, which was itself a protection against exploitation, predation, and even death. Anything that sullies your reputation is a threat to your honor, and such threats are taken very seriously in an honor culture.

Reputation management sits at the center of the value system of all honor cultures, no matter how they might differ in their other particulars. All human beings are concerned with reputation. That's just part of what it means to live together. We care about what other people think of us, and we strive to ensure that what people think of us is closer to our ideal selves than to our poorest selves. Honor cultures take this normal human concern and magnify it. They put it on "cultural steroids." Honor cultures also channel the types of reputations that people strive to attain (and to defend), and they do so in distinct ways for men and women, as we shall see.

So far, I have focused mostly on men in speaking of the impact of living in a lawless and poverty-stricken land, but the ideology of honor has implications for women as well as for men. Men in this social system had to prove they were tough, but women had to be almost as tough as men. While men were off fighting in wars and raids, women were left to do everything else: bearing and raising kids, cooking, and farming the unyielding Lowland soil. However, although the primary reputational concerns for men involved strength and toughness, those for women primarily involved loyalty and purity. Women had to be tough to survive, but they had to be known as loyal to their man and sexually chaste if they wanted to be valued. To be seen otherwise would be to invite dishonor not only on themselves, but also their husbands, their fathers, and their entire families. In such a culture, dishonor is intolerable. If a man can't protect or keep control of his woman, what kind of a man was he? As damaging as cowardice and weakness were for the reputations of men, so were sexual infidelity and disloyalty for the reputations of women.

Coming to America

Why should we be concerned about this one, small land from a time so long ago? The whole of Scotland is only about the size of South Carolina. Could it really be all that important, aside from illustrating how the elements of economic insecurity and lawlessness can come together (maybe with a little wine, some nice music, a little candlelight) to birth an honor culture? Had the Scots stayed in Scotland, the influence of this country's culture would have been as modest as its size. As it happened, they did not stay in Scotland, due in large part to what might be considered an accident of history.

It all started with a particular Scot named James. You've probably heard of him. He's the guy the King James Bible is named after (he commissioned its translation in 1604). Before he was James I of England, he was James VI of Scotland, from the House of Stuart. He ascended to the throne of England in 1603 after Queen Elizabeth died. Soon after he took the throne, James implemented an elaborate and devious plan to subdue the troublesome Irish (and expel a few troublesome people from England while he was at it). His plan primarily involved granting lands in the north of Ireland, in Ulster, to Englishmen and Lowland Scottish landlords, with the understanding that they would encourage their tenants to move there. Some were, indeed, encouraged to go. Others were forced to go—essentially exiled to Ireland. Whatever their motivations, thousands of southern Scots went to Ulster.

In essence, the plan was to provide Ireland with the cultural equivalent of a kidney transplant (you know, something to help process all the poisons from the host body). The English would provide a ruling class and a bit of English sophistication, whereas the rough and war-ready Scots would provide the muscle needed to help subdue the rebellious Irish, bending them to the king's will. Northern Ireland also made a nice place to send religious dissenters against the Church of England, as well as other miscreants from the border region between Scotland and England, so over time it became something of a social dumping ground for King James.

The Lowland Scots took to the transplant idea fairly well. After all, they had next to nothing in their homeland, other than the familiar ache of misery, insecurity, and war (which, admittedly, the new Scot on the English throne helped to diminish; but still, it takes generations just to regrow the forests, not to mention teaching people to read, write, and obey the rule of law).[5] Their new Irish host, however, was not as amenable to the transplant and tried to reject the newcomers. Big surprise here: no one likes to have his lands stolen and given away to foreigners. The fact that the foreigners were frequently uncouth, illiterate, violence-prone

---

5. It is interesting that King James, when he was still James VI of Scotland, instituted a law setting fines for landowners who failed to plant trees on their lands, and he exacted severe punishments for people who cut down or otherwise harmed these new saplings. Specifically, the law stated that "willful destroyers and cutters of growing trees be punished to death as thieves" (cited in Leyburn, 1962, p. 5). James VI was not the first Scottish king to make a law such as this, either. Treelessness had long been a problem in southern Scotland.

Scots made it all the worse. So, James's fabulous idea didn't go over very well with the Irish, and the consequences of this "Ulster Plantation," as it came to be known, are still being felt in Northern Ireland today. I suppose that sort of balances out the whole Bible thing, doesn't it?

Thus, after toiling to make a living in a foreign country, where on the whole they proved to be barely better at farming than they were in their home country, and after weathering a long-running and brutal civil war full of massacres and pillaging, many of these transplanted Lowlanders began to wonder, after a few generations, whether they should start over once again somewhere else—get a truly fresh start this time, without all the history and messiness of Ireland versus England, and Catholic versus Protestant, and Presbyterian versus Anglican. Somewhere like America. That was the hope, anyway.

And so, in several enormous waves of immigration, particularly during the early to mid 1700s, the Ulster Scots crossed the Atlantic and came to America. They came as entire families in many cases, which allowed them to settle quickly and outbreed many other immigrant groups. These Ulster Scots—or "Scotch-Irish," as they were often called in America, as a result of their recent stay in Ireland—brought with them not just their wives and children, but also the beliefs, values, and social scripts of an honor culture that had incubated for nearly a millennium in the strife-stricken Lowlands of Scotland.

Quickly, they became one of the most dominant social forces in the parts of the fledgling colonies where they settled. As historian David H. Fischer (1989) wrote, "So well adapted was the border culture [of Scotland] to this environment that other ethnic groups tended to copy it. The ethos of the North British borders came to dominate this 'dark and bloody ground,' partly by force of numbers, but mainly because it was a means of survival in a raw and dangerous world" (p. 639).

Some Ulster Scots went north into Maine, and some entered the port of Philadelphia and headed west. The latter group was "assisted" in their westward trek by the Quakers, who ran the state of Pennsylvania. Because the Quakers were theological pacifists, they found their dealings with the Indians somewhat complicated by their own inability to take up arms. The Scots had no such qualms, of course, and so they were once again exploited by the powers that be for their skills as fighters. Taking a page out of King James's playbook, the Quakers encouraged them to move westward by giving them cheap lands in western Pennsylvania, effectively using them as a human shield against the Indians (who, like the Irish, didn't much appreciate their lands being invaded by foreigners).

The bulk of the Ulster Scots, though, went southward, which at that time was still considered the frontier of the colonies. Arriving with little but their pride and the shirt on their back, they couldn't afford to buy the most desirable lands in and around established towns along the coast. Instead, they went where land was cheap and plentiful—into western Maryland and Virginia, and down into the Appalachian mountains of the Carolinas (where they once again became herders of sheep, pigs, and goats), eventually making their way into Georgia, Kentucky, and Tennessee, and from there continuing west. In the early days of their migrations southward, the Ulster Scots made up more than 50% of some counties, so vast were their numbers, and so successful were they in these frontier regions.

Lacking much in the way of a national identity—the Ulster Scots carried their pride on their shoulders, but this pride was not really about being Scottish—these displaced Lowlanders found their sense of self and their ties to the past largely through their family relations. Indeed, absent the feudal system that had diluted the clan ways of the Scottish Lowlands, the Ulster Scots seemed to have enhanced the ancient loyalties to extended kinship networks in the dangerous and uncertain world of the American frontier. These revived clans took on great importance to the survival and success of Scottish immigrants.

When they married outsiders, whether German farmers, English merchants, or even Indians,[6] they spread their honor-related beliefs and values like a social virus, from one generation

---

6. A scholar I know who is half Cherokee once told me a story that fits well with what we know of the Ulster Scots. His Cherokee grandmother used to say that, of all the European colonials who came to America, only the Scots were tough enough to marry Cherokee women, which they seem to have done with some frequency. These two cultures, so different in some respects, were also quite similar in ways that made intermarriage between them uncommonly tenable.

to the next. Indeed, trying to withstand the honor culture they brought with them was like trying to face down a tornado. You could try, but you were unlikely to survive the attempt.

Thus, other cultural systems tended to take a back seat to the dominant manner of thinking, feeling, and behaving that the Ulster Scots carried to the colonies. In this way, all the trials and tribulations of the long and terrible history of the Lowland Scots came together—from centuries of warfare, poverty, and lawlessness, to the political maneuverings of kings and statesmen, to their relative lack of national identity and their intense loyalty to kin. It is almost as if a thousand years' worth of history had been orchestrated just to make these Scottish immigrants successful in the frontiers of the New World. If they were like a kidney transplant in Northern Ireland, they were like a heart transplant in America. And this time, the transplanted organ was not rejected.

Earlier in this chapter, I raised the question of what Davy Crockett and Randall McCoy had in common. Both men, it turns out, were descended from the southern Scots, and their lives reflect the cultural legacy of the honor syndrome born in this region. This legacy can be seen in the lives of many other Americans as well, from President Andrew Jackson to George W. Bush, from Sam Houston to George Patton, and from Devil Anse Hatfield to, well, me. My forebears, it turns out, are southern Scots on my father's side, and I grew up steeped in the traditions and habits of this Scottish honor culture in the rolling hills of central Alabama. It was not until long after I had become a social scientist, however, that I discovered this cultural heritage and began to understand its many intricacies as I conducted studies on the ideology of honor.

I can't help telling pieces of my own story while describing how the Ulster Scots brought their honor culture to America. In doing so, I hope to illustrate in a personal way the legacy these Scots have left us—a legacy that still orients us today. This cultural ideology drives us to be ever vigilant when we suspect that the guy we are talking to in a bar has just insulted the virtue of our mother, and it tells us how to respond when a coworker has humiliated us with a post on his Facebook page that left everyone in the office roaring with laughter at our expense. This cultural legacy is the common man's no-holds-barred version of the gentleman's duel, but the former existed long before the careful liturgy of the duel came to be—and has outlasted it. (Although, even today, the oath of office for state legislators in Kentucky contains a promise that the oath-taker has never participated in any duels. Perhaps that oath should be amended to reference bar fights.)

I will contend that to comprehend the American South, and to a lesser extent the West, you must listen to its heartbeat, which is found in the culture of honor inherited from the Ulster Scots. For Americans, doing so not only helps us understand each other, but it also helps us to comprehend many other people around the world whose hearts beat to a similar rhythm. The idea of honor links long-dead figures such as Davy Crockett and Randall McCoy to each other and connects them to more contemporary ones, such as George W. Bush and Osama bin Laden. It likewise unites the ancient warriors in Sparta, terrorist insurgents in the Middle East, inner-city gangs in Los Angeles, college football fans in Alabama, patriot militias in Montana, and police officers in Charlotte, South Carolina. The ideology of honor is the chain that binds all these people together, along with so many others—from cowboys to presidents to terrorists, and everyone in between. Honor ideology is not restricted to any race or ethnic group, although, as we'll see, its influence might be more prevalent in some groups of people than in others, or more geographically distinct among some groups than others. The cultural ideal of honor is a powerful and pervasive force, and we would do well to appreciate how it has helped shape the American psyche and changed the world.

Discussion Questions

1. An old axiom in science is that "nature abhors a vacuum." In what sense did the environment of southern Scotland during the 17th century reflect a kind of social vacuum? What was missing that human nature "abhors?"
2. Can you think of other examples of this sort of social environment from modern times? From other societies around the world?
3. This chapter discussed research on the broken window effect as an example of how sensitive human beings are to

cues of lawlessness. When was the last time you were in a place that had such lawlessness cues? How did it make you feel? Did you behave any differently there than you do in other environments?

4. This chapter presents the argument that reputation management is at the heart of the honor syndrome. What are some of the ways you've seen people strive to manage their reputations? What is the most extreme example of this that you can recall?

For Further Reading

Fischer, D. H. 1989. *Albion's seed: Four British folkways in America.* New York: Oxford University Press.

Peristiany, J. G. 1966. *Honour and shame: The values of Mediterranean society.* Chicago, IL: The University of Chicago Press.

Wyatt-Brown, B. 1986. *Honor and violence in the old South.* New York: Oxford University Press.

CHAPTER TWO

A Penchant for Violence

A RIZONA TERRITORY IN THE YEAR 1881 was a rough place to
live, at once both a place of promise and peril. With ren-
egade Apaches to the north, Mexican raiders to the south,
and a silver mine underneath that was nearing its zenith, the town
of Tombstone had little to endear it to the annals of history, save
for a singular event in the autumn of that year that would eventually make this boomtown famous. That event was the notorious gunfight at the O.K. Corral between Wyatt Earp, his brothers
Virgil and Morgan, and his friend Doc Holiday on one side, and
brothers Ike and Billy Clanton, Billy Claiborne, and Tom and
Frank McLaury on the other.

The "star" of this gunfight, though, was clearly Wyatt Earp. I'm
not sure how many movies have been made about Wyatt Earp in
the past 100 years, but I've seen two of them last year alone. Earp,
like Davy Crockett, is another legend of American folklore—just
a simple man trying to make his way in the world the best way he
knew how. Can he be blamed if that way involved a badge and a
gun? Villains always hate a man with a badge and a gun. And who
among us will weep over a few dead cowboys so righteously slain
by Wyatt Earp and his faithful companions?

In those days, *cowboy* was not a term of endearment. No woman
would ever try to seduce a man with a "come-hither" look and a

call of "Hey there, cowboy," no matter how many times we've all seen them do so in the movies. A cowboy was the nickname given to those who dealt in cattle, and in that part of the country, "dealing in cattle" often meant stealing them, typically from Mexico, and selling them on the black market. When cattle rustling wasn't paying well, cowboys in Arizona Territory sometimes took to robbing Wells Fargo stagecoaches at gunpoint. Such robberies were frequently conducted without anyone being injured, but sometimes a driver or a security agent was killed.

Just such a murder occurred near Tombstone, and Wyatt and his brothers had ridden with a posse to try to bring the culprits to justice. They eventually learned the identities of three of the bandits from one of the cowboys' own friends, but they were never able to catch them. That failure led Wyatt to hatch a plan to lure the bandits into a trap using another cowboy, who agreed to betray his acquaintances for the promise of a fat reward, courtesy of Wells Fargo. The cowboy's name was Ike Clanton.

Ike would eventually begin to have misgivings about the scheme. When the suspected murderers turned up dead in another county, and all hope of cashing in on their heads was lost, Ike became particularly agitated that word of his planned complicity in Wyatt's scheme might get out. He began to badger Wyatt every time he came to town, particularly after a bout of drinking at one of Tombstone's many saloons. Ike seemed especially concerned that Wyatt might have told his friend Doc Holiday about the plan, and Ike felt sure that if Doc knew, others would soon find out as well.

The night before the infamous battle outside the O.K. Corral, Ike was in town drinking heavily, and Wyatt thought he could settle the matter once and for all if he set up a meeting between Ike and Doc to put the whole ordeal to rest. However, when Wyatt and Doc approached the drunken cowboy to assure him his reputation was safe, Ike was already too drunk to be persuaded, and the confrontation that ensued did not go well. At least, it did not go well for Ike Clanton, who ended up face down in the dusty street with a small crowd of Tombstone citizens to witness his downfall. Ike's humiliation would prove to be the primary catalyst for what happened the following day.

In a way, the central role played by Ike's humiliation was fitting, for all of the characters in this notorious gunfight were driven to distraction by their desire to manage their public images. Wyatt was no exception. Indeed, his life-long preoccupation with becoming a man of status and respect (despite several run-ins with the law himself in years past) set the stage for the events of October 26, 1881. His need to be seen as a powerful man who would never back down from a fight fueled his rage and forced his hand, as Ike Clanton continued spewing his drunken threats to anyone who would listen after Wyatt and Doc humiliated him. This need for respect was what led to Wyatt's ill-fated scheme to catch the stagecoach bandits in the first place. Wyatt wanted desperately to be elected county sheriff, one of the most prestigious and lucrative jobs around for a man like him, and to do that he needed to show up Johnny Behan, the current county sheriff who had beat Wyatt in the previous election. He figured that catching these murderers would serve both to humiliate Behan and elevate his own profile before the next election.

Ike Clanton's paranoid antics threatened to ruin all of that. Not only was Wyatt's original plan scuttled, on account of the murderers getting killed before he could get Ike to betray them, but now Clanton was becoming a serious liability to Wyatt's reputation. To countenance a good-for-nothing, drunken cowboy running around town declaring that he was going to kill Doc, Wyatt, and any other Earp he could find was simply unacceptable. Wyatt wasn't just *ready* to fight Clanton. He was eager to do so. He had to prove himself to keep his honor intact.

In this way, Wyatt was driven by the same impulses that compelled Ike, as well as his friend, Tom McLaury. McLaury had heard about Ike's scuffle with the law that day and went to the town courthouse to see if Clanton needed assistance. Outside the courthouse, McLaury met Wyatt, who witnesses say clocked McLaury with the butt of his gun, sending him to the ground just as he had done to Clanton a few hours before. Thus, Wyatt managed to publicly humiliate not just one, but *two* cowboys within less than a day. When these two were joined by their brothers, Frank McLaury and Billy Clanton, and their friend Billy Claiborne, the die was cast. In truth, despite all the retellings of this famous western gun battle, there were no heroes or villains that day outside the O.K. Corral—only nine proud men who felt the social necessity of proving their manhood (Guinn, 2011).

Entrance ramps and merge lanes in Oklahoma are notoriously short—the miniskirts of U.S. roads—almost as if Oklahomans lack the patience to ease onto a busy highway. Do it or don't do it, but don't lollygag about it. No need to take a quarter mile trying to tiptoe into traffic. Drive like you mean it. I don't know if that's really the official policy behind this feature of road construction in this state, but it seems to fit the apparent mentality pretty well.

It was just after dusk, and my friend Collin was in a good mood. His infant daughter was making nonsensical chatter in the backseat of his old, restored Mercedes, and he was taking her home to bed. The cloudless Oklahoma night revealed an array of stars just beginning to appear in the evening sky as he navigated the interstate. Collin had only a short distance to go on this road before needing to exit toward home, so the traffic didn't concern him much as he chauffeured his tiny princess to her castle. The traffic, though, did create a problem for him as he passed another entrance ramp where another driver was clearly trying to enter the interstate. Although this driver had a yield sign, he was not, apparently, the yielding type. Collin could see him just ahead, but cars to the left and behind made it impossible to move over to let this driver get on. The other driver was not happy, which became clear to Collin when the driver honked at him.

Now, depending on where you live, a honk might not carry much meaning for you. I can recall sitting in the passenger seat beside a friend driving in Houston who had moved there from Pennsylvania. When he honked at another driver, I gave him a look that fused shock with consternation. "What'd you do that for?" I had asked him. "You do realize that people here don't honk at other drivers, right? Unless you're trying to cuss them out in car-horn language, in which case, honk away."

Having grown up in Texas, Collin knew exactly what it meant when the driver honked at him. It wasn't a "Hey, your left headlight is broken" honk, or a "Watch out for the cop up ahead" honk. Collin spoke the language of car-honks well enough to know that it meant he should perform inappropriate acts with certain bodily orifices. Which, of course, made him angry. His baby girl was listening, after all.

The pissed-off other driver wasn't finished, either. Once he did manage to get onto the interstate, he sped up and roared past other vehicles until he was right behind Collin's car (almost within orifice range). He then floored it and passed Collin, honking angrily as he did so, only to pull dangerously in front of Collin's car, quickly putting on his brakes to make his exit off the interstate. They were heading the same way, it seemed. Having both exited, they came to a halt at the stop light that crowned the top of the overpass onto which they both sought to turn left. Collin expected to see a hand gesture or two at that point, but he wasn't expecting what happened next. The angry driver *got out of his car*, leaving his own door wide open, and started pounding the pavement toward Collin.

The whole situation felt somewhat absurd. Had this happened to two other drivers in many other states in America, there likely would have been no angry honking, no obnoxious gesturing, and certainly no getting out of cars. But this wasn't one of those other states. This was Oklahoma, and a pair of testosterone-fueled egos were about to collide.

Almost as if he were on autopilot, not fully in control of his own body, Collin found himself getting out of his car to meet the enraged other driver. In moments, they were nose to nose, the angry, middle-aged white man practically spitting as he vented his venomous rage. The strong Oklahoma wind whipped his hair around his face as if it were alive. For just a moment, it looked to Collin like a nest of writhing snakes, and it was at that moment that something changed. Perhaps it was the image of the snakes that reminded him of the famous Gadsden flag and its Revolutionary War motto, "Don't Tread on Me." This motto had served as the inspiration for some research that Collin had recently been conducting on violence and culture; he was, it turns out, a social scientist who studies the social dynamics of human aggression. Whatever it was that made him realize what was happening in that brief moment, he turned away, and without answering the challenges being hurled at him, he quietly returned to his car and drove away, blood boiling and heart pumping violently in his chest, his daughter still cooing and bubbling in the backseat.

Collin's experience is not unique. Indeed, it is the sort of conflict that is played out daily on roads and barstools throughout America. What can make grown men, even well-educated and emotionally stable men, turn into mindless Cretans bent on domination and destruction within the span of minutes? There are several ways to answer this question, but one way is to point out that men, just like women, are products of their environment, which means they are programmed by their culture to respond in particular ways to particular kinds of social situations. That's really what socialization is all about, in the end. We learn growing up that when x happens, you should do y. You should be prepared to do z if you have to, but under no circumstances should you do w.

This type of if-x-then-y formula is what is known as a *social script*. Social scripts provide the building blocks of our lives together, and they permeate our experiences with people and events all day, every day, whether or not we realize it. My friend Collin was perceiving the actions of the angry driver through a framework he had learned throughout the course of many years, and he was following a script for how to respond to the behaviors he encountered in the angry driver. The same was true, by the way, for the angry driver. They were both acting out roles written for them by their culture, just as Wyatt Earp did about 120 years before them. As we shall see in this chapter, honor cultures provide beliefs and expectations that are designed to focus attention, guide interpretation, and drive action, largely in the service of managing and defending reputation. Unfortunately, these beliefs and expectations have a tendency to escalate minor irritations into major infernos. They can even turn a small matter of a missing pig into a family feud of legendary proportions, as the Hatfields and McCoys found out the hard way.

In Chapter 1, I described the beliefs and values of the Ulster Scots, or Scotch-Irish, who immigrated to the United States in massive waves throughout the 1700s, settling in the Carolinas and Georgia, and eventually moving westward into Kentucky, Tennessee, Alabama, and beyond, bringing their culture with them. The United States is currently a very different place than it was during its settlement. Rule of law is well established, and the uncertainty regarding property ownership is no longer the issue that it was during the 18th and 19th centuries. However, the honor-based culture of the Ulster Scots that took root in parts of the American South and West is still alive and well. As we will see in this chapter, research shows that honor-related beliefs and values still influence people living in these regions of the United States, providing the lenses through which people living in "honor states" in the South and West interpret social interactions, and the expectations for how they should respond to their interpretations.

Table 2.1 lists the states in the United States that are considered to be "honor states" by the researchers whose work is described in this chapter and throughout this book, as well as the states deemed to be "nonhonor states." This kind of listing vastly oversimplifies matters, because any breakdown of the world into "two types of *x*" is almost always too simple. As the list below shows, states are generally classified according to their U.S. Census Bureau designation, with southern and western states typically classified as honor states, and northern states classified as nonhonor states, with only a few exceptions (specifically, Alaska and Hawaii).

Part of what makes this two-group classification overly simplified is that states are not homogeneous, as just about anyone who has ever lived in different parts of a state knows. Southern Illinois, for instance, is different from northern Illinois, just as western Pennsylvania is different from eastern Pennsylvania. However, because regional studies typically depend on state-level averages,

Table 2.1 RANKING OF ALL 50 STATES IN ORDER OF THEIR CULTURE OF HONOR ORIENTATION

1. South Carolina	**13. Montana**	**25. Maryland**	38. Iowa
2. North Carolina	**14. Nevada**	**26. Utah**	39. Massachusetts
	15. Kentucky	**27. California**	40. Illinois
3. Alabama	**16. Florida**	~~~~~~~~~~~~~~	41. Michigan
4. Georgia	**17. Arizona**	28. Maine	42. New York
5. Arkansas	**18. Oregon**	29. Missouri	43. South Dakota
6. Mississippi	**19. Washington**	30. Alaska	44. Connecticut
7. West Virginia	**20. Idaho**	31. Vermont	45. New Jersey
8. Virginia	**21. Colorado**	32. Ohio	46. Hawaii
9. Tennessee	**22. Louisiana**	33. Kansas	47. Rhode Island
10. Texas	**23. Delaware**	34. New Hampshire	48. Wisconsin
11. Oklahoma	**24. New Mexico**	35. Pennsylvania	49. Minnesota
12. Wyoming		36. Indiana	50. North Dakota
		37. Nebraska	

States in bold type are categorized throughout this book as honor states; the rest are categorized as nonhonor states.

such as the average homicide rate in a state over a certain period of time, researchers tend to stick with the admittedly simplistic categorization scheme shown in Table 2.1. What is equally problematic with this simple classification system is that not only are all parts of a state lumped together, but also very different states are classified equally as honor or nonhonor states. Surely, California and Washington are less dominated by honor-related beliefs and values than Oklahoma and West Virginia are, right?

This lack of nuance is something that social scientists interested in honor culture need to work on. In one attempt to do just that, social scientist Michael Tamborski and I created a system for ranking all 50 states according to the degree to which their citizens exhibit a wide range of honor-related characteristics, all of which are described in this book.[1] Although most studies on the geography of honor in the United States rely on the simple, honor-versus-nonhonor classification system just mentioned, I think it is useful to remember there are meaningful differences within each of these categories. Some honor states are more strongly honor oriented than others are, for instance. Degrees of honor orientation are like degrees of height. A group of "tall people" is taller, on average, than a group of "short people," but within each group there are meaningful variations in height. This variation, incidentally, is not restricted to the level of states. People within each state also vary in their honor orientation. Simply living in an honor state doesn't mean you have a strong honor orientation, just as living in a nonhonor state doesn't mean you are *not* honor oriented. I return to this individual variation in Chapter 3.

Looking at the state rankings in Table 2.1, we can see some of the variation within each category of honor states and nonhonor states, and this variation makes sense. For instance, it is not surprising that South Carolina is ranked #1 in honor orientation among the honor states; this state is one where the Ulster Scots first settled in really large numbers during the 1700s. From the Carolinas, they migrated southward and westward; but, as they did so, the force of their social norms was diluted as their relative numbers in the population diminished. Thus, California (still categorized as an honor state) is ranked #27, the least honor oriented of the

---

1. This state ranking system is presented in Tamborski and Brown (2011).

honor states. Louisiana is also ranked rather low in honor orientation (#22), although it is not nearly as far west as California. This is likely because of the many other cultural influences on Louisiana early in its settlement by Europeans, especially the French (France is not an especially honor-oriented culture). We can also see that Maine is ranked higher than other New England states, which makes sense in light of the fact that a surprising number of Scotch-Irish immigrants also settled in Maine early on, although not in as high a concentration as they did in the Carolinas.

Now that we have established what researchers mean when they talk about differences between "honor states" and "nonhonor states," it's time to look at what some of those differences actually are. As we will see in this chapter, studies show that honor's emphasis on reputation and defense of self, property, and family results in an extreme *sensitivity* and *reactivity* to honor threats. In other words, people from cultures of honor—particularly men— are more likely to perceive threats in ambiguous social situations and to feel compelled to respond to those threats with aggression and violence. *Not* to do so would be to risk losing what is valued over almost anything: your reputation.

In one of the earliest systematic studies on the culture of honor in the United States,[2] Richard Nisbett and his collaborators (1995) looked at homicide rates around the United States. Their focus was on one type of homicide in particular, though—argument-based homicide, which is the type of homicide that often starts in a bar, on a street corner, or perhaps on a front porch. This is, in fact, the single most common type of homicide around the world.

---

2. What I mean when I use the word *systematic* is that we are not dealing with data from a personal example or even from an anthropological study of a distinct group of people. What we need if we want to have confidence regarding cultural differences are data structured in such a way that we are able to make meaningful comparisons between people or groups. For example, if someone were to claim that the Amish in western Pennsylvania are an unusually happy people, we would want to be sure to have a well-validated measure of happiness administered to a large, representative sample of Amish folk that we could compare using the same measure to a large, representative sample of non-Amish folk. If we have all that, and we find the average happiness level of the Amish group is, indeed, greater than the average happiness level of the non-Amish group, then we can say with reasonable confidence that the Amish are an unusually happy people. The same is true when we compare one part of a single country with another, or when we compare two entirely different countries.

Despite what we might learn at the movies, it's not the stranger wearing a hockey mask that you should fear will kill you some day. If anyone is going to kill you, it will most likely be someone you know. These are the people we are able to betray, and betrayal is a big motivator of violence. These are also the people with whom we are most likely to argue, often just in the course of talking about our favorite football teams or what we thought of the big fight last night or who is most to blame for the state of the economy. And it's these little discussions that can sometimes turn nasty, with someone making a little slur, followed by a little gesture, or a little shove, and then maybe a little suggestion about the virtue of someone's sister or mother. "What was that? Are you talkin' to *me*? Did you just say what I think you just said about *my* sister?" Thus it begins.

Known as *trivial altercations* in the language of police reports, these arguments-gone-wild are the single biggest cause of murder there is. As you can probably imagine, these kinds of (often public) altercations can get out of hand easily when the people involved live in a culture of honor, where not only are men expected to raise the bar when challenged—you don't give as good as you get; you give *better* than you get—but also they aren't expected to stop raising the bar just because things start to get physical, which can happen pretty quickly. A couple of beers doesn't do much to help this process, either. Nisbett and colleagues focused their attention on these argument-based homicides, comparing their rates between honor states and non-honor states, and controlling for a host of statewide characteristics that might incidentally differ between these states as well, such as poverty levels, social demographics, and so forth. These sorts of control variables, as we will see throughout this book, are important for strengthening our sense of what is causing things in studies of regional differences.

What they found was that states in the southern and western regions of the United States (in other words, honor states) exhibited higher rates of argument-related homicide than did states in the North (or, nonhonor states). But it is almost as important to note what they did *not* find. Specifically, rates of *felony* homicides (which occur during the commission of another crime, such as robbery) did not differ between honor and nonhonor states. In short, *other* precipitants of homicides that weren't fundamentally about honor were *not* more prevalent in honor states, but homicides precipitated by insults and arguments *were*. The inference made by Nisbett and his colleagues was that residents of honor states are more likely to respond violently—even to the point of killing—when insulted or threatened, compared with residents of nonhonor states.

But wait! There's more! Not only do honor states differ from nonhonor states in rates of argument-based homicides, but later studies revealed two more important qualifications to this pattern of aggression. First, the difference in homicide rates between honor states and nonhonor states occurs primarily among whites. Nonwhites do not consistently exhibit these differences across state lines. This does *not* mean that nonwhite demographic groups in the United States don't operate according to honor-related norms. It just means that the extent to which they do isn't distributed regionally the way that it seems to be among whites, which is consistent with the notion that honor culture beliefs and values were brought to the United States by the Ulster Scots (among others), who then carried their cultural norms throughout the South and into the West.[3]

A second qualification is that the argument-based homicide differences that Nisbett and colleagues found are even greater in small towns than in big cities. This "small-town effect" might surprise you, especially if you think of big cities as hotbeds of homicidal rage. After all, many people in small towns don't even lock their doors at night, whereas people in big cities can't seem to put enough locks on their doors. How, then, could small towns be a bigger problem than big cities when it comes to homicide rates?

The answer has to do with what else is true about small towns. To put it simply, in a small town, *everyone knows your name, and everyone knows your shame*. If you score the winning touchdown, everyone praises you everywhere you go in a small town. But the converse is also true. If you let down the team, or if you get "called out" by a rival and fail to "show up," or if you show up but you can't stand your ground, then everyone knows that, too, everywhere you

---

3. Other demographic groups also typically adhere to honor norms, such as Hispanics/Latinos.

go. Thus, the honor-related dynamics that feed the cycle of one-upmanship that can lead to violence can actually be magnified in small towns, where the consequences of both honor and dishonor are often greater than they are in big cities. In a big city, a person can usually find ways to blend into the sea of humanity and disappear. The small-town effect offers powerful support to the idea that honor plays a major role in motivating argument-based homicides.[4]

Let's Get Personal

A comparison of regional differences in homicide rates is all fine and good, but it leaves a lot to be desired, despite the important nuances concerning racial demographics and the small-town effect just described, both of which help to support the culture-of-honor hypothesis. As impressive as statistics on real-world violence are, a closer look at behaviors enacted by individual people under controlled conditions would be even more impressive, especially if you are a social scientist and you know how many ways those state-level analyses can wind up being misleading. Yes, there's nothing better than a nice, controlled experiment to convince a social scientist of the truth of an idea. How, though, could anyone create an argument that leads to homicide in the lab?

Actually, no one would propose that we try to create that kind of argument in the lab, nor would anyone be able to endanger participants in a laboratory study by permitting them to harm each other (although a few social scientists got closer to doing just that than they meant to get, as we will see shortly). Ethical limitations prevent us from creating situations in which participants get to punch each other in our studies, but we can still find evidence of a *readiness* to beat up someone, if we know what to look for. Finding clever ways to look for evidence of what people are thinking, how

---

4. Additional data show that the proportion of a county's populace born in the U.S. South is predictive of the argument-related homicide rate in that county. Furthermore, this proportion–Southern-born demographic variable is even predictive of white homicide rates in non-Southern counties, demonstrating that Southern whites who migrate to other regions of the United States could potentially raise the violence quotient in their new communities. See Lee and colleagues (2007).

they are feeling, and what they are prepared to do is, in fact, the specialty of the social psychologist.

Once again, we turn to the work of Dov Cohen, one of the pioneers of scientific studies on the culture of honor. Along with Richard Nisbett, Brian Bowdle, and Norbert Schwarz, Cohen created a situation in which Northern and Southern men—all of them college students—would be insulted by a stranger (Cohen et al., 1996). Across three studies, unsuspecting guys were insulted by a "confederate" (someone working secretly with the experimenters, but seemingly just a random person) who bumped into them as they walked down a narrow hallway and then called them an asshole. The researchers found several important differences between how the Southern and Northern males responded to this insult. If you've never heard of these studies, you might not believe how deep the differences went.

First, Northern guys were more likely to find the incident with the insulting confederate somewhat amusing. For the Southern guys, there was nothing funny about being insulted by a stranger, and they became angry and hostile as a result. This difference appeared to be a result of the fact that the Southerners were more likely than the Northerners to interpret the insult as a fundamental threat to their masculinity, as revealed by participants on a survey they completed shortly after the insult occurred. Second, the Southerners showed *physiological* signs of greater stress (increased levels of cortisol, a stress hormone) and readiness for aggression (higher testosterone levels). It should be noted that, before the insult occurred, levels of cortisol and testosterone did *not* differ between Northerners and Southerners; it was only *after* the insult that this difference emerged. Thus, Southerners were more likely to feel stressed out by the insult (because it threatened their masculinity) and were more ready physiologically to respond aggressively (to restore their masculinity).

Third, Southern participants who had been insulted were more likely to engage in actual behavioral displays of aggressive masculinity. For example, in one study, participants encountered a large male (another confederate, but not the same one who delivered the earlier insult) walking toward them down a very narrow hallway. For the confederate and participant to pass each other, the participant had to give way to the other, much larger man. This situation, as you might realize, is essentially a game of "chicken"—that wonderful game of "who has more guts" that has played out on countless playgrounds, alleyways, sidewalks, and roads throughout history. The glory that accompanies evidence of guts in this game accrues to the one who stands his ground the longest, giving way only at the last possible second, if at all. In this laboratory study, of course, giving way was never really a question. Two objects cannot occupy the same space at the same time, and the bigger object in this instance was most definitely *not* the participant—it was the linebacker heading toward him down that annoyingly narrow hallway. So, what did participants do?

They did exactly what their cultures had programmed them to do, of course. In the absence of an insult, the Southern men politely gave way to the confederate (sooner, in fact, than did the Northerners). "Oh, please, after you, sir." However, *after* an insult, the Southern men waited significantly *longer* to give way to the confederate. They played the game of chicken right up until the end, when the laws of physics dictated they just had to give way. But, by that point, all was well. They had shown that they had *cojones*. They were men again. Their honor had been challenged before, but now it was more or less restored. They had proved their mettle.[5]

There are a few findings from these studies that deserve to be highlighted. One is that men from honor cultures are not *generally* more aggressive, hostile, or dominant than are other men. If they weren't insulted to begin with, Southerners were actually *more polite* than Northerners were. However, Southerners were more likely to perceive the stranger's insult as a personal threat to their masculinity, and they were more inclined to restore their masculinity by way of aggressive and dominant displays. Taken together, these findings reinforce the idea that in cultures of honor, (1) the defense of masculine identity is a particularly important concern, (2) men are hypersensitive to threats to their masculinity,

---

5. Other behaviors were also assessed in these studies, including the firmness of the participant's handshake and the dominance of the participant's behavior during an interview. Time after time, Southern subjects were *not* especially aggressive or dominant in the absence of an insult, but were extremely so *after* an insult.

and (3) these threats can provoke extreme reactions designed to restore a man's honor.

Another remarkable laboratory study was conducted a few years later by Dov Cohen and another set of collaborators. This study examined patterns of *conflict escalation* among Southern and Northern males (Cohen et al., 1999). Cohen and his colleagues sought to compare the reactions of culture-of-honor and nonculture-of-honor men after relatively minor social irritations, rather than overt, in-your-face insults (like the terribly impolite name flung by the stranger in the prior studies). The researchers also wanted to investigate differences in how people tended to resolve their social conflicts. Participants were told they were going to take part in an "art therapy session" to examine the possible soothing effects of drawing. During the course of the study, a confederate (posing as another participant) was instructed to deliver a series of 11 "annoyances" to the real participant, including throwing crumpled wads of paper at him and calling him a somewhat patronizing nickname ("Slick"). The researchers anticipated that Southern men would become more annoyed and would be more confrontational than Northern men would. This expectation was in keeping with previous studies on how men from honor cultures respond to insults. However, the intensity of the actual responses surprised them. Indeed, despite taking multiple precautions, Cohen and colleagues reported that several Southern participants actually managed to make *physical contact* with the annoying confederate in this study!

The general findings of the study were these: Northern participants expressed their irritation *in stages*, sending a clear signal of their growing annoyance to the obnoxious confederate. For the most part, though, they did not actually retaliate. After about the fifth annoyance, Northern participants' irritation and risk of confrontation leveled off and did not escalate further. The researchers inferred that the Northerners chose to ignore the confederate at this point, convinced that any further confrontation would be about as useful as spitting into a headwind. In stark contrast, Southerners initially withstood the repeated provocations with stoicism and an apparent lack of concern, giving *no signs at all* of their increasing ire. However, after a threshold of disrespect was crossed (again, at around the fifth annoyance), Southerners went ballistic. Their reactions were *so extreme*, in fact, the researchers decided the study should be shut down. The goal, after all, was to study the *precursors* of murder, not to produce an *actual* murder in the lab.

This study illustrates how confrontations unfold in cultures of honor. Cohen and colleagues (1999) suggest that politeness norms can explain the initial stoicism of Southerners in their study, and this is no doubt part of the reason for what they found. From their perspective, one of the main reasons that Southerners tend to be so polite is that this helps to prevent or smooth over minor offenses before they become overt conflicts that can turn violent.

Another aspect of the Southern–Northern difference, however, might be that Northerners were *avoiding* a physical altercation by expressing their anger and providing fair warning to the confederate. Anger serves as a social signal to others, often discouraging further provocation in the real world. So, ironically, the Southerners' lack of an initial emotional reaction might have *invited* the escalation of the situation by hiding warning signals to the aggressor that he had crossed a line and an altercation was imminent. This initial concealment of negative emotions deprived the confederate of a chance to stop his irritating behavior and avoid a fight, and it made the surprising attack that frequently followed all the more effective and intimidating. If this interpretation is correct, it puts politeness in a whole new light, doesn't it? This "paradox of politeness," as Cohen and colleagues called it, might help to explain why, in the North, cities that had previously been rated as very courteous were also cities that exhibited relatively low rates of argument-based homicides, whereas in the South, this wasn't the case. In fact, as Cohen and his fellow researchers showed, Southern cities high in courteousness actually have slightly *higher* rates of argument-based homicides compared to Southern cities that were ranked relatively low in courteousness.

Nisbett's and Cohen's seminal research during the 1990s focused on adult violence, as do most other studies on the culture of honor, but retaliatory violence is also greater among children and adolescents in honor states. Recently, Lindsey Osterman, Collin Barnes, and I decided to examine regional differences in school violence (Brown et al., 2009). Consistent with Nisbett and Cohen's findings with adults, we found that school shootings in the United States are also more common in honor states. Specifically, during a 20-year period (1988–2008), 108 prototypical school shootings occurred in the United States, according to our investigation, and of those, 75% occurred in honor states, despite the fact that these states account for just about 55% of the U.S. population. Likewise, we also found that high school students living in honor states were more likely to report having brought a weapon to school during the past month compared with students living in nonhonor states. When you live in an honor state, it's good to come prepared.

Subsequently, Lindsey Osterman and I obtained data from the Bureau of Alcohol, Tobacco, and Firearms (the ATF), which has a Bomb Arson Tracking System that tracks attempted and success-ful school bombings.[6] The good news is that most of these bombs are made by kids who don't know what they're doing (turns out there is a silver lining to the mediocre science education many kids receive these days). As a result, they either get caught before the bombs go off, or they attempt to detonate the bombs, which end up fizzling. The bad news is that *kids are making bombs and trying to explode them at school.* Every silver lining has its cloud.

What we found in our examination of these school bombings tracked by the ATF was consistent with what we had found previously with school shootings. Of 208 attempted or thwarted school bombings reported to the ATF between 2005 and 2010, 147 of them (or 71%) occurred in honor states. Clearly, violence in honor states is not restricted to adults, nor can it be blamed simply on better access to guns in honor states. Past studies have suggested that school violence is often precipitated by rejection and bullying (Leary et al., 2003; Newman et al., 2005). Because social rejection and bullying are forms of reputation threats, school shootings (and bombings) might represent extreme attempts to restore reputation in cultures of honor.[7]

In the Preface, I noted that our analysis of school shootings involved both location and time of year, but so far I've talked about

---

6. We are grateful to the ATF for providing these data on request for our analysis.

7. It's probably also worth noting that surveys show parents in honor states are more likely to believe their children should *fight* bullies rather than reason with them. This is not to suggest that these parents would endorse such extreme forms of school violence as mass murder, but rather that the pervasive cultural scripts that support aggressive retaliation for honor threats might reveal themselves in the behavior of children, just as they do in the behavior of adults (Cohen & Nisbett, 1994).

the location variable only. When we examined which months were the most dangerous for these admittedly rare events, we found an interesting pattern in the data. It appears there are three months in the year when school shooting rates are elevated, particularly if we adjust the counts for the number of days in a month.[8] Two of them are not all that surprising—December and May, the months when most students have to endure the stressful ordeal of final exams, and when they are most likely to be faced with the prospect of having failed one or more classes. The elevated risk that we see in these two months makes sense. But the other elevated-risk month might be less obvious. This month exhibited the greatest number of school shootings of any month of the year, both in terms of raw counts and adjusted counts: February. From an academic perspective, February is not a particularly special month in the life of a student. For college students, at least, there might be a first round of exams during this month, but this also tends to be true in September (for schools that start in August) or October (for schools that start in September). So why February?

We surmised that what makes February "special," leading to its elevated risk for school violence, has nothing to do with the school calendar, but rather with the national calendar. February is the month when we celebrate Valentine's Day. This day is supposed to be a celebration of romance and relationships, but for those who don't have a romantic partner, or whose true love has recently "dumped" them, Valentine's Day is like lemon juice in a paper cut. Perhaps especially for a boy, romantic rejection can strike at the heart of his sense of value as a man, which is so often encapsulated in whether he is recognized as having social status by members of

---

8. Making adjustments to these shooting counts can get very tricky very quickly. For instance, how many days are students typically in school in December and May? The answer depends, in part, on whether we're talking about students in primary school, secondary school, or college, which can vary greatly in the number of typical school days in these months (not to mention whether college students are on the quarter system or the semester system). Likewise, how long do most schools provide vacation days for Thanksgiving? Some schools give a full week, whereas others give only a half week. For our analysis, we adjusted each month for its naturally occurring number of days, except for November (which got 27 days) and December and May, which we gave an average of 21 days. In doing so, we found that December and May tied at second place for the greatest number of school shootings at 14.3. February came in first place at 18.2 shootings.

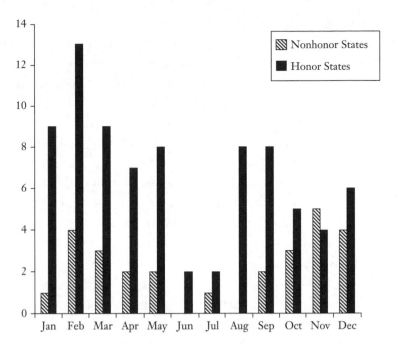

FIGURE 2.1 School shootings by month and state type (not adjusted for number of school days in the month).

the opposite sex. For this reason, we suspect, the month of February appears to be a more dangerous month than either January or March (or almost any other month) for school violence. What is especially remarkable, though, and consistent with an honor-based interpretation, is that this elevated risk in February is restricted to honor states, as shown in Figure 2.1 (the counts shown in Figure 2.1 are raw counts, not adjusted for the number of days in a month).

Honor and the Law

The attitudes and behaviors of individuals living in honor cultures are not the only things that reflect the beliefs and values of the honor syndrome. Even the penal code can do so. As Dov Cohen demonstrated in a series of studies back in the mid 1990s, laws related to homicide are more permissive in honor states, under certain honor-related circumstances. When a man kills to defend his person, family, or property, or to defend his honor, he is more likely to receive a reduced sentence in honor states compared with men committing the same types of crimes in nonhonor states (Cohen, 1996). Specifically, "hot-blooded" murders, such as the shooting of an intruder or a man found in bed with one's wife, are more likely to be acquitted or to result in less jail time in honor states. Such reduced sentences and the laws that enable them show that "we understand" in honor states when someone kills to defend honor. We won't necessarily waive it off with a wink and a nod—we aren't completely lawless, after all—but we'll do as much as we can to demonstrate our commitment to our shared honor values. In our hearts, we *know* that such killings aren't completely bad. We know that if we found ourselves in similar circumstances, we might kill as well, and our social and institutional norms—including our legal systems—reflect that shared understanding.

Of course, there's one aspect of life in an honor culture that makes it much easier to kill than it would otherwise be. I am referring here to the ease with which people in honor states can get their hands on guns. Analyses by Cohen (1996) have shown that gun control legislation is more permissive in honor states than it is in nonhonor states, just as penalties for honor-related violence are. In a recent study, Mikiko Imura, Lindsey Osterman, and I (Brown et al., 2014c) examined how easily people living in honor states can get their hands on a gun. According to national surveys, about 38% of American households report having a gun in the home.[9] However, statewide rates of gun ownership vary widely, from a low of around 9% in Hawaii to a high of more than 61% in Wyoming. Overall, our analyses showed that honor states have significantly more gun owners than do nonhonor states—21% more, to be exact. And this household gun ownership gap gets even bigger if we look only at non-Hispanic white households, among whom the honor-state average is actually 30% higher than it is in nonhonor states.

One last note about guns and violence in honor states is worth mentioning. In the wake of the notorious shooting in 2012 of unarmed teenager Trayvon Martin by George Zimmerman in Sanford, Florida, social scientists have examined the impact of

---

9. This estimate is based on a nationally representative survey conducted in 2001 by the Centers for Disease Control and Prevention as part of their Behavioral Risk Factor Surveillance System.

the now-infamous stand-your-ground laws that a number of states have put in place. These laws extend the so-called "castle doctrine"—the notion that a person's home is his or her castle, where intruders can be rebuffed by any means necessary, including deadly force—to any place where a person has a legal right to be. Thus, these laws free citizens from the legal necessity of retreating when they feel their lives are at risk. They are allowed, instead, to stand their ground.

Between 2004 and 2011, 18 states enacted some type of stand-your-ground law, although the details varied a bit from state to state. Utah already had such a law in place. Of the 19 states in the United States with stand-your-ground laws on the books at the time of this writing, 14 of these (74%) are honor states. More important, studies show that, after these laws are put into place, the homicide rate *increases* (Cheng & Hoekstra, 2012; McClellan & Tekin, 2012). So much for deterrence. One of these studies, by Chandler McClellan and Erdal Tekin of the University of Georgia, is particularly noteworthy because it examines the impact of stand-your-ground laws by race and gender. Their analysis revealed that, after states have enacted such laws, the homicide rate has historically increased, but *only among white males*. There is no evidence of an increase among black males. Although McClellan and Tekin did not discuss the consistency of this finding with other research on the culture of honor, the fit is nonetheless remarkable. When white men in honor states are allowed by law not to back down when threatened, they don't. This legal allowance reflects and reinforces the social *expectation* not to back down when you feel your honor is being threatened. Is anyone really surprised that in such an environment, more people are killed?

Gun laws are more permissive in honor states than they are in nonhonor states, which helps to explain why more people living in honor states own guns. This legal permissiveness coincides with the views of those living in honor states regarding the justifiability of lethal force in protecting one's family, one's property, and one's person. Legislative sympathy toward defense-related violence thus seems to be an extension of the cultural expectation that family patriarchs, in particular, should be willing, able, and equipped to defend their own families without having to rely on legal authorities to take care of matters. And when that pivotal moment comes, when a man is challenged by another man, or when his interests are otherwise threatened, he is allowed to stand his ground. Indeed, his culture tells him that he is *expected* to stand his ground, whatever else the law might say. To do otherwise is to be seen as a coward, which is about the worst thing a man can be called in an honor culture.

Consistent with these legal manifestations of honor culture beliefs and values, there is a wealth of diverse data at state, region, and individual levels suggesting that cultures of honor promote specific types of violence. Legislation coincides with personal attitudes regarding defense-related violence, and defense-related violence is more prevalent in parts of the United States that are heavily influenced by honor-related beliefs and values. But it is worth emphasizing the qualification that I have, by now, made several times over: the *types* of violent behaviors and attitudes that are more prevalent in cultures of honor are related to *defense* and *reputation*. Only in response to honor-related threats is violence endorsed explicitly by people living in honor cultures. Absent such threats, people in honor cultures are often courteous and hospitable. We say, "Yes, ma'am," and "Pardon me," and "Bless your heart." We smile, we nod in polite acknowledgment, and we show great deference to one another. We can be as sweet as molasses. Be careful, though. If you cross us the wrong way, we might just kill you.

Discussion Questions

1. This chapter discussed the essence of a social script. What are some social scripts you have encountered that might either enhance or inhibit people's likelihood of engaging in aggression?
2. If you were trying to come up with a set of metrics to put together to rank the 50 U.S. states in terms of their honor orientations, what metrics would you use? See if your answer to this question differs by the time you finish reading this book!

3. What sorts of problems or limitations might come with even a nuanced ranking of honor states and nonhonor states? What sorts of methods might you use to try to overcome some of these problems and limitations?
4. The "paradox of politeness," as Dov Cohen and his colleagues (1999) called it, is a remarkable feature of Southern life. How else might this paradox manifest itself in daily life? In business? In politics?

For Further Reading

Brown, R. P., L. L. Osterman, and C. D. Barnes. 2009. School violence and the culture of honor. *Psychological Science* 20:1400–1405.

Cohen, D., and R. E. Nisbett. 1994. Self-protection and the culture of honor: Explaining southern violence. *Personality and Social Psychology Bulletin* 20:551–567.

Cohen, D., R. E. Nisbett, B. F. Bowdle, and N. Schwarz. 1996. Insult, aggression, and the southern culture of honor: An "experimental ethnography." *Journal of Personality and Social Psychology* 70:945–960.

Chapter Three

Boys to Men, and the Women Who Love Them

T HE MAN SITTING ACROSS the table from me at the quaint Mexican restaurant weighed, I guessed, about 375 lb. I'm pretty good with numbers, although I figured that I might easily be off by 50 lb in either direction. With someone that size, it's hard to estimate with any accuracy. I was silently praying that our food would come soon, because that would give us something to talk about. This was only the second time we had met, and we had very little in common, except that we both loved his daughter.

As the waiter brought out our food on platters twice the size of my head, I breathed a quiet sigh of relief at the helpful distraction, but my relief was to be short-lived because our meal did not rescue me from my discomfort. This man—Thomas was his name—was toying with me the way a tiger toys with a rodent before biting its head off. He was enjoying my suffering, and he was about to intensify it substantially.

"Have I ever told you about my cousin Lilly?" he asked, taking a large bite of chalupa as he did so. Thomas had never told me about his cousin. What does "ever" even mean the second time you meet someone? It turned out that the story of his cousin would have been a strange thing to have talked about.

"No, I don't think you did. I love that name, though. I've often thought about using that name if I ever have a daughter." No response to that comment. He just kept chewing. I wondered if my indirect reference to procreation, a requisite to having a daughter that one could consider naming Lilly, was really the best idea at this moment. A small bead of sweat began to form at the end of my nose. Did anyone else realize how warm it was in the room? My enchiladas needed salt, I thought, but it was possible I had just temporarily lost the ability to taste. I couldn't be sure.

The mariachi band had started to sing again, just a few tables from where we sat. Their enthusiasm for an old woman's birthday forced me to lean forward to hear Thomas's story. He wiped both hands on the two napkins he had spread across his voluminous lap, so I knew he was about to continue.

"Lilly is my youngest cousin. She was always beautiful, so she never knew a lonely Saturday night." I grinned knowingly. Too knowingly? Dial it back, Brown. I was walking a tightrope here, stretched across a large, deep canyon. You can't walk too fast or too slow on a tightrope; either error could be the end of you.

He continued, "Lilly got married young, and I was never very fond of her husband. I couldn't have told you why. He just didn't feel right. Several years later, I learned why." At this point, he paused, as if waiting for me to ask what he had learned.

"Why was that?" I asked obligingly.

"One night, Lilly showed up at my sister's house with a black eye, a swollen lip, and a broken wrist," he answered, pausing again and staring at me intently. He took another bite of chalupa and, after swallowing, wiped his mouth slowly with one of his napkins before going on. This man was a master of the pregnant pause. "After my sister called me and told me what Lilly told her, some of the cousins and I got our baseball bats and some ski masks and paid her husband a visit." He paused again to let the implication sink in. "He had to go away for a while after that."

The mariachi band was circling now, like a pack of wolves around a wounded calf. Please, God, don't let them sing! I needed to think. How should I respond to this story? I had no schema for this, no precedent on which I could draw for wisdom. There was a reason he was telling me this story, and I needed to figure it out quickly.

"The reason I'm telling you this story," he said, leaning in as much as his rotund belly would allow, "Is simply this. If you ever hurt my daughter, I've still got my bat in the back of my truck." He leaned back in his chair then, and I worried, but half hoped, that it would break, which might allow me to dart out the back door unnoticed.

If I lacked a precedent before, I was really at a loss now. I reached into the depths of my soul, trying to imagine having a daughter and facing off with a 22-year-old boy who naively believed he was her equal. "I can respect that," I said. It was all I could come up with. I thought about adding "sir" to the end of my affirmation, but I worried I would sound like a kiss-up. Looking down at my plate, I realized that somewhere during my future father-in-law's tale, I had ground my entrée into a pile of goo with my fork. Hoping that my handiwork might not have caught his attention, I coolly scooped up a mound of the remains and shoved it into my mouth. "Great enchiladas!" I proclaimed authoritatively. I should have finished chewing first.

"She's so pretty. She's like an Egyptian princess, Dad!" So said my son, just six years old when he made this exclamation of adoration. The "she" he was talking about was his violin teacher, Maria, and she was, indeed, striking. She had the dark and exotic features reminiscent of a Catherine Zeta-Jones, or a Mila Kunis, except that she was barely 5 ft 2 in. (in heels). Of course, to a six-year-old, 5 ft 2 in. is towering, so her petite stature failed to register with my son. He just thought she was the bomb.

My son was as disappointed and disconcerted as my wife and I when Maria had to stop my son's lessons for a while because of a medical emergency. Finding a great music teacher who can really connect with a young child, perhaps especially a young boy, can be more than a little challenging, so we were desperately hoping we would be able to continue lessons with Maria. A mutual friend later told us that Maria had broken her jaw and was laid up for weeks in recovery, sipping soup through a tiny straw. We never asked *how* she broke her jaw. We just knew that we had to take a hiatus from violin lessons for a little while. Eventually, she was back in the saddle, and our lessons resumed as if nothing had ever happened. Being one of the most sociable people I know, my wife always made a point to speak with Maria after lessons, and a casual but genuine friendship slowly grew between them.

About a year after Maria's unexpected hospitalization, my wife called me at work. She was very upset. Her tone was not frantic exactly, but as soon as she started talking I knew that I needed to turn away from my e-mail and give her both halves of my brain. I could feel the blood in my face first leave and then return in a rush as my wife recounted how Maria had called her in a tearful panic. She needed help. Her husband, Ted, who had recently returned from his second deployment in Iraq, had thrown her against a wall like a rag doll and choked her, threatening to do worse. As soon as she was able, she had fled their small apartment and gone to the most public place she could find across town. That was when she had called my wife.

As we soon learned, Maria had found out about Ted's "indiscretions" with another woman and had confronted him about it. This was not the first time he had cheated on her, either. The first time she discovered his affair, she had also confronted him, and their ensuing fight ended with her in the hospital—with a broken jaw. After this first attack, he had promised to reform and to be faithful to her, and she had agreed to take him back. Perhaps her forbearance was driven by her fear of his rage. Perhaps it was more genuine than that. In any case, Ted's promises of eternal fidelity fell a little short of forever, and this time she wasn't going to look the other way. But would she survive her new-found resolve?

The events in these stories happened almost 20 years apart, and although the first story is mildly humorous in hindsight, the common denominator isn't funny at all. In fact, it's one of the least funny subjects imaginable. According to the U.S. Department of Justice, domestic violence is a reality suffered by about 25% of American women at some point in their lifetime, and approximately 1.5 million women in the United States are raped or physically assaulted each year by their current or former romantic partners (Tjaden and Thoennes, 2000). In addition, approximately a half-million women each year are stalked in the United States by a current or former romantic partner. These are just estimates, however, because no one really knows exactly how prevalent domestic violence is. Like child abuse, domestic violence (or "intimate partner violence," as it is often called) is a crime that occurs mostly behind locked doors, where prying eyes cannot peer.

Victims of domestic violence can be men or women, but they seem to be women much more often than men, and when men are the perpetrators, the consequences are typically much more severe.[1] Women who are victims sometimes make excuses for their partner's behavior, if he is, in fact, a current partner (many victims of domestic violence are attacked by ex-husbands or ex-boyfriends). "He really does love me. He gets so jealous sometimes, that's all." Or, "He has such a short fuse these days, with all the stress at work. I just need to be more supportive while he works through a few things." The narrative details might differ from case to case, but the excuse-making itself is all too common. For those of us who are not victims of abuse, such rationalizations might be puzzling. Why would anyone put up with such mistreatment, much less *make excuses* for it, we wonder?

And yet, we all make excuses for our partners and loved ones, don't we? Isn't this part of what makes relationships "work"? We overlook or downplay our partner's faults, and we "accentuate the positive," as the old song goes. Research even suggests that happy relationships are those in which partners exhibit such "positive illusions," including the belief that the relationship itself is getting better and better over time, despite the fact that it really isn't. It's only when the little illusion grows into a grand delusion that this formula goes bad, as is the case when one partner abuses the other. A carefully crafted story, though, can cover up an act of abuse, just like a heavy coat of makeup can cover a black eye. The trick is in the application.

Culture and Definitions of Masculinity and Femininity

What does it mean to be "a real man"? What would it mean to be "a real woman?" Have you ever asked yourself either of these

---

1. One review of the evidence suggests that, although men and women engage in various forms of physical aggression at roughly the same frequency in relationships, when men are the perpetrators of domestic violence, the consequences tend to be much worse (Archer 2000).

questions? My guess is that the first question might have occurred to you or have even been posed to you at some point, but probably not the second question. That question is more likely to sound weird if you say it out loud. Try it. "Are you a real woman?"

One of my favorite movies is *Lars and the Real Girl*, starring Ryan Gosling in the title role (as Lars, not the real girl). Lars is a young man with an attachment problem. Having suffered through the loss of both of his parents, he struggles to get close to anyone, especially women. That's why, after a coworker mentions that it is possible to buy a life-sized, anatomically correct woman (in actuality, a sex doll, although sex does not appear to be foremost on Lars's mind), Lars decides that he should buy himself a girlfriend. So he does. Awkward hilarity ensues as Lars pushes her around his small town in a wheelchair (she got a disease in the tropics that has left her paralyzed, he explains). He seems caught in a delusion that she is a real person who is in love with him, and the people in his life who truly do love him go to great lengths to oblige his delusion.

There is a touching scene in which Lars asks his brother (the only living person to whom he feels somewhat close) how he knew he had become a man. "Was it, you know, the sex thing?" he inquires, as his brother nervously folds his laundry. Although denying that "it" had anything to do with "the sex thing," his brother struggles to articulate when it was that he knew he had become a man, or what it was that had made him so. How *did* he know he was a man? The scene is awkward on several levels, in part because his inability to answer this question seems to trouble Lars's brother more than a little.

For a time, all men are boys, until they grow up. Periodically, magazine articles complain about the extended adolescence that today's American men seem to be enjoying, to the chagrin of their parents (with whom they most likely live). To some, this might suggest that a number of today's American men are not actually men at all. They are just tall boys with facial hair and lots of credit card debt. This is not how things are supposed to be, we know in our heart of hearts. Boys are supposed to become men. They are supposed to grow up and make that magical transition. But *how*? How does one turn into *a real man*, and how does a boy know when this transition has happened? Lars is not the only one who wants to know the answer, is he?

Cultures throughout time, all around the world, have provided answers to this important question. Typically, the answer has involved painful, difficult rituals—"rites of passage," as they are often called. A boy becomes a man when he can hunt, making his first kill all by himself. A boy becomes a man when he has slain a member of a warring tribe, counting coup on his enemy. A boy becomes a man when he can endure the ritually inflicted knife wounds of his tribesmen without crying out. The details of the rituals vary, but the common threads are that these rites of passage involve public displays of strength, bravery, toughness, and resilience. The *social* proof is key. You can't just *claim* to be a real man; the title must be bestowed upon you by others. A man is a man only if others say he is. For Christmas one year, a relative gave me a drink coaster that said, "The truest measure of a man is how tall he stands in the eyes of his family." I'm still not sure what this person was trying to communicate with this gift. Was it an affirmation or a subtle denunciation of my standing in her eyes? In either case, this slogan underscores the point that manhood is measured socially, and some biological males can be found wanting.

When the title of "manhood" has been earned, it can, unfortunately, be lost again. That is the nature of things that must be earned, isn't it? A man can be socially demoted through acts of cowardice or weakness, which nullify the acts that originally proved his manhood. Thus, real men shun all signs of cowardice and weakness. That's why if someone dares you to do something, guys know they have to do it, no matter how dumb it might be. Not to do it might be interpreted to mean you are afraid, that you are a coward. Your male peers will then call you a girl, a wimp, or a variety of more focused epithets related to female body parts (I'll have more to say on this subject in Chapter 9). Real men can't stand to be associated with femininity. Real men don't wear lace. They don't carry purses, nor do they feel comfortable holding them for their girlfriends or wives, even momentarily. Real men don't eat quiche.[2] Real men know these things and they follow the code.

---

2. Believe it or not, there is actually a study on this one: Gal and Wilkie (2010).

What about "real women"? What does it take for a girl to transition to a woman, and how does she know when she has crossed over from one to the other? Unlike manhood, womanhood worldwide is defined not socially, but *biologically*. A girl becomes a woman when she begins to menstruate, signaling that her body is preparing itself to bear children. When that happens, she is separated from the boys of her childhood and is given new responsibilities and new restrictions, but no one asks whether she is "a real woman." To be a woman is to be a real woman. One of the only ways that her status as "real" might ever come into question is if she is never able to conceive. In that case, the biological basis of her womanhood might be questioned.

Through advances in modern medicine, we seem to have created a new threat to womanhood: the mastectomy. When a woman develops breast cancer, one of the ways that doctors try to keep it from spreading is to remove the cancerous breast. Sometimes this is done to both breasts. And, more recently, with the advent of genetic tests that can indicate whether a woman is *likely* to develop breast cancer at some point, the practice of *preemptive* breast removal is occurring. When she learned she shared her mother's genotype, actress Angelina Jolie made headlines for taking this radical step against the disease that claimed the life of her mother. Women who have mastectomies typically report that the experience is nothing short of traumatic, as if a key part of their womanhood is being stolen from them. Sympathetic as I am to this sense of loss, I can't help associating this experience with women of ancient times whose sense of womanhood was undermined by their infertility (or presumed infertility—no one seems to have ever questioned the fertility of the men involved). We seem unable to escape the belief that womanhood is fundamentally about biology, about the physical body, no matter how modern we think we are.

In this way, womanhood differs from manhood. Manhood is not about *biological* proof so much as *social* proof. Nature cannot bestow the status of manhood on a boy the way it does womanhood on a girl. Society, not nature, decides that a boy has become a man. This fundamental difference sets the stage for cultural beliefs and values to enter into the picture, to establish the rules for what it takes to prove one's manhood. Culture provides the details for the rituals—the schemas and scripts—that must be followed for the social status of manhood to be conferred on a boy (see Vandello et al., 2008).

Part of the essence of the honor syndrome lies in how it defines what it means to be a man or a woman of worth.

In Chapter 2, I described how honor cultures promote aggression through creating schemas and scripts that people learn and internalize. By faithfully following a rule that says, "If someone insults you, you'd better be prepared to fight," you might avoid being seen as a target for exploitation. Other people will think twice before "calling you out" just to build their own credentials as "tough guys" or to try to dominate you and take what is yours. If you don't follow this script, your reputation is likely to take a serious hit, assuming that others view your nonaggressive reactions as an indication that you are afraid or weak.

In the same way, honor cultures teach the schemas and scripts that define what it means to be "a real man" and "a good woman." Real men in honor cultures are tough and strong and intolerant of disrespect. They build and promote their reputations on these qualities, and they defend them at all costs. Good women are faithful and loyal to their families and spouses above all, and they are careful to protect their virtue. If necessary, they call on the men in their lives (husbands, brothers, fathers, or cousins, if need be) to follow the masculine honor scripts for aggression to defend their feminine reputations for purity and loyalty when threatened.

The next twist in this story is that these same social schemas and scripts teach women who are in abusive relationships to remain loyal, to "stand by their man," as the old Tammy Wynette song goes, as long as that abuse can be construed as somehow fitting the honor code—in other words, if their man's violence is seen as part of his own conformity to this code. How would the honor syndrome lead a man to behave violently toward his romantic partner? Isn't such behavior seen as dishonorable? The answer, it seems, is no—not if his violent behavior springs from jealousy or because he senses that another man might be threatening the integrity of his home through the fidelity of his woman. A man's worth and his woman's sexual fidelity and purity are intimately intertwined in honor cultures. As the old Arab proverb puts it, "A man's honor lies between the legs of a woman."

To demonstrate this link between men's honor and women's faithfulness, Joseph Vandello and Dov Cohen (2003) conducted an experiment in which they staged a fight between an engaged couple in a waiting room. During the fight, a man and woman, posing as participants for a psychology study (in actuality, actors), got into an argument that ended with a physical altercation. The disagreement began when the woman indicated she needed to "go over to John's" house after the study was over so she "could pick up a few things." John, it turns out, was her ex-boyfriend. This news did not go over well with her fiancé, who grabbed her wrist and violently stripped her car keys from her hand. When she attempted to take her keys back, things really heated up. The young man shoved her against the wall, pinning her there, and made it clear that she was not to go over to her ex's house. After asserting that he would see her at home, he stormed off, her car keys still in his possession. All the while, the *real* participant (not an actor) was sitting on the other side of the room about 15 ft away, in earshot and in full view of the entire affair.

Composing herself, the woman came and sat down next to the real participant and began a carefully scripted interaction. This is where the experiment diverged for different participants, depending on what condition of the study they had been randomly assigned to experience. To some participants, the young woman was contrite and demure, making excuses for her fiancé's behavior, saying, "He gets so jealous sometimes. I guess it was kind of my fault, huh?" and "He really cares about me. I guess that's just how he shows it, you know?" To other participants, the woman behaved in the exact opposite manner, showing anger rather than submissiveness, asserting her intentions to "give him his keys *and his ring* back." The question the researchers wanted to answer with this study concerned how participants would feel about this woman when they later got the chance to evaluate her. Would they have more respect for the contrite or the assertive woman, and would their reaction to her depend on whether they themselves came from an honor state or a nonhonor state?

The researchers found several pieces of evidence that people from honor states (1) were more tolerant of the abuse and (2) appreciated the contrite victim more than the assertive one. First, people from honor states were more likely to verbalize their tolerance for the abuse than were people from nonhonor states. This tolerance showed up in their words to the woman after she sat down, as they affirmed the victim's self-blame, encouraged her to stay in the relationship and to try to work out their problems, and even suggested that jealousy can be a good thing. After all, a guy who doesn't get jealous couldn't *really* be in love, could he?

Second, when participants were later asked to give their impressions of the woman (under the guise of the study being about first impressions), participants from honor states had a more positive impression of the contrite victim than of the assertive one. Participants from nonhonor states showed the opposite pattern, reporting a more positive impression of the *assertive* woman than of the contrite one. In an honor culture, a woman who stays loyal in the face of jealousy-induced violence is considered strong and good. Outside of such cultures, a woman who stays in an abusive relationship, regardless of what is motivating the violence, is more likely to be seen as weak and troubled.

What these results suggest is that women such as my son's violin teacher, Maria, might be more likely to be encouraged by friends and family to stand by their abusive husbands or boyfriends if they live in honor regions or honor subcultures in the United States than if they live elsewhere. They might even feel socially stigmatized if they assert their right to live free of fear and violence by leaving their attackers. We know when the people around us approve or disapprove of our behavior. We "get the vibe" when others believe we aren't doing what they want or expect us to do, when we fall short of some cultural ideal. And as much as Americans love to think of themselves as courageously independent nonconformists, the reality is that no one—man or woman—is truly an island, free of concern for what others think. Concern over the opinions of other people is part of what makes us human. It's part of our DNA to be socially minded and, hence, socially concerned. So, we should not be at all surprised when victims of abuse who live in an honor culture stay with their abusers. They are simply following the social script given to them by the world around them.

But do these same social scripts actually increase the likelihood of male domestic violence? Anecdotal and survey evidence suggests this might be true, as do carefully controlled studies comparing the perceptions of people from prototypical honor societies with those of people from nonhonor societies. For instance, in one such study, researchers compared the responses of people from Chile (an honor culture) to the responses of people from Canada (a nonhonor culture) who listened to an audiotape of a man describing how he punched his wife in the face during a fight. More important, the fight was either about her spending too much money on clothes and makeup, or about his perception that she had been flirting with another man at a party (because this was an experiment, some people heard the first reason and other people heard the second). People from Chile were more accepting of his behavior and had more positive views of this man when his violence was based on jealousy than when it was about money, whereas Canadians showed no such pattern. Indeed, Chileans actually saw the guy as *a better husband* than Canadians if his violent reaction came in response to his wife's perceived flirtations, but not if it was in response to her spending habits (Vandello et al., 2009).

Powerful as these results are, one might still wonder whether honor-based values and beliefs would motivate such relationship violence among men in the United States. Although these studies clearly show that people from an honor culture differ in their views and responses to honor-related relationship violence (compared with people from nonhonor cultures), this does not indicate that honor *actually promotes greater relationship violence*. Is there any evidence for such a connection among American men? Unfortunately, there is.

The FBI's crime statistics, gathered from police reports all around the country, give us a tool for exploring whether violence toward women is greater in honor states than it is in nonhonor states. These data don't capture all crimes committed in every state, of course—only reported crimes. Furthermore, if what you want to know is *who* committed those crimes, these FBI data are limited even more by whether anyone *knows* who committed them. In many cases, we don't know the perpetrator of a crime. Still, these crime statistics can allow us to compare various crime rates across the country to determine whether there is any evidence of the sorts of differences we would expect based on what we know about regional difference in honor norms. As we've seen already with respect to regional differences in violence between men (such as in argument-related homicides), we should only expect to find

Table 3.1 RAPE AND DOMESTIC HOMICIDE RATES
(PER 100,000 RESIDENTS) AMONG WHITES IN HONOR STATES
AND NONHONOR STATES, ADJUSTED FOR STATEWIDE
CONTROL VARIABLES

RAPE		DOMESTIC HOMICIDE	
HONOR STATES	NONHONOR STATES	HONOR STATES	NONHONOR STATES
55.02	41.93	0.91	0.56

large regional differences among whites as a result of the immigration patterns that created regional differences in honor-based norms in the first place.

In a recent study, my fellow investigators and I looked at FBI rape data (more specifically, arrest rates for forcible rapes) for adult males from 2008-2009 across all 47 US states that report these crimes to the FBI (Brown et al., in review).[3] As always when making state-by-state comparisons, we also gathered data on things such as poverty, unemployment, church attendance, and other variables that tend to differ from one state to another across the United States to account for these sorts of regional distinctions. We then compared rape rates between honor states and nonhonor states, controlling for these other statewide differences, and we found a striking pattern. As shown in the left column of Table 3.1, average rape rates differed significantly between honor states and nonhonor states, controlling statistically for statewide differences in economics and the like. *But, these differences occurred only among whites.*[4]

In a follow-up study (Brown et al., in review), we took the same approach to investigate domestic homicide rates, again using FBI crime statistics to do so. By "domestic homicide," I mean murders of women committed by a husband, ex-husband, boyfriend, or ex-boyfriend. The "ex's" play an important role in domestic

---

3. Note that Florida, Illinois, and Minnesota do not report statewide incidences of rape to the FBI's Uniform Crime Reports, so data from these three states were not included in this analysis.
4. Rape rates among blacks—although generally greater, on average, than among whites—didn't differ significantly between honor states and nonhonor states, although if anything they were somewhat greater for blacks living in *nonhonor states*.

homicides, which comes as a surprise to many people. It would be comforting to believe that women who escape from unhealthy, abusive relationships are always safe, as if leaving a bad relationship is like entering your country's consulate in a foreign land. Sadly, such images don't reflect the reality faced by many women in abusive relationships, whose husbands or boyfriends know where they work and who their friends and family are. In some cases, these men even retain joint legal custody of children and thus are able to keep in contact with their victims. Even when women are able to escape to new cities or states, their abusers sometimes follow them, despite great efforts by women to hide their identity. There are few things more terrifying than being stalked by an angry former lover. There are few things more dangerous, too.[5]

The right column of Table 3.1 shows the average domestic homicide rates by white men in honor states and nonhonor states. These averages have been adjusted statistically for a host of other statewide differences. Consistent with what we see with rape rates, domestic homicide rates are substantially and significantly higher, on average, in honor states than in nonhonor states. This difference is even greater than the difference for rape rates. On average, white domestic homicide rates were more than *62% higher* in honor states compared to nonhonor states.

These state-by-state comparisons are important and informative, but as is always the case with such macrolevel analyses, we are forced to make a large leap from these data. We know honor states differ from nonhonor states in terms of both rape and domestic homicide rates, and we know these differences are not explainable in terms of obvious things such as poverty or rurality (because we can control for these variables statistically). But these differences might be the result of something that we missed, something not included in our models that nonetheless differs between honor states and nonhonor states, and that causes these higher rates of

---

5. Social scientists Martin Daly and Margo Wilson (in their 1988 book, *Homicide*) have noted that jealousy is one of the leading causes of homicide worldwide—across cultures. Such homicidal jealousy can be sparked by sexual infidelity during a relationship, but it can also result when one partner leaves the other. For women, there is no other factor that even comes close to leaving a lover as a risk factor for murder, other than infidelity.

violence toward women. It would be powerful if we could some-how measure people's actual level of endorsement of honor-related beliefs and values to determine whether people who endorse the ideology of honor are more likely to commit rape or domestic homicide than are people who reject this ideology.

Those sorts of data would, indeed, be ideal, but they don't exist, and they probably never will. Fortunately, we can at least get in the *neighborhood* of this ideal, as long as we are willing to substitute some other outcome for *actual* rapes or murders. As a substitute, consider sexual objectification.

Many years ago, as a middle school student, I can recall trav-eling with my school's track team for an out-of-town race. Tired of how they felt they were being "looked over" by some of the guys, a couple of girls on the team decided they would return the favor to show all the guys how it felt. I can still remem-ber the sensation of having these girls stop and look me over from head to toe every time they spoke to me, or I to them. It was weird, to say the least, and more than a little uncomfort-able. That was the point, of course. As middle school girls, they were already terribly body-conscious, and running around in those skimpy little track uniforms wasn't helping matters much. They felt constantly objectified by guys, many of whom prob-ably weren't even aware of their own behavior and certainly weren't aware of how it made these girls feel. There are few things about middle school boys that could be reasonably called "subtle," including how they tend to gaze at middle school girls.

To feel sexually objectified is to feel that other people see you as less than fully human. You aren't a complete person, with thoughts and feelings, hopes and dreams, intellect and soul. You are a crea-ture at best, and an inanimate object at worst. You are a "thing," the purpose of which is merely to give pleasure to others. The people doing the objectifying might deny all this, but they can protest all they want. *You know how they make you feel.* And if that's not enough, social science research has affirmed these feelings, showing that when people objectify others, they fail to see them as fully human, at a very subtle level below conscious awareness, but not so subtle that we can't measure the perception.

However, objectification doesn't have to be outside of aware-ness. In fact, researchers have devised scales to measure men's tendencies to objectify women sexually. We administered one such scale to a group of more than 100 college men (Brown et al., in review). Items on this scale included statements such as, "It's not a big deal when a man touches a woman's butt at a party or bar," and "When I first see a woman, I am likely to notice particular body parts, such as her legs, hips, chest, and so on." Men read these and other similar statements (26 in all) and indicated how much they agreed or disagreed with each one. Their responses were then averaged over all the items to produce their sexual objectification score. As a related consequence of the ideology of honor, we also gave people in this study a measure of their beliefs about the appropriateness of men having power over women in everyday life and decision making.

In addition to these scales, men also completed a set of other measures, including a scale we developed to measure how much people endorse the beliefs and values of an honor culture. This scale has nothing to do, on the face of it, with sexual objectification of women. Rather, it has items such as, "A real man doesn't let other people push him around" and "A man has the right to act with physical aggression toward another man who insults his mother." (See Appendix A for examples of this and several other honor ideology scales used by social scientists.) In fact, one of the drawbacks to this scale is that it fails to reference masculine virility, one of the common features of masculinity in honor cultures. Honorable women are pure and chaste. Honorable men ... well, not so much. The fact that this particular honor ideology measure doesn't mention anything at all about sexual conquests or attitudes toward women, besides the importance of a man confronting another man aggressively who flirts with his wife, makes using this scale to predict sexual objectification kind of conservative. It would be remarkable if high scores on this measure were related to high scores on a measure of sexual objectification. To be even more conservative, we decided to throw in a few other measures shown in previous research to predict sexist attitudes (such as authoritarianism, religiosity, and the like).

What we found was consistent with the regional differences shown in Table 3.1. Specifically, men who scored high in honor ideology also tended to report higher levels of sexual objectification and stronger beliefs that men should have power over women, independent of other personality differences that might also be related to these attitudes. It seems that in regions of the United States dominated by honor norms, white men are more likely to rape women and to kill their (ex-)wives and (ex-)girlfriends. And even among intelligent, educated young men, the extent to which they embrace the beliefs and values of the honor syndrome predicts their levels of sexual objectification of women and related patriarchal attitudes. The evidence for this dark link between honor ideology and misogyny fits together like the pieces of a puzzle, forming an image we'd rather not see. However uncomfortable this picture might make us feel, the data are consistent, compelling, and convicting.

These findings are also consistent with a very different analysis by historian David H. Fischer, whom I've already referenced. Fischer is perhaps best known for his book, *Albion's Seed*, on the four dominant streams of British immigrants who came to the United States primarily during the 17th and 18th centuries, including the Ulster Scots. In describing the enduring cultural legacies of these four different groups, he notes that attitudes toward women have exhibited an impressive degree of consistency from the early days of immigration well into to the 20th century. For instance, Fischer notes that of the 10 states that failed to ratify the right to vote for women in the years immediately after World War I, every single one of them was an honor state. Almost the exact same pattern occurred half a century later with the Equal Rights Amendment during the 1970s. Of the 14 states that failed to ratify the Equal Rights Amendment, all but one were honor states. Times change, but some things remain the same. Culture, it seems, has remarkable staying power.

Maria, my son's violin teacher, had a rough road ahead of her. She had to get a friend's help to sneak back to her apartment one day, after her husband had left for work, so she could get some of her clothes and other belongings that he hadn't thrown away yet. She also had to stay in hiding for a while until he cooled off, after which she began the laborious process of trying to get legal protection and a divorce. This procedure proved to be more complicated than it should have been, primarily because she and her husband were both from California but were living in Oklahoma while he was deployed at an Air Force base outside of Oklahoma City.

Why does all of this matter? California and Oklahoma have very different laws when it comes to divorce, with the laws in California much more generous to wives in divorce cases than the laws in Oklahoma. This fact meant that Maria was very motivated to get her divorce processed in California, which necessitated that she prove her legal residence in that state. Her husband, Ted, was equally motivated to prove his legal residence in Oklahoma. Abuse in relationships, it turns out, doesn't just have to be physical to be a pain.

Discussion Questions

1. If domestic homicide lies at one end of an abusive relationship, what lies at the other end? In other words, how might such relationships begin, and what role, if any, might the ideology of honor play during the early stages of relationships that end in homicide?
2. What sorts of messages do you think women in honor cultures (or even in nonhonor cultures) receive that inhibit their efforts to get out of abusive relationships? Where do these messages come from?
3. Recent attention has been given to reports of sexual abuse in the U.S. military. In what ways might honor ideology function within the military to influence the occurrence of and responses to such abuse?

For Further Reading

Vandello, J. A., and D. Cohen. 2003. Male honor and female fidelity: Implicit cultural scripts that perpetuate domestic violence. *Journal of Personality and Social Psychology* 84:997–1010.

Vandello, J. A., D. Cohen, R. Grandon, and R. Franiuk. 2009. Stand by your man: Indirect prescriptions for honorable violence and feminine loyalty in Canada, Chile, and the United States. *Journal of Cross-Cultural Psychology* 40:81–104.

Chapter Four

Lay Down Your Burdens

J UST SO WE'RE CLEAR, I don't cry easily. Sure, I occasionally get a little misty over a well-done OnStar commercial. I might even be heard getting the sniffles when they "move that bus" on an old episode of *Extreme Home Makeover* (it's just allergies, really). But I don't weep. Weeping is for little kids who get separated from their moms at the mall, or refugees from civil wars when they finally reach the safety of a Red Cross camp. Not that there's anything wrong with crying, mind you. I just don't normally do it.

That's why the briny rivers of woe pouring down my face were so surprising to me. I guess I had been saving them up for an appropriate moment. Had other drivers taken notice of me and seen the wretchedness of my countenance, they would certainly have changed lanes, and maybe even called 9-1-1. "What's my emergency? Well, there's this guy driving down I-35, just south of Waco, and he's ... well, he's crying. Like, really crying. It's a wonder he can even see where he's going. Someone ought to, you know, stop him or something." I truly was a menace to other drivers as I sped down the Texas interstate. It's not an exaggeration to say that it is a miracle I survived the trip.

The source of my anguish was the death of my friend's father, Robert. It was not because it was so unexpected, although it *was* unexpected. No one saw this coming. And it was not because Robert was so young or because he had seemed fine the last time I saw him, although he was, and he had. What was so shocking and, I think, what magnified my grief was that Robert had taken his own life. And now we had to bury him, and I had to drive. Eight hours of driving, six of which I spent balling my eyes out, and two of which I spent drinking to stay hydrated. Weeping is surprisingly fluid draining. I had no idea.

About two years later, I was on my way to another funeral, also for a friend's father. He, too, had taken his own life and, once again, no one saw this coming. I had never met Bill, but what I learned about him stood in stark contrast to what I knew about Robert. There were a few similarities. Neither man was old—one in his late 40s, the other in his late 50s. Both spent most of their lives in helping professions (one as a pastor, the other as a fireman), and each man had started a second career late in midlife as real estate agents. Both had been married only once, and both had two children, now young adults. They were both grandfathers. They were, obviously, both men who had committed suicide.

But these similarities, more demographic than idiographic, were the only connections I could see between these two men. Robert was artistic and cultured, a fan of Broadway show tunes who had an eye for beauty. Bill was more of a "man's man," prone to reminisce about high school football games after a beer or two, and he had attended college on a baseball scholarship. Although both men had been in the business of rescuing others, Robert did so quietly, counseling the grief-stricken and sitting vigil at hospital bedsides, whereas Bill did so dramatically, pulling children out of burning houses or administering CPR to patients on the way to the emergency room. Where Robert derived immense pleasure from an afternoon nap and the daily ritual of a phone call with his daughter, Bill's great love seemed to be winning, being the best at whatever he was doing. Robert lived comfortably, although not extravagantly; Bill had amassed serious gambling debts that he had tried (for the most part successfully) to hide, which was one of the factors in his impending divorce.[1]

---

1. I have changed the names of these two men to protect their identities. Reputation matters, both for the living and the dead.

So what, if anything, could possibly connect the deaths of these two men? As we shall see in this chapter, the fact that both men spent most of their lives in honor states might be an important part of the answer to this question. In this chapter, I describe the link between the culture of honor and well-being, exploring the dynamics of mental health and mental health care at both the individual and the institutional levels. The picture in this chapter is one of a struggle *within* for people living in honor cultures, more so than a struggle between egos in face-saving brawls, although this internal struggle is, ultimately, a sociocultural one.

From Depths of Woe

How and why might the dynamics of honor cultures be related to suicide? This is not a simple question to answer. In Chapters 1 and 2, we saw how honor cultures breed insecurity and interpersonal violence. This violence is triggered often by seemingly trivial provocations, but in an honor culture, a provocation is a call to action. The word *provocation*, after all, means "to call forth," and when a man in an honor culture is called forth, as when someone questions his bravery, his word, or his sister's virtue, he must answer the call. To do otherwise is to invite exploitation and ridicule, possibly putting himself and his family at risk. This sensitivity to provocation sets a man on the edge of a knife (which he should carry with him at all times, preferably strapped to his hip, right next to his pride). It can place a man at odds with his fellow man, and sometimes with his woman, too.

On the surface, suicide does not seem to fit well within this cultural landscape. Suicide is about retreating, not advancing. Suicide is about looking for an escape hatch, not marching to victory. Odes are not written to commemorate the taking of one's own life in despair. What glory could come from killing yourself? What honor? Why not dishonor, in fact?

To find the connection between honor culture and suicide, we must first consider *why* people commit suicide. Thomas Joiner, a clinical psychologist and researcher at Florida State University, has written extensively on this subject and is one of the world's foremost experts on the predictors of suicide. As the son of man who took his own life, Joiner takes the subject of suicide rather personally. Psychology research, as they say, is often me-search.

Joiner has spent his career delving into the underlying motives for this mysterious act. He has conducted dozens of studies on suicide, running the gamut from simple surveys of "normal" college students, to in-depth interviews of hospitalized suicide attempters, to linguistic analyses of suicide notes left behind for loved ones. What Joiner has found in his years of research is that three factors appear to be central to understanding the motives and circumstances that facilitate the taking of one's own life.[2]

The first of these factors is a feeling of burdensomeness. From survey data to suicide notes, people who attempt suicide report feeling a sense of being a burden to others, more than anything else. This sense seems to correspond to their feelings of depression, the single most common emotional precursor to self-destruction. Whether the sense of burdensomeness is a cause or consequence of depression is hard to say. Suicide notes reveal this feeling of burdensomeness through statements such as, "I know that you will all be better off without me," and "I can help you more in my death than I ever could in my life," which are almost formulaic of this genre. People who kill themselves are looking for a way out, yes, but not just for themselves. Rightly or wrongly, they view the act of suicide as a way to reduce the burden they believe their life represents for the people around them, both family and friends.

The second factor that Joiner describes is a relative sense of disconnectedness. This factor might seem to be at odds with the first factor. How, after all, can you feel that you are a burden to the people around you if you also feel socially disconnected? If you aren't close to other people, who are you trying to unburden through your death? These two factors are, indeed, somewhat paradoxical, but suicide is rarely driven by clear and logical thinking. Suicide notes often reveal such contradictory thought processes, such as when the suicidal person admonishes a spouse to make sure to pay the car insurance right after reflecting on the unbearable strain of existence. These factors aren't actually contradictory, though.

---

2. People interested in this topic should read Thomas Joiner's excellent book, *Why People Die by Suicide* (Joiner, 2005).

Disconnectedness is not the same as total isolation. A person can feel disconnected while surrounded by people, working alongside them in an office, perhaps, and even attending the occasional going-away party for a colleague.

Similarly, people who commit suicide often have friends, family, and other loved ones in their lives. They have social connections, but something sets them apart from others. Their social connections are broken by forces not obvious to most of those around them. They can stand in the midst of others and feel like castaways. When this feeling is paired with a sense of burdensomeness, the result is emotionally catastrophic.

The result of this combination, though, is not necessarily suicide. These two emotional factors are *necessary* motivational forerunners to suicide, according to Joiner, but they are not *sufficient* by themselves. What is needed to translate these two feelings into self-destructive behavior is a tolerance for pain that inures a person to the natural disinclination people feel toward suffering and death. When you see someone cut himself with a knife by accident, you wince empathetically, don't you? We learn to associate knives with pain, and we handle them with care accordingly. The same is true for guns, and for other potentially lethal objects, and even for heights. It takes experience and guts to peer over the edge of a balcony without automatically and instinctively pulling back. The instinct for self-preservation kicks in normally, as if to say, "Hey, watch out for that! Warning, warning! Danger, Will Robinson!" This powerful instinct must be overcome for a person to commit suicide.

Thus, says Joiner, many people who die by their own hand have built up to that big moment with numerous smaller moments in which they got used to cutting themselves or holding themselves under water or taking an extra pill or two, or maybe three this time. They push the boundaries. They grow calluses over their instincts. This callousness is crucial to move from feelings of burdensomeness and disconnection to actually killing yourself. We have lots of feelings we don't act on; often, that's a good thing. Sometimes this failure to act is intentional, such as when we bite our tongue to keep from saying what we really think about a boss's new tie or a loved one's new haircut. Sometimes this failure occurs despite our best intentions, such as when we fail to start that exercise program we've been talking about for so long. The same is true with suicide. You can feel the desire without going through with it. Desire must be coupled with ability, and that ability is acquired through experience, according to Joiner's research.

Lindsey Osterman and I (Osterman and Brown, 2011) suspected there might be a connection between these factors and honor culture. If our suspicions were correct, then suicide rates ought to be substantially higher in honor states compared with nonhonor states, particularly among the demographic group that previous research has shown is most prone to be a carrier of honor ideology in the United States: white males living in nonmetropolitan areas.

Consider the first of Joiner's risk factors: the feeling of burdensomeness. In previous chapters I described the nature of identity in honor cultures. What it means to be a real man and a good woman in a culture of honor is strictly prescribed and painstakingly reinforced from birth to death. Men and women know the roles they are expected to play and the characteristics they are supposed to exhibit. Failure to do so leads to dishonor and can damage a reputation beyond repair. When that happens, the one who fails is not the only one to suffer. His or her family also enjoys the sting of a sullied reputation. Personal honor is intimately connected to collective honor. Some failures, of course, can be compensated for through redoubled efforts to prove one's worth as a man or a woman of honor. Some cannot. Some failures just scratch the surface of a person's reputation, whereas others cut much deeper. It is the latter type that is the most pernicious, and its possibility hangs in the air interminably, like a Lowland Scottish fog that refuses to be burned off by the sun's rays. The possibility of such deep dishonor never goes away, for what must be earned can necessarily be lost. Under such an existential weight, then, is bred the sense of burdensomeness that Joiner's research has pointed to as the first ingredient in the suicide formula.

Next, consider Joiner's other emotional risk factor: the sense of social disconnectedness. Although honor cultures tend to be more collectivistic than individualistic, being part of a collective is not necessarily the perfect antidote to feeling disconnected. As I already noted, this feeling is not simply about knowing lots of people, or even having a family, although having a family certainly helps. It's more psychological than physical, and it involves being known deeply, feeling accepted unconditionally, trusting and being trusted. Cultures of honor might interfere with this feeling of being known, through their rigid rules regarding masculinity and femininity, and their unyielding pressures to perform, to earn the right to be respected. Part of being respected in honor cultures, especially for men, is proving you can do what must be done without crying out for help. One should be charitable, but one should never *need* charity. You can give aid and comfort, but you really shouldn't seek it. I'll return to this point shortly. It is sufficient for now to note that enduring feelings of social intimacy are not likely to be fostered by the typical honor culture.

Then there's the third risk factor: the one that translates feelings of burdensomeness and disconnectedness into self-destructive behaviors. Recall that earning a reputation for strength and toughness, particularly for men, involves acts of social proof, and the more dangerous or painful the act, the better. Might this dynamic lead to a dulling of normal sensitivities to pain, a weakening of the instinct to flee danger or recoil from the dark abyss of death?

Finally, let's not forget a little fact that I mentioned back in Chapter 2: honor cultures tend to be full of heavily armed people. Being armed at one time meant having a sword, but the more common armament these days is the handgun. It's hard to say how many handguns there are in the United States, but as I noted earlier, honor states have looser restrictions on the owning and carrying of guns than nonhonor states, and research has shown that people are more likely to have a gun in the house if they live in an honor state. Indeed, surveys suggest that almost 40% of households in the United States have at least one gun in them.[3] Because a large proportion of suicides in the United States are committed with guns, and because people who use guns are more likely to be successful in their suicide attempts, this by-product of honor culture might facilitate death by suicide indirectly. Thus, we have good reasons to expect that suicide rates might be higher in honor states than in nonhonor states.

---

3. This estimate is based on a nationally representative survey conducted in 2001 by the Centers for Disease Control and Prevention as part of their Behavioral Risk Factor Surveillance System.

So, is that in fact the case? To answer this question, Lindsey Osterman and I examined suicide rates tracked by the Center for Disease Control and Prevention (CDC) from 1999 to 2007 for whites and nonwhites, for men and women, and for people living in metropolitan and nonmetropolitan areas. Before comparing these suicide rates, we also gathered a host of control variables to try to ensure that any differences we might observe were not a result of factors unrelated to honor culture, as with other studies that I've already described. For instance, we assessed statewide levels of economic deprivation (such as poverty, unemployment),[4] an estimate of a state's tendency toward collectivism, average yearly temperature (which other researchers have found is related to aggression against others), and the percentage of people who have at least one gun in their home, using survey data collected by the CDC.

In addition to these somewhat obvious control variables, we also added another that few researchers tend to assess: access to medical care (specifically, the percentage of the population living in what's known as a "health professional shortage area"). We included this last variable because all causes of death tend to be magnified by lack of access to medical care for reasons that have nothing to do with culture. If you don't have easy access to a doctor, even a little infection can kill you. That's not culture. It's just biology.

What we found matched quite well with our expectations. Suicide rates among white men and white women were much higher in honor states than in nonhonor states, as shown in Table 4.1. This difference remained even after we controlled for all the variables I mentioned earlier. The difference among men was greater in absolute terms than it was for women, but it was statistically significant for both groups—about one and a half standard deviations in magnitude. This difference was significant but much smaller among black men than it was among white men, and it was nonsignificant among black women.

---

4. This economic deprivation index was a composite of statewide poverty rates, unemployment rates, median income (reversed for consistency with the other variables), and educational attainment. Although these facets all capture something a little different from one another, they fit well together from a statistical perspective, and, collectively, they perform more effectively than any of them could alone—kind of like members of a family.

Table 4.1 SUICIDE RATES (1999–2007) PER 100,000 RESIDENTS
IN HONOR STATES AND NONHONOR STATES, ADJUSTED
FOR STATEWIDE CONTROLS

VARIABLE	HONOR STATES	NONHONOR STATES
White men	25.5	19.2
Black men	12.0	8.9
White women	6.3	4.4
Black women	2.2	1.7

What was equally interesting to us was that, consistent with research on homicide rates, the difference in suicide rates between honor states and nonhonor states was especially great for whites living in nonmetropolitan areas. This finding could be counterintuitive, insofar as small towns are places where "everybody knows your name." If anything, these should be places where people feel socially connected, right? Well, that might be true, but as we saw in Chapter 2, smaller towns are also places where everybody knows your shame. Thus, reputational concerns get magnified in small towns, not minimized. Small towns put honor concerns on high alert.[5]

We've established now that suicide rates are higher in honor states than in nonhonor states, especially among white males living in nonmetropolitan areas. But, this pattern is pretty high level, like looking down on people from 10,000 ft. Is there any other evidence about how honor-related dynamics might be linked to the suicide risk factors that Joiner has found?

It turns out that there is, in fact, more to this story. Again, in research that I conducted with Lindsey Osterman, we examined statewide depression levels (which I have already mentioned is a well-known precursor to suicide) as well as prescription rates for

---

5. Another interesting finding from this study was that the metro versus nonmetro effect was actually *reversed* among black males. In other words, suicide rates weren't significantly different for black men living in small towns, but they *were* different for black men living in big cities—the reverse of the pattern we found for whites. This difference, we think, underscores the argument that this is a product of cultural factors, rather than simply geographic or economic ones. It also suggests that regional differences in honor culture dynamics that we see among whites might be replicated to an extent among blacks living in the inner city, for reasons already noted in Chapter 1. This speculation, however, awaits more systematic research.

antidepressants. If life in an honor culture is truly replete with social and existential burdens, as I have argued that it is, then people living in honor states ought to be at a higher risk for experiencing depression (although they might be reluctant to admit it, because that itself might be a sign of weakness, leading to dishonor).

Of course, where depression levels are high, we should also see high rates of doctors prescribing antidepressants in response, shouldn't we? If you break your arm, then you go to the doctor to get a cast. If you have an ear infection, then you go to the doctor to get an antibiotic. If you are depressed, then you go to a doctor to get an antidepressant. That would seem to be the most rational response to emotional distress, wouldn't it? But for the same reason that people might be reluctant to admit feeling depressed, people also might be reluctant to seek help from a family doctor or a psychiatrist. Furthermore, people who feel depressed might even be urged by family members *not* to seek medical help, for the dishonor of one person can stain everyone in a family, just as the honor of one can lift the status of the others.

To assess the emotional side of the burden of living in an honor culture, we examined survey data on statewide rates of major depressive episodes, defined as having experienced at least five out of nine key symptoms of depression within the past year. These data were collected in 2004-2005 as part of the National Survey on Drug Use and Health by the U.S. Substance Abuse and Mental Health Services Administration (also known as SAMHSA), and they included several hundred thousand respondents across all fifty states. Unfortunately, these rates are reported for each state in the aggregate, without specifying gender or race, so we had to make comparisons across all our variables of interest at this same aggregate level for the sake of consistency. This was unfortunate, because we know that honor dynamics around the United States are more powerful within certain groups (such as white males in small towns). We also examined data on antidepressant prescriptions for each state for the nearest available years (2006–2007) (Mark et al., 2007). Finally, we looked at statewide suicide rates across all demographic groups for the year 2005, in keeping with our aggregate depression data, and used the same control variables described earlier, matched in time as closely as possible.

What we found was remarkable. Despite the reluctance that people in honor states might feel toward admitting on a phone survey that they felt depressed, statewide depression levels were modestly, but significantly, *higher* in honor states than they were in nonhonor states. But, that's not the most interesting part. Although depression rates were higher in honor states, antidepressant prescription rates were *not*. In fact, when controlling for depression levels (in other words, statistically equating all the states for their emotional health), antidepressant prescription rates were significantly *lower* in honor states. This means that, despite the clearly felt need for emotional help, people living in honor states were *less* likely to receive help, at least in the form of antidepressant medications.

This combination makes for the perfect storm with respect to predicting suicides. We discovered that statewide depression levels were unrelated to suicide rates across nonhonor states, which we might expect if people with depression in these states were getting the help they need, including (but not limited to) antidepressant medications. In contrast, statewide depression levels were *strongly* associated with suicide rates across honor states. Thus, if a lot of people living in an honor state experience a major depressive episode in a given year, suicide rates in that state are likely to be higher than normal. This pattern is exactly what we should expect to see if people are not only *more* emotionally distressed, but also *less likely to seek professional help* for their distress.

Before leaving the subject of suicide, I will mention one more aspect of this mysterious behavior that appears to be linked to honor. People who commit suicide typically have to build up to the act, as I noted already. The inclination to end your own life runs up against the powerful instinct for self-preservation, and for the former to win over the latter, a person needs practice. This practice often involves slowly building up a sort of psychological immunity to self-harm, taking small steps toward the ultimate end of suicide. These acts are often interpreted as "cries for help," especially by the suicidal person's loved ones, but they are more likely simply to be dress rehearsals for the final show. The methods that suicidal people choose, either during the build-up or the final act, are not typically the focus of anyone's attention, however. Loved ones left behind don't really care all that much *how* a person died, as much as they care about the fact of the death and the *why*. This isn't to say that *how* is completely unimportant, but it seems to get lost in a sea of details surrounding the death more often than not. This is also commonly the case among those who study suicide and who hope to understand it better.

But *how* really does matter. It matters, first and foremost, because some methods are more effective than others. Jumping out of a plane without a parachute is a pretty reliable way to die, for instance, whereas taking too many sleeping pills is not nearly as effective. Thus, overdosing on pills is more likely to be part of the dress rehearsal than is jumping from a plane. Consequently, the methods used in attempted suicides might reveal how far along a person is in the process of becoming immune to the idea of self-destruction.

The methods people use might also reveal an important cultural "signal" relevant to this whole honor–suicide dynamic. With this in mind, Mikiko Imura, Lindsey Osterman, and I examined the methods people used to kill themselves (Brown et al., 2014c). We weren't looking at people who attempted suicide but failed; rather, we looked only at those who succeeded in ending their lives, in part to ensure we were examining only those people who were equally far along in the process of commitment—people who really wanted to die and were ready to make it happen.

What we found was that both men and women from honor states were much more likely to use guns to end their life compared with men and women in nonhonor states. As with so many other behaviors, this pattern only occurred among white men and women, though. More important, this difference was found even when we controlled for the greater availability of guns in honor states that I've already mentioned.

What does this pattern indicate? Well, it could indicate several things. Besides the fact that using a gun is one of the most lethal means available to most people for committing suicide—stomachs can be pumped for pills, but a gunshot to the head is not something from which a person is likely to recover—we think the choice of a gun is also evidence of a greater desire to demonstrate courage and toughness, even in death, among suicidal people from honor states. Any means of killing oneself is, by definition, violent, but people who use a gun to commit suicide, it could be argued, are choosing a method that is *especially* violent, compared with, say, taking a bunch of sleeping pills or sitting in a closed garage with the car running.

This argument, although speculative, is consistent with the ancient Japanese ritual of *seppuku*. This ritual involved a man stabbing himself in the stomach, which was believed to be the seat of the soul, to cleanse his dishonor through pain. After doing so without crying out (at least, not excessively crying out), the ritual would be completed through his beheading. The endurance of the self-inflicted pain, though, was really what restored the man's honor. Perhaps, in a way, something similar is happening among people who commit suicide in honor states in the United States. It's less formal than *seppuku*, to be sure, and it doesn't involve the assistance of other people in a ceremony, but maybe there is a culturally bound sense of "rightness" to the use of a gun in the commission of suicide that derives from a similar way of thinking.

In sum, having a *sense of shame* is good and right in an honor culture. *Feeling ashamed* is a natural consequence of living in a social system driven by powerful reputational concerns and strict rules for how those concerns are handled. Having to cope with that shame on your own is simply another of these natural consequences, it seems, and some people, some of the time, are less able to cope effectively than others. When coping fails, suicide might feel like a reasonable way to solve their problems, or at least to escape from them.

From Individuals to Institutions and Back Again

If people living in honor states are less likely to seek professional help when they experience depression, then it stands to reason that honor states might be less likely to invest a lot of money in training mental health professionals and in building mental health facilities. After all, it doesn't really matter how distressed people are if they are unlikely to seek help. You can't make people go to the doctor for their mental health needs if they don't want to, and they might not want to if they have been culturally programmed to feel that seeking help is a sign of weakness, a source of dishonor.

What would be the point of investing a lot of money in mental health services in such an environment? We should spend money on the things that people really want, such as sports arenas. Feeling down? Go watch a ball game. That'll pick you right up, and you don't have to get an injection, take a pill, or talk about your feelings to a shrink. Plus, when was the last time you got a freshly baked pretzel and a cold beer at the doctor's office?

We wondered if states characterized by honor culture norms exhibit this sort of reluctance to invest in mental health services, and the answer, it seems, is yes (Brown et al., 2014b). Table 4.2 shows the average number of mental healthcare professionals (psychologists and psychiatrists) per 100,000 residents, average state expenditures for mental healthcare per capita, and the average number of mental health hospitals per million residents, as a function of the honor status of each state. All three of these indices demonstrate a lower level of social investment in mental healthcare among honor states, by large and statistically significant margins. Overall, nonhonor states invest 30% to 40% more in mental healthcare compared to honor states.

Furthermore, these investment levels are adjusted for statewide differences in economic deprivation, rurality, collectivism, and religiosity. So, these differences in mental healthcare investments are not simply about the population being more spread out or being more religious in honor states (perhaps getting help

Table 4.2 INVESTMENTS IN MENTAL HEALTHCARE AMONG HONOR STATES AND NONHONOR STATES, ADJUSTED FOR STATEWIDE CONTROLS*

VARIABLE	HONOR STATES	NONHONOR STATES
Mental healthcare professionals per capita[†]	43	56
State expenditures for mental healthcare per capita	$88	$126
Mental healthcare hospitals per capita[‡]	3.8	4.4

*Such as rurality and wealth.
[†]Rates shown are per 100,000 residents.
[‡]Rates shown are per one million residents.

for emotional needs from their churches), nor are they the result of poverty, education, and the like, which are all captured by the economic deprivation variable. These differences in investment appear to be rooted in cultural values. We invest in what is really important to us.

But these investment deficits create something of a vicious cycle. The beliefs and values of honor cultures can create intense emotional vulnerabilities, as people constantly strive to earn and maintain their social status, defending their reputation at all costs. Like Bill, who I described briefly at the beginning of this chapter, they have to win, for losing honor can't be tolerated. Losing the honor of one's name, one's reputation, means everything, and in an honor culture your name is on the line every day of your life. To make matters worse, when you feel the sting of distress, you aren't allowed to seek professional help for it. You can probably mention your problems in passing to your Uncle Willy, and he might even give you a little sage advice about what to do about the blues (pretzels and beer, for starters). But don't think about spilling your guts to a therapist. Just deal with it. Man-up, cowboy.

This reticence can also extend to one's children and *their* mental health needs. In a national survey of parents (primarily mothers) conducted by SAMHSA, parents were asked whether any of their children had experienced any serious emotional or behavioral problems from a list the surveyors gave to them. In addition, when parents answered in the affirmative for one or more children, they were then asked whether they had taken their kids to seek help from a professional therapist or medical doctor. Perhaps it wasn't surprising to find out that parents living in honor states were significantly less likely to report they had gotten help for their children who needed it than were parents from nonhonor states (Brown et al., 2014b).

But wait. Might this just be part of a broader reluctance to seek help? This seems like a reasonable possibility, for the reasons already discussed. Solving your problems on your own, rather than asking someone else for help, appears to fit the cultural mandate of the honor code. Maybe parents in honor states simply don't take their kids to any kind of doctor, and there is nothing special about mental health professionals. Fortunately, we can find out if this is the case using the same survey data from SAMHSA, because it turns out their survey also asked parents how many times in the past year they had taken their kids to see nonmental health doctors as well. The data show there is absolutely no regional difference using this variable. Parents in honor states took their kids to the doctor just as frequently as parents in nonhonor states did. Thus, the apparent reticence to take their kids to see a mental health professional seems to be something specific to *this type of doctor*, consistent with the idea that honor cultures promote the stigmatization of mental healthcare and mental health needs.

Not long ago, a friend of mine confided that he and his wife had recently taken their son to a neurologist in an attempt to figure out why he had so many little "tics." I am not referring, of course, to the kind that bites your dog or gives you Rocky Mountain spotted fever. I mean the kind of tic that makes people look at you funny because you twitch, turn, grimace, or grunt for no apparent reason. What my friend and his wife had discovered about their son's tics was that they were caused by a disorder known as Tourette syndrome (or TS). This medical condition is named after a 19th-century neurologist who first surmised that it was caused by a biochemical problem in the brain. However, 100 years worth of misdirection from the Freudian psychoanalytic crowd caused thousands of people with TS to seek emotion-focused counseling to uncover what was believed to be the real cause of TS—the shortcomings of their parents, especially their mothers. Freud and his followers blamed moms for many things.

Backed up by the facts of science, I assured my anxious friend that his son's disorder was not the fault of his (or his wife's) failures as a parent, and he seemed somewhat relieved to hear this. He still seemed uncomfortable, though, and I couldn't help wondering whether his discomfort was at least in part a result of his concerns about being stigmatized as the father of a boy with a neurological disorder. As I pressed him cautiously about this possibility, he rejected this notion right away. Rather, he told me, he was concerned with how other people would treat his son if his condition became widely known. For this reason, he seemed reluctant to take the business card of a therapist that I held out to him. "Call this woman," I urged him. "She's a friend and she works with kids all the time. She's great. Really." He took the card, but I'm not sure if he was just being polite.

If we take my friend's assertions at face value, not only was his son's disorder *not* the result of bad parenting, but his own reluctance to seek treatment for his son was *also* not a reflection of bad parenting. It was a reflection of my friend's awareness of the realities of life in Oklahoma, an honor state, where people are hypervigilant to signs of weakness, and where a neurological disorder was likely to be seen as just such a sign.

If you find that the beer-and-pretzels approach to your psychological problems falls a little short, you might decide to look for something more medicinal in nature (and lower in carbohydrates). That decision, however, is not the end of the story, because the culture that created the conditions that led, at least indirectly, to your distress is also the culture that determines how much to invest in mental healthcare services. You might decide that you *want* to get professional help, but that doesn't mean that help is available. Do you see the perniciousness of this cultural syndrome? You can't just change people's willingness to seek help, and you can't just throw money at the problem to build more mental health facilities. One without the other is little more than folly. The culture itself must be changed at its foundations. Psychiatrists aren't going to last long in a state where no one goes to see a psychiatrist. They'll just move. Or they might change careers and sell pretzels. Either way, their professional services are neither given nor received.

I would be remiss not to mention before closing this chapter that none of the data on suicides that I have described here goes quite far enough to make an airtight case for the link between the ideology of honor and self-destruction. Although there is another important indicator of this link that I discuss in Chapter 7 the fact remains that just knowing there is a higher suicide rate in honor states doesn't tell you exactly *who* is committing those suicides. Yes, we can see that whites, especially white men living in small towns, seem to be particularly vulnerable, but we can't know from these aggregate numbers whether the excessive number of suicides in honor states is the result of people who embrace the beliefs and values of the culture of honor, or of people who reject these beliefs and values.

For all the reasons I have talked about in this chapter, we might conclude that it's the former group—people like Bill, the fireman, the "man's man." But, it could also be Robert—the sensitive, artistic guy who loved Broadway musicals. Guys like Robert might feel the mismatch between their own beliefs and values, and those of the broader society, and this mismatch itself could be one of the main sources of their distress. Thus, a culture of honor might lead to more suicides among its Bills, its Roberts, or both. Because of the nature of suicide and the difficulty of tracking people prospectively to see which "type" of person is more likely to self-destruct, we cannot yet be sure which is the case. This remains a mystery, and one that I hope future researchers feel inspired to resolve. Given that about twice as many Americans die each year from suicide as die from homicide (in a country with one of the highest homicide rates in the developed world), this seems to be a mystery worth investigating.

Discussion Questions

1. What are some other "signs of weakness" related to health (either mental of physical) that might be stigmatized in an honor culture?
2. What kinds of people do you think might be at the greatest risk for suicide in an honor culture? Why?
3. How could the honor-based stigma associated with seeking help for mental health needs be reduced?
4. What role do you think family and friends might play in encouraging or discouraging people living in an honor culture from seeking help for their mental health needs?

For Further Reading

Brown, R. P., M. Imura, and L. Mayeux. 2014. Honor and the stigma of mental healthcare. *Personality and Social Psychology Bulletin* 40:1119–1131.

Joiner, T. 2005. *Why people die by suicide*. Cambridge, MA: Harvard University Press.

Osterman, L. L., and R. P. Brown. 2011. Culture of honor and violence against the self. *Personality and Social Psychology Bulletin* 37:1611–1623.

CHAPTER FIVE

Reckless Abandon

FLYING DOWN THE UNLIT country road, I hung on for dear life. I don't use that expression lightly, either. I had the sense at that moment that my life was on the line. I was perched on the front wheel cover of a four-wheel ATV, one of four helmet-free passengers being driven by our friend David. His mantle of thick red hair framed the giant grin on his face, his teeth illuminated by the pale green light of the speedometer and the sliver of a moon glancing down at us from above. There were no streetlights along this lonely stretch of dirt and gravel, and David had turned off the ATV's lone headlight.

We were headed, ironically enough, to an old graveyard. The idea was that we were going to sit around and tell ghost stories while perched atop crumbling headstones. Inevitably, someone would slip away in the middle of someone else's story, only to reappear with a crash and a scream meant to stop the hearts of the rest of the troupe. That was the plan, anyway. I felt almost certain we were going to our own graves that night.

All we would need to do was to hit a large enough pothole of the sort that riddled this little dirt road. Or, a sufficiently large piece of road kill—a possum, perhaps, or maybe a half-scavenged raccoon. Yes, half a raccoon would do nicely; a full-grown coon is about the size of large beagle. A corpse of that size would be enough to catapult us all into the air, and without the headlight on, we would never see the carcass in time to avoid it. I had to get him to turn on that headlight.

I began to reason with him, trying as best I could to be heard over the roar of the engine and the wind that whipped our faces. I wanted to sound cool, not panicked, so I kept my tone as level as I could at first. "That's real funny, David. Ha ha. It's time to turn the lights back on now," I said. My tone was meant to convey both my lack of concern and my disdain for his childish behavior. It didn't work.

"What are we? Ten-year-olds?" I asked rhetorically, raising the stakes a bit. "Turn 'em on now, seriously." Nothing. He might even have sped up a little.

"David, really, you're being kind of immature here, don't you think? What's going to happen if we hit something?" Draw him into the process. Get him to reason through his actions. Don't just boss him around. He won't take kindly to being bossed around.

"Maybe *you* feel okay about all this, David. *You've* at least got something to hold on to. The rest of us don't. Are you really that comfortable putting our lives in danger like this? Are you?" I was getting desperate and it was coming out in my voice. We were going to die this night—all of us. I couldn't see anyone else's face in the dark. One of my friends was on the other wheel cover, and the remaining two were facing backward, away from me. I imagined them looking longingly toward the distant light of the lake house from which we'd come. David's lake house. David's ATV. David's way.

I started to get angry. He wasn't listening to me, although I knew he could hear me just fine. I was practically screaming in his ear at this point. He just didn't care. Surely he could tell I was scared out of my wits. Surely he could see that his behavior was unnecessary and uncool, but by that point I'd pushed him too far. He couldn't back down now. My language got harsher, along with my volume. I won't repeat what I yelled in his ear next. My mother might read this, after all.

Adolescent males have always done stupid things, taking risks for which one can hardly see any reward. We build ramps over ditches to jump our bikes, and when that is mastered, we add some exciting broken glass to the ditch (I did that one). We jump off roofs with sheets as parachutes (which, incidentally, has *never* in the history of bed linens actually worked; I did that one, too). We race one another in our cars, we have drinking contests—sometimes right before racing one another in our cars—and we speed down country roads with our headlights turned off. This is the way it's always been and probably the way it always will be.

This kind of excessive risk-taking, common to male-dom as it is, can be found in even greater degrees among people living in honor cultures. Why would that be? What could possibly be seen as "honorable" about such silly risk-taking? And wouldn't the self-defeating nature of such behaviors eventually get weeded out of the gene pool? We'll return to this last question shortly; but first, let's explore why there might be a link between excessive risk-taking and honor-related motives, and whether there are any systematic data to support such a link (besides my own childhood anecdotes of recklessness).

Living Dangerously

A recent song by country singer Chris Cagle expresses nicely one of the primary motivations behind young men engaging in reckless acts of stupidity. The refrain of the song captures the essence of Cagle's thesis: "'Cause the chicks dig it." He notes that "pain hurts, but only for a minute," and he urges his listeners to "throw caution to the wind . . . then sit back and watch your life begin." It's basically the redneck version of *carpe diem*.

Even so, this is just one song by one country music artist. It hardly makes for a strong evidence base to back up the claim that one of the effects of the honor syndrome is excessive risk-taking. Is there any better evidence for this argument?

In a recent set of studies, Collin Barnes, Mike Tamborski, and I attempted to assess this possibility (Barnes et al., 2012). We began with the idea, discussed back in Chapter 2, that men in general feel the need to demonstrate and prove their manhood, but this facet of maleness is magnified by the beliefs and values of honor cultures. To be a "real man," after all, is to live on an eternal proving ground, for the moniker of masculinity is socially conferred. It must be earned. Overt, public acts that show how tough, brave, and strong you are make for the best forms of social proof, and acts of aggression are typical of this category of evidence. But, beating people up for looking at you funny or for calling your sister inappropriate names isn't the only way to prove that you have *cojones*. Maybe jumping off the roof with a sheet would work.

Unfortunately, no one seems to keep good records of bed-sheet jumping. However, the fine folks at the CDC do keep track of the reasons people die every year (bless them), and those data can be used to test the possibility of a link between honor culture and recklessness, at least when that recklessness leads to an early death. To be more specific, the CDC reports a category of causes of death labeled as "external causes," with subcategories that include transport accidents, falls, accidental electrocutions and drownings, contact with venomous animals, and the like. This category doesn't include homicides or suicides or diseases such as cancer. It's basically roof jumping, with a grown-up twist.

Excluding exposure to forces of nature, such as floods and tornadoes, we assessed accidental death rates, for whites and nonwhites, in all 50 states.[1] We then assessed accidental death rates separately for white men and white women, just as with the analyses of suicide rates discussed in Chapter 4, and we compared these accidental death rates between honor states and nonhonor states.

Before describing what we found, it is probably worth noting the sorts of variables for which we had to control in our state-by-state comparisons, as I have done in prior chapters. Rurality is, once again, a fairly obvious control variable, to the extent that the sorts of reckless behaviors we are talking about might be just the sorts of things that people living out in the middle of nowhere, bored out of their skulls, might do to pass the time. Average yearly temperature and economic deprivation (that composite variable I've mentioned before that includes poverty rates and unemployment levels) were two other such control variables, for the same

---

1. More specifically, we examined causes of death associated with International Classification of Diseases-10 codes V01 through V99 and W00 through X59, excluding X30 through X39 (which refer to exposure to forces of nature).

reasons that they usually show up in analyses of regional differences in violence and aggression.

For our analysis of accidental deaths, though, we also added a few unusual control variables to the mix to be especially careful not to confuse the honor status of each state with other incidental characteristics that might have nothing to do with the culture of honor per se, but that might produce the very differences for which we were looking. Specifically, we added the percentage of each state's population living in what health officials call a "health professional shortage area," in case people living in honor states might be more likely to die, not because they are more reckless, but simply because they are less likely to have good access to medical care. Because our accidental death rates contained a component involving automobile-related deaths, we also added the average state speed limit, the number of cars per capita, the number of miles driven each year per capita, and the number of police officers per capita. Whew. That ought to have covered our bases fairly well.

But wait! What if people living in honor states are more likely to die of accidental causes, despite all these control variables, but for reasons having nothing to do with culture? What if, for reasons we haven't captured with any of these control variables, people living in honor states are simply *more likely to die*, period, from any and all causes? We've already seen they're more likely to die from homicide and suicide, after all, and this "accidental causes" category is pretty nonspecific. How might we control for such an "unknown, pervasive death factor," the UPDF, without controlling for a cause that is itself linked to honor culture? We settled on a final control variable for our analyses that we thought would do the trick of capturing this UPDF: cancer-related death rates. Statistically, cancer makes for a nice control variable because it covers an unfortunately common cause of death that you don't have to do anything to experience. People get cancer all the time, everywhere, and anthropological data suggest they always have. So, this served as our final control variable.

Table 5.1 shows what we found. Notice the range of accidental death rates across states. They varied enormously from state to state, from an average low of about 23 deaths per 100,000 people each year to a high of about 60 deaths per 100,000 people each

Table 5.1 ACCIDENTAL DEATH RATES PER 100,000 RESIDENTS
AMONG WHITES IN HONOR STATES
AND NONHONOR STATES

GENDER	HONOR STATES	NONHONOR STATES
Both Sexes	42.0	36.9
Men	61.1	47.5
Women	27.4	23.3

year (among whites). In a state the size of, say, Ohio, that higher death rate amounts to almost 6000 people dying each year just from accidents. In fact, accidents are among the leading causes of death for Americans each year, typically ranked around number five, just behind strokes.

As you can see from Table 5.1, whites in honor states exhibited higher accidental death rates than did whites in nonhonor states, after we controlled for all the variables mentioned previously. The size of this difference, in statistical terms, was quite large—almost a full standard deviation. Furthermore, it held for both white men and, interestingly, white women. In contrast, it did not hold for nonwhites, consistent with previous studies on region-based culture of honor outcomes that I've already discussed.

The finding that white women living in honor states seem to die of accidental causes at higher rates than white women in nonhonor states piqued our curiosity a bit. Were these women just "collateral damage" in the reckless rampages of the men around them, or were they, too, behaving foolishly and throwing caution to the wind one time too many? To try to answer this question, we decided to administer a survey to male and female college students at the University of Oklahoma. As part of this survey, students completed the honor ideology measure I described earlier, as well as a measure of how often they engaged in a host of risky behaviors—from skydiving and bungee jumping to binge drinking and unsafe sex (Weber et al., 2002). What we found confirmed the pattern we saw with death rates across states. The more that women endorsed the beliefs and values of the honor culture, the more frequently they also reported "living dangerously" across a wide variety of life domains. It appears that women aren't just passive victims of reckless men.

Sissified

Lying flat on my back in my physical therapist's office was one of the most refreshing experiences of the day. Physical therapists have a knack for propping you up in all the right places to provide just the support an aching body needs. In my particular case, I was in need of some relief from neck pain. I chose to blame my pain on my years of pole vaulting as a younger man—every vaulter I know has some kind of neck or back problem—but I realized that the source of my discomfort could just as easily have been age. Getting old sucks.

I lay there while my therapist massaged and rotated and prodded and pulled and iced, and it wasn't long after my breathing had become slow and regular that he decided to ask me what I thought about the recent settlement the National Football League (NFL) had reached over the class-action lawsuit brought on behalf of a bunch of former players. The players claimed the NFL had ignored years' worth of evidence concerning the long-term consequences of large men running into each other with their heads. As one physician put it, it turns out that getting tackled by an NFL linebacker is equivalent to being in a head-on car crash, in terms of what the impact can do to your brain.

"So, I was listening to The Sports Animal this morning," he began. The Sports Animal was a popular radio program that he, and many people around the state, tuned in to on a semireligious basis. "One of the commentators complained that, with this settlement by the NFL, the rules will change in professional football to 'make things safer,' which will mean that college football will probably change as well, and that will result in rule changes in high school and even pee-wee football all around the country. And before you know it, football will have become 'sissified.' What do you think about that, Dr. Brown?"

I suspect my therapist had some idea what I might think about that, based on our prior conversations about what I study, and that he might have been looking for a little affirmation of what *he* thought about the commentator's remarks. I was happy to oblige.

"'Sissified,' huh? So, this guy, whose job is to sit in a chair and talk into a microphone about other people who play a game for a living—a game that is pretty much one of the roughest games in the civilized world, one that regularly puts huge men in the hospital, from which those men typically retire in their 30s because their bodies can't take any more abuse ….” I trailed off then, for dramatic effect. “This guy is afraid that football will become a game for sissies? *Really*? I wonder if he's like some of those coaches I've heard about who think it's a good idea to have eighth grade football players run into each other at top speed, head first, over and over, to toughen them up.”

“Exactly,” my therapist replied. I had apparently given the correct response to his question. He was feeling affirmed, and that's always a good state of mind for someone who is manipulating your cerebral vertebrae.

He went on to recount his own horror stories from his high school football days, stories of young players experiencing the after-effects of what we now would recognize as traumatic brain injury. We know that such injuries, even those classified as “mild,” accumulate over a person's lifetime, the same way that small amounts of mercury ingested through polluted fish accumulate in the body, leading to chronic health problems when those levels get high enough. I was properly appalled at his stories, and at the reactions of his coaches and their little euphemisms for these concussive injuries. “Billy got his bell rung, did he? Ha! Well, shake it off, boy, shake it off! Take five and we'll get you back on the field when you can see straight.” Spit, scratch, continue.

Yep, there's no more manly response to traumatic brain injury than to “shake it off.” That's what a concussed brain needs most, after all—more shaking.

This commentator's ranting about football becoming “sissified” is a great example of what can happen when people steeped in the ideology of honor are allowed to have a microphone. This ideology, as we know, tells men to be brave and strong and tough. If you “get your bell rung,” you should shake it off. Don't complain about it. Just get back on the field.

It seems that a lot of former NFL players are beginning to think differently about the wisdom of this approach. Is anyone seriously suggesting these guys are just being a bunch of sissies? When the NFL “concussion scandal” broke, a journalist asked famed former NFL quarterback Troy Aikman whether he would “do it all over again” (meaning, play football) knowing what he knows now about the long-term health consequences of concussive head trauma. He answered unequivocally, "No way. I'd play baseball instead." These are not the words of a coward or a wimp or someone who is full of sour grapes over a failed football career. Aikman led the Dallas Cowboys to a remarkable three Super Bowl championships in his 12 seasons as quarterback, and he was elected to both the College Football Hall of Fame and the Pro Football Hall of Fame. Despite all this success, he wishes, in retrospect, that he had accepted the baseball contract offered to him by the New York Mets when he graduated high school. That's quite an indictment, especially coming from someone like Aikman.

Echoing this strong sentiment, then-current San Francisco 49ers linebacker Chris Borland announced his retirement from professional football in spring 2015 at the ripe old age of 24. His reasons? Concerns about the long-term effects of repetitive head trauma. Apparently, Borland puts more value on his well-being than on the social accolades (including money) that come to someone who is successful in the NFL.

Reckless behaviors lead people living in honor states (especially men) to their deaths at unusually high rates. "Hey, y'all! Watch this!" is their battle cry. It comes before they fall off, go under, get bitten, or slip out. They need someone to watch them, because they do what they do as social proof of their mettle. But is that the whole story when it comes to risk-taking? Could there be a positive element to this pattern of excess?

Hail to the Chief

Do you know what the single best predictor of the winner of Presidential elections has been during the last 100 years in America? You might be thinking that political party would make a good predictor. That would be reasonable, but wrong. Across the 28 Presidential elections we've held in the United States since 1900, we've put Republicans in office barely more than half the time. So, clearly political party is not a great predictor of who wins. Scanning the portraits of the past 20 Presidents, I am surprised at how much hair they all have (having lost much of mine, I find myself feeling a great fondness for the nearly bald Eisenhower). But hair can be dismissed as well. Surely the other contenders for the job had just as much hair, and anyway, something like hair is clearly too trivial to make a difference to voters. I guess I still have a chance.

Although no one, to my knowledge, has actually tested the hair hypothesis, an equally trivial characteristic of the winners of presidential elections for the past 100+ years is both easily observed and oddly effective as a predictor. More than two to one (20 of 28 times, or 71%, if we're just counting the popular vote; 19 of 28 otherwise), the man most likely to be elected is *the taller of the candidates*. The height advantage isn't quite as pronounced if we look at all contested presidential elections since Washington (before the days of cameras and televisions), but it's still there, trivial as it might seem to be as a resume builder for the leader of the free world. Perhaps a taller President is in a better position to see the communists coming?[2]

There is another odd characteristic that is a good predictor of who will be elected to the Presidency. It turns out that among the 43[3] men who ascended to this high office, as many as 22 can trace their ancestors back to the border region between southern Scotland and northern Britain, and most of these were Ulster Scots.[4] Of the first 24 men who became President, either because

---

2. One reason to focus just on the presidential elections since 1900 is that precise records of each candidate's height (both the winners and the losers) are not consistently available for earlier elections. Although some scholars enjoy debating exactly how large of an advantage accrues to the taller candidate, the most striking trend I see in this debate is for *all* contenders in Presidential elections, both winners and losers, to be taller than the average American. Incidentally, the same is true for other politicians, including members of Congress (where we have much larger samples from which to draw when testing this height hypothesis).

3. Although Barak Obama is known as the 44th President, only 43 different men have ever ascended to this high office. Grover Cleveland was President twice, but not consecutively, so he gets two separate Presidential numbers.

4. I have consulted multiple sources for this information, some of them more reliable than others. Thirteen Presidential pedigrees seem indisputable to me: Andrew Jackson, James Polk, James Buchanan, Andrew Johnson, Ulysses Grant, Chester Arthur, Grover Cleveland, Benjamin Harrison, William McKinley, Theodore Roosevelt, Woodrow Wilson, Richard Nixon, and Bill Clinton. Another nine seem to be less certain but highly probable candidates as having a meaningful heritage from the borderlands of southern Scotland or northern Britain: John Adams, John Q. Adams, James Monroe, Dwight Eisenhower, Harry Truman, Jimmy Carter, Ronald Reagan, George H. W. Bush, and George W. Bush. Of course, the real

they were elected to the office or they took over from the Vice Presidency, at least nine, and possibly 12, were descendants of people from this border region. Now, you can immediately tell this genealogical factor is still not as good a predictor as height. Twenty-two is slightly more than 50% of 43, so it's not even close to playing the role that height has played in Presidential elections, at least during the past century.

Even so, 22 is statistically much higher than we would expect by chance alone. Considering that, in 1790, the Ulster Scots comprised approximately 10% of the entire U.S. population, we might expect only four or five of the 43 U.S. Presidents to be descended from Ulster Scots, unless other factors related to being descended from Scots is somehow related to being elected President (such as wealth, which *is* related to becoming President, but tends to work *against* the Scots, at least during the early days of America). Statistically speaking, the odds of America electing a Scot as President 22 times rather than just four or five times are quite small (roughly 1 in 100,000).[5] And yet, there they are.

What can account for this greater-than-chance number of U.S. Presidents descending from the Ulster Scots? Is it something in their genes? I think the answer to that question is an emphatic *no*. A thousand years of environmental pressures on a fairly isolated gene pool is probably enough time to produce some unique genetic characteristics among the Lowland Scots, although I am not aware of any evidence supporting this possibility. Even so, multiple migrations since 1600 and a plethora of intermarriages

---

trouble with calling any of these men Scots is the question of how many people in one's ancestry must hail from Scotland for one to be counted as Scottish. This is the same problem we run into with *every* social categorization system, including what it takes to be considered white, black, or Asian. In the end, we tend to rely on self-identifications in these matters, although that is not always true (recall the 1/64 rule in pre-civil rights America).

5. A chi-square goodness-of-fit analysis comparing the observed frequency of 22 of 43 Presidents to an expected rate of only 10% (based on an estimate of the Scotch-Irish representation in the U.S. population in 1790, which might be conservatively high) gives a chi-square value of 80.95, which is highly significant ($p < .001$). Even if we were to consider only the 13 U.S. Presidents who have an indisputable borderland heritage (most able to trace their ancestors directly to the Ulster Scots), the result is a proportion that differs significantly from chance: a chi-square value of 19.56, with $p < .001$.

would almost certainly be enough to dissolve any such genetic effects if they ever existed.

I would suggest, however, that the same cultural influences that lead people in honor cultures to engage in excessively risky behaviors—some of which can get you killed—might also promote the kind of risk-taking required for leadership, or for entrepreneurship more generally. I was discussing the research on risk-taking and accidental deaths once with a journalist, and he pressed me on how bad I was willing to say this risky proclivity really is. Aren't there some positive aspects to taking risks, he asked? Absolutely there are! If people never took any risks, no new companies would be built, no new educational programs would be initiated, no innovations of any kind would occur. In short, there would be nothing new under the sun. It takes a little dose of crazy to start something new. Being married to a small-business owner has shown me that much. The right kind of risk-taking can go a long way, when it's paired with wisdom, grit, and resources. Perhaps the high proportion of U.S. Presidents with an Ulster Scot heritage is a case in point.

A Medal for Your Mettle

Another positive side to high levels of risk-taking comes from a study that Collin Barnes, Kevin Dodd, and I recently conducted (Brown et al., 2011, unpublished paper). After a talk I gave at Baylor University on the culture of honor, a social psychologist named Jo-Ann Tsang asked whether there was any evidence of increased valor on the battlefield being shown by soldiers from honor states. There wasn't any such evidence at the time, but my collaborators and I found a way to examine this possibility by analyzing data on recipients of the Congressional Medal of Honor (CMH), which is given (often posthumously) to soldiers who display high levels of bravery and selflessness in war. In many cases, this bravery leads to their own death in the service of their comrades because the recipients of the CMH typically risk their lives trying to save their fellow soldiers. These risks can be so extreme, and the odds of success so low, they might sometimes be considered suicide missions. There is a fine line between suicide and selflessness, and the psychological distinction between the two might be even finer than most people realize.

In our analysis, we focused on the CMH given to soldiers during World War II, in part because the timeline for this war was well-defined and relatively compact (only about four years long compared with the meandering Vietnam conflict or the ongoing wars in Iraq and Afghanistan), and in part because more CMHs were awarded during World War II than during any other war in American history. Thus, we were able to create a sufficient database of medals attributed to each of the 50 states.[6] Because of institutional racism within the U.S. military at that time, medals were awarded only to white males during World War II, although seven CMHs were awarded by President Clinton a half-century later to black servicemen in long-overdue recognition of their wartime heroism. This systematic, institutional racism actually worked to our advantage in one respect, however, because it allowed us to compare award rates across states as a function of a very specific demographic group—the white populations present in each state according to the 1940 U.S. Census numbers. For statistical reasons, this fact makes for a pretty "clean" analysis, as far as such data go.

What we found in our analysis was consistent with our expectations. Specifically, soldiers from nonhonor states received a lower number of medals (an average of 3.17 per million white residents) during World War II compared to those from honor states (an average of 4.73 per million white residents). In other words, soldiers from honor states received these awards for bravery at a rate *about 50% higher* than the rate for soldiers from nonhonor states. This difference remained when we controlled statistically for each state's unemployment rate, and even for contemporary differences between honor states and nonhonor states in recruitment levels into the army (which are, in fact, higher among honor states).[7] Thus, as we suspected, the very cultural

---

6. I realize that Alaska and Hawaii were not actually states during World War II, but people still lived there in 1940, even if they were only territories. Thus, we included them in our study.

7. This contemporary recruitment difference is noteworthy because, unlike during World War II, there is no longer any legal requirement for military service for Americans. Thus, any differences we might see in recruitment rates today are *voluntary* differences, capable of reflecting people's beliefs and values.

forces that seem to lead to higher levels of suicides and excessive risk-taking on the home front can also come together on the battlefield to drive soldiers from honor states to exhibit incredible degrees of bravery against the enemy and in service to their fellow soldiers.

This finding, of course, does nothing to diminish the very real acts of valor shown on the battlefield by soldiers from nonhonor states. It merely reflects what we think is a cultural influence that can contribute to the kind of excessive risk-taking needed to rush headlong into enemy fire to take out a bunker or to rescue a fallen comrade. You'd have to be almost crazy to do what so many of our soldiers, men and women alike, have done in this regard—including many soldiers who have never been recognized formally for their bravery. Once again, a little excess in the right circumstances can be a good thing.

Just when I had given up hope of surviving this midnight ride to the graveyard, we were there—the old tombstones grinning up at us from among the tall weeds. Gravel and dried up flowers crunched under our heels after we pried our fingers from the sides of the machine that only moments before we felt would almost certainly drive us to our deaths. David was elated, of course, no less by the thrill of the ride than by his success at ignoring my demands. Though relieved, I was also enraged. The others had to separate the two of us at that point. We did not tell ghost stories that night. We did not enjoy an evening of raucous adolescent fun. The fun was over before it had even begun. David and I rarely spoke again after that night. I couldn't forgive him for what I perceived as his childishness in risking all our lives for a personal thrill, and he couldn't admit that he might have crossed a line in putting us all in danger. Humility and forgiveness do not come easily for people living in the embrace of the honor syndrome.

In this chapter, we have seen how aspects of honor culture norms can lead to excess levels of risky behaviors that do not always end the way my ride with David did, with the only casualties being a bruised ego or a friendship. Proving that you aren't chicken, that you have no fear of death's sting, can sometimes get you killed, and other people can be collateral damage in your inglorious plunge to the pit. But we have also seen that this same proclivity for risky business can, under the right circumstances, also lead to happier endings, including social recognition and awards, or even the main chair in a big, oval-shaped office.

Less extreme outcomes on the happy end of this continuum might include winning the mate of your choice in the dating game or starting a company that the world's more cautious types would only dream about, if they dared to dream of such things at all. Let's not forget that some dreams are little more than fantasies (my financial advisor pointed out that distinction to me recently—a painful lesson, to be sure). As Michael Wallis (2011) notes in his biography of American–frontier icon Davy Crockett, Crockett had no shortage of such fantasies. He spent his adult life jumping from one financial opportunity to the next, always sure that *this* time would be different from the last. He amassed huge debts that he never paid off, even with the sale of his autobiography (which earned him around $2000—an enormous sum in those days). Some might have said that Crockett was tenacious, persistent, or full of grit. I think the reality is that he just couldn't let go of a reckless venture until there was nothing left to hold on to. He wouldn't hesitate before jumping in, and he couldn't pull out when things went bad, for fear of looking timid (on the front end) or weak (on the back end). In the end, Crockett repeated the pattern of his father, differing primarily in that he simply fled his creditors—to the Alamo, where they'd never find him—rather than using his children as indentured servants to pay his debts. A lifetime of wise and well-reasoned risk-taking can certainly pay off, but a lifetime of impetuous recklessness typically leads to ruin.

My own risk-taking friend, another David, survived his immature driving days and eventually became a successful entrepreneur. Today, he is the owner of, no kidding, a deep-sea diving company. I laughed out loud when I discovered this fact, as I always suspected he would end up swimming with the fishes. Admittedly, I thought this would be a metaphor, not *literally* what he would do for a living. I wonder if he ever takes his clients into sunken ships and turns off the lights.

Discussion Questions

1. This chapter describes some of the first positive dimensions of honor ideology. Can you think of others, regardless of whether they are linked to risk-taking?
2. What other sorts of excess might be associated with honor ideology, and how might gender roles influence the types of excess valued in honor cultures?
3. This chapter briefly references military service. In what ways do you think the military might function like an honor subculture? In what ways might it be different?

For Further Reading

Barnes, C. D., R. P. Brown, and M. Tamborski. 2012. Living dangerously: Culture of honor, risk-taking, and the nonrandomness of "accidental" deaths. *Social Psychological and Personality Science* 3:100–107.

Chapter Six

Lineage

"OYEZ, OYEZ, OYEZ!" CRIED the garishly dressed town crier, as long-pent-up cheers resounded to the twittering flashes of photographers' cameras. Holding the parchment dramatically in front of him, he announced the arrival (at 8 lbs 6 oz) of His Royal Highness the Prince of Cambridge, the newborn son of William and Catherine, the Duke and Duchess of Cambridge. This child, who for a brief while became known only as "Baby Cambridge," was now third in line to inherit the throne of Britain (and potentially about $1 billion, give or take), pushing Prince Harry, the younger son of Prince Charles and the late Lady Diana, into a distant fourth place.

Expectations for the coming of Baby Cambridge were high; the nation of Britain was riding a fresh wave of enthusiasm for the royal family and, indeed, the entire concept of the monarchy, which had taken a beating during the 1990s. The wedding of William and Kate had proved to be a magnificent boon to the royals, and it wasn't long afterward that royal watchers began to rumor about a possible majestic conception on the horizon—or perhaps not just on the horizon. Was that a "bump" that Kate was seen shielding with her fabulously stylish clutch? And why didn't she join that toast with a glass of champagne, choosing to drink water instead? So the rumors went, until eventually they were confirmed, and thus began the countdown to the big day—the day of Baby Cambridge's bursting forth into the world of his inheritance, full of castles, balls, charity dinners, and paparazzi.

When he vacated his cozy little womb and the world learned the constitution of his genitalia, the next phase of international angst began: what, oh what, will this new baby boy be named? Royal names often take a while to be determined, for reasons I honestly don't understand. Gestation still takes a little more than 9 months, even if you are a future king, so didn't William and Kate (and the many royal parents who have gone before them) ever stop to discuss possible names? Were they worried that picking a name in advance would "jinx" the pregnancy or something? Why did they seem so flummoxed by the question of a name? "What? We have to name it? Egad! No one told us. Someone surely ought to get fired for missing that one!"

Top picks among professional British bookmakers were James and George, and I admit I was rooting for James, personally. But even if James were not chosen as the child's first name, it could always win a second, third, or even fourth seat on the name train, for as all true fans of British monarchs know, most royals have multiple first names (no last names), such as Arthur, Philip, Henry, Charles, and Edward, which connect them to their royal ancestry or denote some person of importance in the esteem of the child's parents, or possibly in the esteem of the currently reigning monarch. For William and Kate, that reigning monarch was Queen Elizabeth II, whose father had been a George (a name he assumed when he inherited the throne unexpectedly from his older brother, who had abdicated his privilege for the love of a woman). This noteworthy great-great-grandfather was one of the reasons that George had garnered one of the top spots on the bookmakers' lists and, before long, the world was relieved to learn that, in fact, George had been selected as the child's first name, followed by both Alexander and Louis. Whew! We could at last stop calling the poor child Baby Cambridge. That was quite a relief, even if my favorite name had not made the final cut (or the second or third cuts, for that matter).

Naming babies is not always this complicated or this political, but even for lowly commoners, choosing a name for a new human being can be something of a chore. There are, of course, books one can consult, and all a mother-to-be need do is raise the question at a gathering of relatives to receive an onslaught of advice. My wife and I learned the hard way not to solicit such input from relatives when one of our top picks (for our first child, a boy) was demolished by my wife's mother, who apparently had known someone with that particular name that she hadn't much liked. This news left us somewhat crestfallen, since our shortlist at the time really was rather short. With a last name like Brown, your options are limited, especially for boy names. Many traditional names sound boring, or like they might be pseudonyms, such as John or Peter or Michael. And forget about James, or any other famous (or infamous) celebrity whose last name had happened to be the color of dirt.

One of our dilemmas, to make matters worse, was that the male names on my side of the family were less than stellar. From the grandfather rolls there was a Robin (not bad, but it conjures up images of a caped sidekick) and a Rudolph (not even good, and the Christmas connotations are too obvious even to bother mentioning). My own father's name is Jerry, but there's the mouse to consider. That left us turning to my wife's side for possibilities, and there we found a couple of contenders, but none for which we were in complete agreement. Certain stronger candidates were associated with, shall we say, less than admirable individuals, causing us to have more than a few late-night squabbles well past the hour when conversations are really constructive. During one of these poorly timed dialogues, my wife pulled out a little paperback book that her best friend had given her called *Don't Name Your Baby*. This book mimicked the standard baby-name books in form, but instead of extolling the meaning and historical significance of each option, it mocked each name and explained why any child saddled with such a moniker would surely end up as either a stripper or a seller of gently used goods. Although hilarious, this book was not particularly helpful at that point in our quest.

What saved us, ironically, was the realization that we didn't have to be chained to the pedantic limitations of only a first and middle name. What if, like the British royals, we were to pick *several* middle names, using a family name that we liked from my wife's side and pairing it with the name of someone we truly admired and respected, which together we would combine with a first name that we liked but that had no other significance for us beyond its suitability to our tastes? It was, for us, an epiphany of the first order—a light bulb moment that may well have saved our marriage. The first middle name we selected, the name associated in our minds with someone worthy of admiration and emulation, was Graham, to be paired with the family name Thomas.

Years later, I was standing in the living room of the Rev. Dr. John Graham, the man whose last name my wife and I had chosen as one of our first son's (three!) names. I was staring at a large painting of an ancient warrior, decked out in full Scottish garb, plaid kilt and all.

"Who is that?" I asked my host.

"That," he replied, "Is a portrait of James Graham, Earl of Montrose, my great-great-great-great-great-great-great-great-grandfather." I later figure out that, technically, he needed about 11 "greats" in that sentence, but it isn't polite to question someone's "greats" when they are telling a story.

The Earl of Montrose, he told me, was a really interesting and complicated guy. As a southern Scot, educated at St. Andrew's University during the early 1600s, Montrose had sworn in a written covenant to protect Scotland's Presbyterian Church from the meddling might of the Church of England. However, Montrose was unusual in that he also considered himself a royalist, one who respected the right of the King of England, then Charles I, to rule over Scotland. Royalists in Scotland (for reasons you might recall from Chapter 1) were often considered traitors by Scottish nationalists, so as both a Covenanter and a Royalist, Montrose was a man of many layers. He would eventually fight both against, and later for, King Charles (actually, two King Charleses—both I and II), experiencing imprisonment and exile before finally being hanged in the town square of Edinburgh at the ripe old age of 38. A complicated man indeed.

Now, my wife and I do not really consider James Graham, Earl of Montrose, to be the namesake of our first son. That honor rests on the shoulders of the man who told me the story of the Earl, the 11-times great-grandson of the Scottish general, John Graham. Still, I can't help enjoying the subtleties and intricacies of this ancient forebear of our dear friend. I like a man who is willing to be hanged for his principles, who shows both loyalty and tenacity. For someone raised in an honor culture, these are truly qualities to be admired.

What the tale of my son's naming illustrates is the mix of motives and values that can be involved when parents name their babies. Do parents value currently popular names or avoid them? Do they strive to recognize their own parents or their parents' parents and, if so, are the father's forebears more important or the mother's? Does birth order matter? Or the sex of the child? Innocuous as it might seem to pick a name for a baby, the fact that multiple motives and values are at work in the process provides us with an opportunity—a window, if you will—into the sometimes subtle, inner workings of honor cultures. Or any culture, for that matter.

What's in a Name?

Teachers encounter a lot of different names over time. When I attempt to learn the names of my students, I must admit the number one problem I face is the quantity of repeated names among even a group of 30 to 40 students. I am never surprised to have four Jennifers or six Sarahs in a single class. But sometimes, you run across the unusual cases, and those you tend to remember. One of my favorites is Feather Feathers. That's Feather (first name) Feathers (last name). Another all-time favorite is Meredith Meredith. I actually decided to ask this young woman what the story was behind her name, and she happily obliged my curiosity. As a young girl, Meredith's parents got divorced. When her mother remarried a man with the last name of Meredith, he got on so well with his new wife's daughter that he decided to adopt her legally, leading to her new name, Meredith Meredith. Life can be funny sometimes, even amid tragedy.

You might think that how parents choose their kids' names is random and unpredictable, and to an extent that's true. According to a recent study, though, unusual names are not completely random occurrences. Rather, a very powerful cultural factor has been implicated in the frequency with which parents give strange, exotic, even completely invented names to their children. That cultural factor is individualism, which reflects the importance that some cultures place on personal uniqueness, autonomy, and differentiation. Individualistic cultures have "pet" sayings such as "To thine own self be true" and "Have it your way" and "Just believe in yourself." Individualistic cultures despise conformity and uniformity, and they prize self-esteem, standing out, and "personal authenticity."

Not surprisingly, the United States has been ranked in previous research as the most individualistic nation in the world (followed closely by Australia and Great Britain), with Central and South American nations anchoring the opposite end of the spectrum as highly collectivistic nations. Only in a highly individualistic country would the government try to recruit people to join the military—a nonindividualistic institution if ever there was one—with the slogan, "An Army of One." What does that even mean? If you could really have an army of one, what would be the point of anyone else enlisting?

Although the United States is arguably the most individualistic country on the planet, there is still variation within it. Some parts of the United States are more individualistic than others, and different ethnic groups that live in the same region vary with respect to this dimension, as well. Using a wide range of social indicators reflecting the different ways that individualism might manifest itself, such as the number of people who drive to work alone instead of carpooling, and the prevalence of single-person homes versus multigenerational homes, researchers have even quantified which states are the most and least individualistic in the country. The top three most individualistic on the list are Montana, Oregon, and Nebraska, with other western and midwestern states following close behind. At the bottom of the list (the collectivistic end) are Hawaii, Louisiana, and South Carolina (Vandello and Cohen, 1999).

States with larger Hispanic, Asian, or black populations were somewhat more likely to fill up the bottom of the list, whereas states with larger European/white populations tended to score the highest in individualism, although racial and ethnic demographics were not the only important factors. Indeed, according to an idea known as the *voluntary settlement hypothesis*, western states in the United States tend to be more individualistic than eastern states in large part because more individualistic people tended to push farther and farther westward as the continent was being settled by European immigrants (Varnum and Kitayama, 2011). Individualistic people like their autonomy and freedom. They like to have space to move around and do as they please. Thus, the West was a good fit for individualists during the early days of colonization, and the difficult, sparsely populated frontier tended to reinforce the individualistic values of autonomy, self-sufficiency, and so forth.

Why is all this important? Among the many consequences of individualism, there is a tendency of individualistic parents to choose unusual names for their children. If I value independence and uniqueness, then I might choose to give my sons and daughters names that will help them to stand out from the crowd, rather than blend in with an ordinary name. This desire, incidentally, is overtly stated as one of the most common motives American parents give for why they chose the name they did for their child, according to a popular parenting website (see www.babycenter. com). Anyone, after all, can be named John or Jill, but I've never met anyone named Jedi or Jeevika (both are actual names chosen by at least two different sets of parents in 2012, by the way).

Now, maybe I don't want my kids to get beat up *every* day at school ("Let's see if you can use your Jedi mind trick to find out who pulled your underwear over your head, kid!"), so I might decide to go ahead and use a more common name.[1] Still, I might spell it in an uncommon way. I might change the "a" in David to an "e" (someone did that), or I might exchange the "r" in Trisha for a nice "w" (someone did that, too). And these are exactly the sorts of decisions that parents make with greater frequency in more individualistic, western states in the Unites States, where parents are substantially less likely to use a popular or common name for their kids. Similar patterns have also been found in other countries with a recent history of European colonization, such as Canada and Australia (Varnum and Kitayama, 2011).

---

1. Another consequence of odd names can be social rejection, as evidenced in a recent study on Internet dating websites (Gebauer et al., 2012).

According to Stanley Lieberson, a sociologist from Harvard, and Freda Lynn, a sociologist from the University of Iowa, many western countries have shown a profound trend toward using more and more unique names during the past 100+ years (Lieberson and Lynn, 2003). Consider the following statistics cited by Lieberson and Lynn. Throughout the 17th and 18th centuries in England, the three most common boy names were chosen for about *half* of all boys born, with only a slightly lower level of concentration for girl names. Specifically, about half of all boys born in England during this period were named William, John, or Thomas, and just under half of all girls born in England during the same 200 years were named Elizabeth, Mary, or Anne. So, if you ever get the sneaking impression that a lot of people you read about in history books from this part of the world seem to have had the same name, it's because, well, they did.

By the 1800s, this incredible level of name concentration was already beginning to decline, but even in 1850, around 75% of all girls still received one of the top 20 names (with nearly 25% receiving the *single* most popular name in any given year during that time). By 1990, slightly less than 40% of all girls born in England received one of the 20 most popular names, with only about 4% receiving the single most popular name (the comparable figures for the United States were about 23% receiving one of the 20 most popular names, with slightly more than 2% receiving the single most popular name). Similar patterns also occurred in other countries as diverse as France, Hungary, and Germany (Lieberson and Lynn, 2003).

Likewise, tabulations of all male colonists in the first English–speaking colony in America (Raleigh, NC, first settled in 1587) show that of the 99 males in the first cohort, there were 23 Johns, 15 Thomases, and 10 Williams—so, about 50% of all the men, in other words, received one of just three popular names (Stewart, 1979). As was true for girls, this high level of name concentration declined rapidly during the 20th century, such that by 1990, only about 34% of boys born in the United States received one of the 20 most popular names, and only 3% received the single most popular name.

According to Lieberson and Lynn (2003), these dramatic changes in name concentration levels reflect changes in the degree to which people pay attention to currently popular trends when they name their babies. Clearly, parents still do follow trends, but they appear to be less chained to popular opinions about the "right" names than they used to be. This freedom from bondage to the rule of popularity is, in Lieberson and Lynn's view, a subtle indication that the United States and other countries they have studied are becoming more and more individualistic in their social norms. People, at least in some countries, seem to be marching to the beat of their own drummer more than ever before, which, when you think about it, has some rather profound implications for human relations. At its heart, though, this change is a *cultural* change, a shift in social influence that drives people—perhaps beyond their conscious awareness—to be more attracted to some names and less attracted to others.

The role of individualism, and changing levels of individualism over time, is a well-studied influence on naming trends. The question I turn to next is whether a different dimension of culture can play a role in how people decide what to name their children. Of course, that cultural dimension is the one that is the focus of this book: the honor orientation of a society. As we delve into this question, we will see that although the answer is yes, it is also more than that, for the *reason* honor ideology is associated with naming preferences reveals something profoundly important about the nature of honor ideology itself.

Of Patronyms and Patriarchs

David H. Fischer, the Pulitzer Prize–winning professor of history at Brandeis University, is a scholar I've referenced several times already in this book. Fischer has documented, perhaps better than anyone else, the lifestyles and social norms of the southern Scots that they brought with them when they immigrated to the United States, either directly from Scotland or by way of Northern Ireland (the Ulster Scots). A central feature of Scottish life was that families were organized into clans—extended family networks headed by a family patriarch, typically a grandfather. This patriarch was the family leader, and if important decisions needed to be made that affected members of the clan, those decisions usually were made by him.

The Scots, it turns out, are not the only people to have organized themselves into clans headed by a patriarch. This sort of social system is actually quite common throughout history, all around the world. And it seems to be particularly common in societies with economies based on the herding of sheep, goats, pigs, or cattle, which—before the advent of agriculture—was what *most* economies were based on.

In modern America, people are unlikely to think of their families as being patriarchal clans and, indeed, compared with the "patriclans" of more traditional societies, today's American families really aren't nearly so patriarchal or so clannish. Nonetheless, the echoes of the Scottish patriclan might still be heard, if you listen carefully, wherever honor norms are alive and well. One subtle way in which this echo might resound is in the names that parents give to their children.

Along with my colleagues Mauricio Carvallo and Mikiko Imura, I decided to investigate baby-naming practices to determine whether the patriarchal system of the Scottish patriclans might somehow live on within contemporary America (Brown et al., 2014a). People who study names use the term *patronym* to refer to names that come from a male forebear (for example, a son named after his father or grandfather). Likewise, they use the term *matronym* to refer to names passed down from a female forebear (such as a daughter being named after her mother or grandmother). We wondered whether parents in honor-oriented regions of the United States might be more likely to use patronyms, but not matronyms, compared to parents in nonhonor-oriented regions. The basis for this idea comes from the social organization of the Scottish patriclan. In such a system, as historian David H. Fischer (1989) noted, sons tend to be named after grandfathers (first) or fathers (second), connecting newborn males to previous generations of the male-dominated patriclan. However, no such tradition exists for daughters, who historically were often married off in strategic alliances with other clans in honor cultures. In such a system, there really wasn't much point in naming a girl after her female ancestors. The important connection for her would ultimately be to her husband's family, more than her own.

Fortunately for my colleagues and me, the U.S. government keeps a close watch on many aspects of social life, including the name of every child born in every state in the union who receives a social security number. It occurred to us that we could use the Social Security Administration's records to create a unique, if indirect, indicator of the use of patronyms and matronyms (or "namesaking," for short).

The logic of our namesaking measure was simple. If parents in some parts of the country are more prone to use family names for their children, then popular names in one generation ought to be unusually popular in the next generation (or the one after that) as well. In other words, if the babies born in 1960 start having babies around 1984 (who then start having babies around 2008), and if Stephen and George, for instance, were especially popular names in 1960, then babies born in 1984 and 2008 might be expected to be more likely to be named Stephen or George if they lived in a region guided by honor norms (such as in the South or West). That's namesaking.

Using this reasoning, we scored each state for the frequency with which the top 10 most popular names in 1960 also made it to the top 10 lists in 1984 and 2008, giving a state an extra "bonus" point if a top 10 name in 1960 made it onto *both* subsequent top 10 lists. We did this separately for boy names and girl names, and analyzed these scores according to whether each state is considered an honor state. As in other such studies of regional differences described throughout this book, we controlled statistically for all sorts of other differences between states, such as the racial and ethnic makeup of the population; the tendency of people to be religious, poor, or rural; and so forth. What we discovered was that honor states in the South and West exhibited substantially higher namesaking scores for boy names (but not for girl names) compared with nonhonor states in the North.

This result was just what we had predicted, but we wanted to verify our indirect scoring index to increase our confidence that it really meant what we thought it meant. The problem with such subtle, indirect measures is that if a bird doesn't quack like a duck (it only whispers, "quack"), it's hard to have confidence that it is, in fact, a duck. What we needed to increase our confidence were detailed birth records for each state that showed the baby's name

Table 6.1 NAMESAKING SCORES FOR NORTH CAROLINA
AND MINNESOTA BASED ON THE TOP 10 NAMES
IN EACH STATE IN 1960, 1984, AND 1998

VARIABLE	NORTH CAROLINA (%)	MINNESOTA (%)
% of Top 10 Boy Names		
Matching fathers	20.7	12.0
% of Top 10 Girl Names		
Matching mothers	1.2	2.5

along with both the mother's and father's names. Such records are not obtained easily, though, and even when they can be obtained, birth certificates in some states do not even include father's names. That's good news for privacy advocates, but the good news for us was that two states—Minnesota (a nonhonor state) and North Carolina (an honor state)—do, in fact, have birth records that we could access that included fathers' names. This made it possible to examine actual birth records for the 10 most popular boy and girl names in each state to determine whether the names of sons and their fathers, and daughters and their mothers, matched more often in North Carolina than in Minnesota.[2]

Table 6.1 shows what we found. As you can see, averaging across the years 1960, 1984, and 1998 (years chosen to match, as closely as the available records could, the years we used to create our indirect namesaking measure), boys given one of the top 10 names in North Carolina were named after their father slightly more than 20% of the time. Boys given one of the top 10 names in Minnesota, however, were named after their father only about 12% of the time. Girls were much, much less frequently named after their mothers in either state. This painstaking analysis of detailed birth records gave us greater confidence that our indirect namesaking measure was capturing what we hoped it would.

---

2. By "matched," I mean simply that a child's name is the same as either the parent's first or middle name, or was extremely similar to it (e.g., a boy named Jon with a father named John). If we only consider exact matches, or what we refer to as *legacy naming*, the differences shown in Table 6.1 are just as strong. Specifically, the rate of legacy names for boys in North Carolina was about seven times higher than it was in Minnesota.

These data support our hypothesis of greater use of patronyms, but not matronyms, in honor states than in nonhonor states. But it's still indirect—even the analysis of actual birth records—insofar as our comparison remained at such a macrolevel (the level of statewide differences across regions). What we needed next was a more direct comparison at the level of people. Thus, in a final study (Brown et al., 2014a), we administered a scale that assessed honor beliefs and values to a group of college students and asked them a set of very simple questions about how likely they would be to use their own name, their father's (or mother's) name, or their grandfather's (or grandmother's) name in the naming of future sons (or daughters).

What we found was that more honor-oriented men were more likely to say they would prefer to use a patronym for their sons. We found no such trend among women when it came to using patronyms for their sons, nor did we find a link between matronyms and honor ideology endorsement among either men or women for their future daughters. The fact that we found the expected link between honor ideology and patronyms among men but not among women makes sense in light of the age of our participants. Although male college students could easily imagine using their own name (or a father's or grandfather's name) for future sons, female college students would probably be hesitant to pick their own father's or grandfather's name for their future sons. Better to wait until they had a husband, in case they might want to use *his* name or in case *he* might want to use his father's or grandfather's name.

This study provided very nice evidence supporting the association between honor ideology and patronym use that we found in our study of regional differences in namesaking. What really made this survey study important, though, is that we included one other measure in addition to the measures of namesaking and honor ideology. This last measure assessed patriarchal attitudes among our respondents. By "patriarchal attitudes," I mean things like believing that men ought to be in charge of decision making in a marriage, and that it's always better for men to work and for women to stay home—you know, all barefoot-and-pregnant. Using a statistical technique called a *mediation analysis*, my collaborators and I were able to determine that the *reason* honor-oriented men showed a peculiar preference for patronyms was that these men also held particularly powerful patriarchal attitudes. In other words, the men in our study who espoused the ideology of honor wanted to use their own name, or a male family name, for their future sons *because* their honor beliefs and values led them to feel that men are, and should be, more powerful—and perhaps even more important—than women.

Does this sound impossibly archaic? Keep in mind that the results I just described were found among *college students*—not exactly the bastions of old-fashioned values. And yet, what they told us across our surveys fit the notion that the ideology of honor is, at heart, a patriarchal belief system, promoting the use of male family names for sons, but not female family names for daughters, because of those same patriarchal beliefs.

I recently came across a national survey conducted by Gallup (Newport, 2011), in which parents were asked whether, if they were to have only one child, they would prefer a boy or a girl (or had no preference either way). As you think about this survey question, do you feel, in your heart of hearts, that most Americans would say they had no preference? What most parents want more than anything is for their children to be healthy, right? If so, the sex of their unborn children probably pales so much in comparison that it would be hard for many people to come up with a preference, wouldn't it? No, it wouldn't. This poll showed that, although many parents don't report any particular preference, men (but not women) would prefer to have a son over a daughter at a rate of more than two to one: specifically, 49% of men prefer to have a son, and only 22% of men prefer to have a daughter (Newport, 2011).

Name That Town

Before we leave the topic of names, there is one last finding that bears noting when it comes to the honor syndrome. I have noted that using patronyms when it comes to picking names for boys is a way in which the patriarchal values of honor cultures are reflected. More than a decade ago, Michael Kelly, a social scientist at the University of Pennsylvania, likewise observed that honor states in the United States are significantly more likely to have town names that include violent words (such as *gun, kill,* and *war*) compared to nonhonor states (Kelly, 1999). A few examples are Murderer's Creek, Cut and Shoot, Gun Point, Cutthroat Gulch, and Gun Barrel City. In fact, when Kelly examined all the towns he could find that involved a violent word, 80% of them were in honor states.

Most people grow up in a town they did not name, or they move to a place because of a job change or out of love. My wife's uncle, for instance, lives in Truth or Consequences, New Mexico, locally known simply as "T or C." I do not make fun of him for the ridiculousness of his town's name; he bears no responsibility for it. It was given that name long before he arrived. Now, if he were to start a business, such as a catering service, and he named it something equally preposterous, such as "Maggot's Munchies," then I would feel not only a sense of allowance, but actually a sense of *duty* to ridicule him for his decision. Thus, business names, most of which are much more recent in origin than town names, provide a nice test of the role that honor plays in contemporary life. That is why it is especially instructive that Kelly (1999) examined the relative prevalence of violent images in business names. As with place names, he discovered that violent business names are decidedly more common in honor states, excluding businesses related directly to violent activities, such as gun dealers (which we would expect to be more prevalent in honor states), or businesses named after the town in which it was located (such as War Taxi, located in War, West Virginia). Indeed, Kelly found that 68% of businesses with violent names were located in the South or West.

Kelly himself summed it up well:

If so inclined, a family in Alabama could have their television serviced at Warrior Electronics, their dog housed at Gunsmoke Kennels, their home addition built by Bullet Construction, and their children taught at Battleground School. A Texan could be born in Gun Barrel City, pray at Battle Ax Church, fish at Bullet Creek, dine at Shotguns Bar-B-Q, work at Outlaw Avionics, and be interred in Battle Creek Cemetery. Of course, northerners can also encounter places or businesses with violent names, such as Bloody Pond, New York, and Shotgun Willie's Saloon in Massachusetts. In a nation like the United States, one does not have to travel far to see violence highlighted.

However, such opportunities are rarer in the North than in the South and West (Kelly, 1999, pp. 15-16).

I have argued, in this book, that the honor culture norms of the Ulster Scots have remained influential in honor states in America for the past few hundred years, which is largely why the types of behaviors described throughout this book are still seen. How, though, are these honor-related beliefs and values, these schemas and scripts for social life, transmitted from one generation to the next? Other chapters (such as Chapters 2, 3, 7, and 9) address this important question from other angles, but I want to end this chapter by speculating that *naming itself* could be one such mechanism. Names, after all, don't just give us a quick way to indicate to whom we are speaking (such as Bill, not William) or where we are going (for example, Tuscaloosa, not Montgomery). Names can also provide a subtle means for a society to express and even teach its values. What I've suggested in this chapter is that how people name things that are important to them—such as their towns, their businesses, and their children—reflects their most cherished values, whether those values are of individualism (for example, being unique and standing out) or those of the honor syndrome (for instance, being aggressive and honoring male ancestors).

Thus, names can serve as a mechanism for transmitting those cherished values, a mechanism so subtle it could go easily unnoticed. This isn't to say that *the values themselves* go unnoticed, although these, too, might be embraced unconsciously (as we will see in Chapter 9). However, if the *mechanism* that transmits the values goes unnoticed, staying beneath the radar of social consciousness, then overt challenges to those values might not be enough to change them. This is why it is important to consider the more subtle channels of communication that societies use to teach their beliefs and priorities to successive generations. Not to do so would be akin to taking away your children's laptops to keep them from e-mailing their friends, but not confiscating their cell phones. The messages are still delivered, even if the delivery device is smaller.

The subtlety of these sorts of norms, incidentally, can be illustrated by returning briefly to my own experience with naming my sons, part of which I referenced earlier in this chapter. My wife and I had a sense that we ought to use a family name, but why? Did anyone sit us down and tell us we had better choose a family name for our sons, or they would be very disappointed in us? Were we concerned that we might be disinherited if we didn't use a family name? No, and no. We just knew that we should. It *felt wrong* not to do so.

The family names we ended up using were a grandfather's name for our first son, and my own name for our second son. This pattern, it turns out, is exactly the pattern of patronyms normative among the southern Scots. Well, maybe not *exactly*, insofar as we used these family names as middle names (which the ancient Scots didn't even have), and the grandfather whose name we used was the "wrong" grandfather—my wife's father, rather than mine. But these exceptions aside, the conformity of our choices to the Scottish naming norms is remarkable and freaky. Among the Scots, first-born sons were typically given the paternal grandfather's name, in essence connecting the weakest member of the clan (who one day might himself be its patriarch) to the strongest member of the clan. Second-born or subsequent sons were often given the father's own name (which itself was typically the name of a previous, likely dead, forebear).

Reflecting on these naming traditions, I recently realized that I myself was named in this fashion; my middle name is the first name of my paternal grandfather, Rudolph. It took me a while to realize this because my middle name isn't Rudolph; it's Paul. However, my paternal grandfather was never called Paul—for reasons I will never understand, he chose to be known by the name of one of Santa's reindeer—so I forgot that Paul was his given name. My wife and I did not know that we were following a Scottish naming norm, and we certainly did not *consciously* decide to do so. And yet, follow it we did. Somehow, it just felt right. That's how these social norms and values often work, it seems—with the quiet force of "it just feels right."

Discussion Questions

1. What reasons have you heard parents give for the names they chose for their children? Do you believe these reasons? Why or why not?

2. What other examples can you think of that might be subtle instances of honor ideology exerting its influence on social life?
3. What might be some of the implications of a society's use of patronyms for boys but not matronyms for girls? Does this difference matter?

For Further Reading

Brown, R. P., M. Carvallo, and M. Imura. 2014. Naming patterns reveal cultural values: Patronyms, matronyms, and the culture of honor. *Personality and Social Psychology Bulletin* 40:250–262.

Kelly, M. H. 1999. Regional naming patterns and the culture of honor. *Names* 47:3–20.

Lieberson, S., and F. B. Lynn. 2003. Popularity as a taste: An application to the naming process. *Onoma* 38:235–276.

CHAPTER SEVEN

The Honor Circle

I's A DAY LIKE any other. Nothing special. You took your morning walk or your morning run or your morning joddle (the love-child of a jog and a waddle, in case you are wondering). Wiping the perspiration from your brow, you grab your first cup of coffee in your favorite mug and sit down to scan the paper while eating a bowl of cereal. It's a good day.

This was how the day began for me when it happened. I had put the paper down—there was nothing that seemed worth reading that morning—and turned my attention to the *Today Show* on NBC, hosted back then by Katie Couric and Matt Lauer. Matt had just started to interview a guy named Richard Hack who had written a book about billionaire Howard Hughes. The interview was interrupted almost before it had really begun. Something had happened. Something big. I put down the cereal bowl whose milky remains I had just lifted to my lips.

The image of what seemed like a very small plane crashing into the World Trade Center in Manhattan was burned into my brain that morning, as it was for millions of Americans and people around the world. What had at first looked like a small plane turned out to be a large jet filled with passengers. It also turned out to be only the first of two planes that would crash into the World Trade Center that morning, the second following the first a short time later, dispelling all doubt that this was just an accident. America had been attacked.

The honor syndrome relates to this infamous day in several ways, as we shall see in this chapter and the next. Honor ideology can motivate people to engage in extreme acts, both good and bad, in the service of their groups. On the good side are acts of heroism and self-sacrifice. On the bad side are acts of terrorism. But honor ideology can also lead to a suite of *reactions* to terrorism that are capable of feeding the cycle of intergroup violence, for honor is not merely a solitary pursuit. It is a collective endeavor, in which people bind themselves to one another in an "honor circle." The honor circle becomes an extension of the people in it, so the reputation of the circle becomes the reputation of everyone in the circle. In this way, the individual and the group become one.

Thinking about terrorist groups is difficult for most of us, though. We've never met a terrorist (as far as we know, anyway), and we can't imagine ever joining a jihadist group. Perhaps we should start with something a little more mundane if we wish to understand the nature of the honor circle. So, let's talk football.

When I mentioned I was visiting from out of state and said the word *Oklahoma*, the doctor's ears perked up immediately. His first question following the revelation of my origins was not "Who are you visiting?" or "How has your trip to the great state of Alabama been so far?" Instead, it was "What do you think about the game?" He didn't specify which "the game." He didn't have to. I knew he was talking about the bowl game scheduled for the next week between the University of Oklahoma and the University of Alabama. Oklahoma was ranked number 11 in the Bowl Championship Series (BCS) poll. Alabama was ranked number three, and if not for its miraculous loss to Auburn, Alabama would be the team playing for the national championship instead of the Auburn Tigers.

I pondered my options. My "doctor" wasn't really a *doctor*, actually. He was a physician's assistant, and he seemed to have a small chip on his shoulder. I, in contrast, had no chips, only the flu. Should I pronounce my confidence in my Oklahoma Sooners, perhaps with a comment about how it would be the blood of the Alabama players that would color the Tide crimson? Or should I play it cool, leaving the Sooner football team to do my talking for me? I *did* want good medical care, and I wasn't sure how deep this man's partisanship ran. I'd already waited three hours in the waiting room. He had the power to make me wait some more.

"I'm not really sure," I replied cautiously. "I think it could go either way." It was an honest response, I suppose, if a bit tautological.

"I think it's *definitely* going to go Alabama's way," he asserted with a hint of disdain. He hardly looked up from his clipboard. No doubts with this guy. Here was a true believer.

"Well, we'll see," I said. Dare I allude to that fantastical catch at the end of the Auburn–Alabama game that had given Auburn its unexpected victory? What a beautiful catch, destined to overshadow the famous "Punt-'Bama-Punt" fiasco of 1972 that I had grown up on. I wasn't out of harm's way yet, though, so I played it safe once again.

My caretaker went on to confess that he had actually married an Auburn fan, and that he didn't just want his team to *beat* Oklahoma. He wanted Oklahoma to suffer an *embarrassing* loss. "After all," he explained, "I've got to recruit against them for next year."

This was one of the most remarkable moments in our strange interchange in this tiny room in this modest doc-in-the-box in Hoover, Alabama, two days after Christmas. As my body was wracked by an involuntary dry heave, I marveled over this man's degree of personal identification with his favorite college football team. *He* was going to have to recruit against my team—against every team— for the next football season. *He* was a physician's assistant, not a sports recruiter. This delusion went deep, and this man needed to be handled with care, as do all full-throttled partisans in a culture of honor. It wasn't just his favorite team's honor that was at stake in the upcoming bowl game. It was *his* honor, too. That the man and his group were psychologically intertwined was not unprecedented. We were, after all, in the heart of the American South, the hotbed of America's long-standing honor culture. I had grown up here, so I knew it well. You can never be sure how far such a man might go to assert his supremacy when his honor is on the line, and this man had access to needles, drugs, and things that can make incisions.[1]

---

1. My caution might well have saved me some unnecessary suffering in that moment. But it would be my Sooners who would later reclaim my pride in their victory over the Crimson Tide at the Sugar Bowl.

The Alabama–Auburn rivalry was a vicious one, as I well knew from my youth. The week of the Iron Bowl (when Alabama played Auburn each November) was one of my least favorite weeks in the entire year growing up, second only to the first week of school in the fall. That's really saying something, considering the Iron Bowl was played the week of Thanksgiving. This rivalry, which started back in 1893,[2] split friends as well as families. My best friend in grammar school was an Alabama guy, which was unfortunate, as his allegiance clashed with that of my Auburn–loving family. Husbands and wives that I knew who rooted for opposing teams would hardly speak to each other for days after this game. It was ugly. It was not just a game to some people. It was war, and it was religion, which made it a holy war.

You aren't really allowed *not* to pick a side in this state, and polls show that a whopping 86% of Alabamians identify with one of these two teams. Some fans have even taken to acts of notorious vandalism, such as the poisoning of a 130-year-old grove of trees in Auburn back in 2010 by rabid Alabama fan Harvey Updyke, Jr.[3] Updyke did some jail time for his crimes against tree-manity, after which he fled to Louisiana in self-imposed exile. He might be a fan, but he's no fool. Okay. Maybe he *is* actually a fool, but he's not stupid enough to stick around in a state filled with Auburn fans after what he did.

I do not believe that the fierceness of this college football rivalry is an accident, as you might imagine. I think that part of its viciousness is, in fact, a consequence of culture. To the same extent that players and fans feel united as an honor circle and bound together in a common cause, they likewise feel antagonism toward their enemies—particularly their archrivals. The ferocity of their loyalty to one another thus finds its complement in the ferocity of their hostility toward members of the opposing team. The Crimson Tide players come to hate the Auburn Tigers, and Auburn fans see red when they encounter Alabama fans. The team's honor is *their* honor. But this is, after all, just one football rivalry, and in scientific terms, that's nothing but an anecdote. Is there any other evidence for the potential role of the ideology of honor in sports? As it turns

---

2. Auburn won that first game, by the way. War eagle.
3. Yes, he was a junior, a patronymic namesake. Coincidence? Or destiny?

out, there is, and the evidence concerns excessive aggression and poor sportsmanship. Harvey Updyke, Jr., is not alone.

Now, sports junkies keep track of a great deal of sports statistics. I imagine that if one were so inclined, the number of left-handed, red-haired Major League pitchers born in February between 1911 and 1993 could be gleaned from the archives. People keep a lot of strange data, just in case someone might need them. It's basically the same approach my mother has taken to, well, everything. She's not a hoarder, mind you, but she has a gift for holding on to things far longer than most human beings ever would. "You just never know when you might need it" is her mantra.

However, one statistic that I've had a great deal of difficulty tracking down concerns penalties for personal fouls and unsportsmanlike conduct in college football. These penalties are assessed against teams after overly aggressive or otherwise inappropriate behaviors, such as hitting a player after he is already out of bounds or threatening to decapitate a referee. So, these are penalties for unnecessary aggression in a sport that is more or less the personification of aggression. Why that particular statistic is so difficult to find, I'm not really sure, although I imagine that it has simply seemed unimportant to the people who track the goings-on of the gridiron. Maybe it feels unseemly to mention it. Maybe people don't want to insult anyone by pointing out their misbehavior. I don't really know.

With some digging, however, one can find sports junkies who manage to keep track of these penalties. Marty Couvillon, for instance, has a website (www.cfbstats.com) that reports more college football stats than you can shake a stick at, if you are inclined toward stick shaking. He has catalogued the games with the all-time highest number of such penalties between 2005 and 2010, and his list is broadly consistent with an honor-based perspective on the Alabama–Auburn rivalry. Of the 19 games in these six seasons with 10 or more penalties for personal fouls and unsportsmanlike conduct, 16 of them (or 84%) involve a team from an honor state. Furthermore, 13 of these 19 high-penalty games (or 68%) involve opposing teams that are *both* from honor states.

Similarly, sports blogger Lew Patton (2013) has looked at such penalty data across the 10 football seasons spanning 2003 to 2012. According to Patton, the data in Table 7.1 are the 20 teams from the BCS with the most and least penalties per game for personal fouls and unsportsmanlike conduct throughout this 10-year period.

There are multiple ways to "cut" these data, but what's most relevant to this chapter is the fact that of the 20 "dirtiest" teams noted in Table 7.1 (that's Patton's label, by the way, not mine), 17 (85%!) are located in honor states. In contrast, only eight (or 40%) of the "cleanest" teams are from honor states, if we exclude the regionally diverse military academies from the honor-state count, all of which show up on the clean list (an interesting fact in itself). Several teams on the dirty list were recent additions to the BCS rolls, so their data cover only a few seasons. Three of

Table 7.1 COLLEGE FOOTBALL TEAMS WITH THE MOST AND LEAST PENALTIES FOR PERSONAL FOULS AND UNSPORTSMANLIKE CONDUCT (2003–2012)

20 TEAMS WITH THE MOST PENALTIES	20 TEAMS WITH THE FEWEST PENALTIES
University of Texas at San Antonio	Wisconsin
Massachusetts	Navy
Idaho	Connecticut
South Alabama	Alabama
Pittsburgh	Vanderbilt
Texas Tech	Minnesota
University of California at Los Angeles	Northwestern
Utah	Ball State
Oregon State	Army
Florida State	Rutgers
Oregon	Virginia
Purdue	New Mexico State
Utah State	San Jose State
Arizona State	Temple
Texas State	North Carolina State
University of Southern California	Boston College
Florida Atlantic	Air Force
University of Nevada at Las Vegas	Wake Forest
Texas	Ohio State
Washington State	Rice

these four recent additions are located in honor states (specifically, University of Texas at San Antonia, South Alabama, and Texas State), and one is not (Massachusetts). However, if we omit these four teams and include the next four on the list, the conclusion remains unchanged; of the next four dirtiest teams, three are in honor states (Troy, Florida International, and Baylor) and one is not (Toledo). In sum, a much greater proportion of teams with the highest number of penalties per game for personal fouls and unsportsmanlike conduct comes from honor states in the U.S. South and West compared with the proportion of teams with the lowest number of such penalties.

But it gets even more interesting (at least if you are a data nerd, like me). Using data from school websites,[4] we can compute the percentage of each football team's roster composed of players hailing from honor states, and then we can use this "honor roster" as a predictor of the number of penalties for personal fouls and unsportsmanlike conduct per game that each team earned, which is an even more nuanced analysis than simply counting "clean" and "dirty" teams. Collin Barnes, Kevin Dodd, and I (unpubl. data) have done this for penalties earned for the 2011 and 2012 seasons, using honor roster data from 2011. As in other studies I've discussed throughout this book, we also controlled for a set of statewide (and in this case, school-specific) variables that might lead to a spurious association, such as state levels of economic deprivation and rurality, whether the school is public or private, and even the team's total percentage of wins from 2005 to 2011 (an index of its competitiveness). Details of this analysis, which has not heretofore been published, can be found in Appendix B.

The results are perfectly consistent with what I've already described from Marty Couvillon's report of the penaltiest games in college football ("penaltiest" might not actually be a word, but it should be). Specifically, the greater the proportion of a team's roster that comes from an honor state, the more penalties per game that team earns for personal fouls and unsportsmanlike conduct. This outcome could just be construed as yet another instance of the kinds of aggression I discussed in Chapter 2, but I think this is

---

4. My deepest thanks to Kevin Dodd for mining these team rosters for this analysis.

actually a somewhat different beast from run-of-the-mill interpersonal violence. This is excessive aggression in an *intergroup context*, a competition in which individual glory is subjugated in part to collective glory. Individual honor is served by the group's honor, and sometimes in football the players seem to think that promoting their team's honor means behaving badly toward the other team, taunting them, hitting them after the play is over, or tackling in a manner designed to inflict the maximum physical damage possible.[5] That type of mentality appears to be more prominent in teams filled with players from honor states.

The Patriot

Every good citizen makes his country's honor his own, and cherishes it not only as precious but as sacred. He is willing to risk his life in its defense and is conscious that he gains protection while he gives it.

—As cited in Hoit (1890, p. 218)

This quote is attributed to Andrew Jackson, seventh President of the United States. Jackson was the first man of full Scottish descent to ascend to the Presidency, although, as noted in Chapter 5, certainly not the last. His parents, Andrew and Elizabeth, were Ulster Scots who immigrated to the United States a few years before his birth in 1767. The senior Andrew Jackson died tragically just weeks before his son was born. Following the Scottish tradition, Andrew and Elizabeth named their first two sons (Hugh and Robert) after other male forebears, only giving their youngest son his father's name after the senior Andrew's death.

President Jackson was born and raised in the Carolinas, and practiced law in the western part of North Carolina, which later would become part of the state of Tennessee. His work as a frontier lawyer helped him rise politically, eventually being elected as

---

5. Football, of course, is not the only sport in which group-based honor concerns can lead to excessive aggression. Baseball, which is not nearly as violent a sport as football, has also been shown to have an honor-based misbehavior element, as demonstrated by research conducted by Timmerman (2007), who analyzed statistics on batters hit by pitches.

a representative of Tennessee to the new U.S. Congress. He was also a successful businessman and farmer, a shining example of a common man rising above his inherited station in life to the highest levels of social influence.

However, it was his skill as a military commander that brought Jackson fame. His military service began at the age of 13, when he fought in the American Revolutionary War against the British. He went on to serve in the Tennessee militia and fought against Chief Tecumseh in the War of 1812 and, subsequently, against Tecumseh's Creek Indians, when he commanded the likes of Davy Crockett and Sam Houston. It was during this time that he earned the name "Old Hickory" from his troops, who respected him for his toughness and bravery in battle (with a few exceptions, including Crockett himself, who deeply resented Jackson). Indeed, his victories during the War of 1812, especially at the Battle of New Orleans, may well have been the single most important factor in elevating him to the office of President 16 years later.

Despite the respect he earned on the battlefield, from friend and foe alike, Jackson also earned a reputation for retribution against those who spoke against him. Indeed, not only did he have multiple politicians and judges arrested for condemning his declaration of martial law after the Battle of New Orleans, he also had six of his own men shot for the same "crime." It seems that, in Jackson's mind, to speak against him was akin to treason. And treason is not something easily countenanced by those who embrace the honor code. For Jackson, a personal betrayal and a collective betrayal were emotionally equivalent, for his country's honor was fused with his own.

In this way, Jackson's mentality is reminiscent of the mentality of many sports teams in honor-oriented regions of the United States that view opposing teams as enemies, and whose fans celebrate their teams' victories as their own. In honor cultures, the honor circle connects the individual to the collective in an almost familial way. The honor circle becomes a "band of brothers," an extension of the self.

Consider the following thought experiment. Imagine you got up one morning as you do on every other morning, going through your regular routine—shower, make the bed, greet the family (preferably *after* the first cup of coffee, which helps to put some civility in your greeting). On your second cup of joe, you crack open the paper, where you are met with an alarming headline: The Statue of Liberty Has Been Attacked! You scan the first page for details, sloshing your coffee on the paper in your earnestness. The attack, it turns out, was the work of terrorists from Afghanistan, possibly linked to Al Qaeda. Their viciousness claimed the lives of more than 250 people, many of them tourists, and more than a few of them children. Adding insult to injury, the head of Lady Liberty had been blown off by the attackers, its twisted and charred remains lying in disgrace at her feet.

How would you feel if this were to happen? Would partisanship disappear in such a moment? Would all Americans rally as one nation in response to this threat, this national outrage, this foreign attack on one of the most beloved symbols of our democracy? Or would cultural ideologies surface and guide people's interpretations and responses to the attacks, leading some to respond with greater malice than others?

This is the very question that Collin Barnes asked in a study several years ago, along with Lindsey Osterman and me (Barnes et al., 2012). We posed a scenario like the one just described to a sample of nearly 200 white men from around the United States. Besides measuring these men's endorsement of the ideology of honor, we also measured a variety of other characteristics, including their levels of religiosity, conservatism, and other personality characteristics that have been shown in previous studies to predict responses to intergroup conflict.[6]

After describing the terrorist attack against the Statue of Liberty (and presenting a fictitious picture of Lady Liberty with her head blown off), we asked these men a set of questions to gauge their mental states and feelings in response to imagining this event. First, we provided them with space to write about their thoughts and feelings for as long as they wanted to do so. We later had a pair of judges (who didn't know anything about our study's purposes) read these open-ended responses and code them for their levels

---

6. These characteristics included trait aggression, right-wing authoritarianism, and social dominance orientation.

of hostility and anger. Next, we presented our study participants with four additional scenarios designed to be much more ambiguous than the attack on the Statue of Liberty. Let's call these the *stranger-danger scenarios*. One of these scenarios, for instance, read like this:

> You are standing in line at the post office when a dark-skinned man dressed in Middle Eastern garb walks in carrying a large, seemingly unmarked package. He is breathing hard, sweating profusely, and keeps looking at his watch.

We asked participants to read each of these four ambiguous scenarios and to rate how suspicious and threatening the person in the scenario seemed to them. These responses were designed to capture participants' levels of vigilance to danger. Last, we asked participants to rate their support for severe interrogation techniques, even if those techniques cause lasting psychological or physical harm, as well as their support for America's "war on terror." We designed our measure of support for the war on terror to be rather extreme, in part to see how far people might be willing to go in their responses to perceived national threats. For instance, in one item we asked whether people believed it was appropriate to engage in "preemptive attacks on countries that are suspected of harboring or supporting terrorists." In another item, we asked whether respondents believed that the United States "should use nuclear weapons to defend its interests" against terrorists.

The results of this study were remarkable. Across all the measures described, participants with strong honor ideology scores expressed greater hostility in their open-ended responses to the fictitious terrorist attack, as well as greater suspicion and vigilance in response to the ambiguous stranger-danger scenarios, and more support for the war on terror. In other words, men who endorsed the ideology of *personal honor* also appeared to feel a sense of *collective honor threat* after imagining an attack on a preeminent symbol of America, and they were more willing to support a policy of preemptive strikes and even *nuclear* retaliation after contemplating this fictional attack. The nation's honor was *their* honor, and it was sacred. Those who violate what is sacred must pay with blood.

Desecration

I was standing at the counter of the glass-cutting shop in the heart of Oklahoma City. The shop sold small panes for windows and large panels for doors, and I marveled at the irony that such a dusty, cluttered store would deal in something as delicate and clear as glass. I could hear the shopkeeper rummaging around in the small room behind the thin plywood wall that separated us, opening and closing file cabinet drawers looking for a record of my order. Things here were done with carbon paper, not computers, so a physical record had to be located before our business could proceed.

As I leaned against the counter, I saw him through a small window, shuffling deliberately from one side of the room to the other, checking his piles and drawers. Then, I noticed a faded decal on the window itself. I hadn't seen it at first because my eye had been drawn to the movements of the old man several feet behind the glass. The decal was a picture of John Wayne superimposed on a large American flag, and I immediately recognized his eye-patched character "Rooster Cogburn" from the 1969 film *True Grit*. What a classic film, one of Wayne's best. He wasn't really much of an actor, but somehow that never seemed to matter. He just pulled it off, especially when cast in a role like Rooster Cogburn.

I looked more carefully at the decal. There were words written next to his head, and I could only make them out by leaning uncomfortably into the counter. They said, "Now, just why in *the hell* should I have to 'press 1' for English?!" I found it easy to imagine these words sauntering out of John Wayne's mouth, dripping with a slightly intoxicated disdain. Then I noticed a sign taped just to the left of the decal, this one much newer than the first. It was a list of local gasoline stations that didn't buy their oil from Middle Eastern suppliers. "Buy American," the sign said.

Psychologists since around the 1940s have connected a certain personality type to a tendency to stereotype others and to reject outsiders, especially foreigners. This type of person is said to be high in authoritarianism, a social pathology that is perhaps best exhibited in the 1970s comedy *All in the Family* by the show's main character, Archie Bunker. Authoritarians fear the unfamiliar, and they find safety in dogmatic adherence to rules and social order.

They are quick to judge and slow to change their views, even in the face of strong opposing evidence. This seemed to me to be exactly the type of person responsible for the pair of images I saw in the glass shop. Together, they declared that to be a true American, you had to speak English (preferably without a foreign accent), and you displayed your patriotism by avoiding gas stations supplied by America's enemies in the Middle East.

Besides being fueled by authoritarianism, could these sentiments also flow from the ideology of honor somehow? There is no direct link between xenophobia and the honor syndrome, and none of the items in any honor ideology measure I have seen (or used in my research) has anything to say about people's feelings toward strangers, foreigners, or anything of the kind. To my knowledge, no one studying honor ideology had ever connected these attitudes to honor cultures. Perhaps they are unrelated.

But then again, perhaps not. After all, in a world with limited resources and fierce competition for global control, both economically and militarily, foreigners might be seen as threats, or potential threats, to the nation's honor. Just as a schoolyard bully can beat down his rivals, so, too, might America's enemies wish to beat us down, limiting our influence in global affairs and even threatening our security. It was just such people who attacked us on 9/11. Similarly, immigrants flooding across the border were a threat to national security and to the security of American jobs. It's not hard to imagine the following diatribe coming from a person steeped in the ideology of honor:

> They come over here and they take jobs from honest citizens, and they use our schools and our hospitals and other social services, but they don't pay for them because they don't pay taxes. They defile our country's good name and exploit our generosity, leaching our wealth and resources. They are like cattle-rustling thieves. Isn't our failure to secure our borders against them a stain on our country's honor?

Collin Barnes and colleagues (including me) decided to test these ideas in another series of studies conducted with both college students and a more nationally representative sample of adults in the United States (Barnes et al., 2014). In one study, we administered various measures of personality (including an index of authoritarianism, among others) along with a measure of honor ideology. We wanted to determine whether honor ideology could predict hostile attitudes toward immigrants and aggressive stances on border control. To this end, we asked respondents the extent to which they believed that "illegal immigrants are a growing problem," and that "we should protect the United States from illegal immigrants just as we would our own homes." Furthermore, we asked people whether they would support the electrification of fences along the U.S.–Mexico border to help discourage people from crossing over illegally, and whether they thought that border patrol officers should be allowed to "rough up" anyone they catch trying to cross illegally.

Across multiple samples of respondents, we found that honor ideology did, indeed, predict these anti-immigrant and aggressive border security attitudes, above and beyond other personality variables such as authoritarianism. Thus, honor ideology endorsement did not appear to be simply another manifestation of a pathological personality or "cognitive style." Rather, honor ideology is something that is learned over time and transmitted culturally, through socialization.

But we also got a glimpse into why honor ideology is related to these hostile attitudes toward immigrants. Two additional factors seem to be at work in connecting honor ideology to these attitudes. The first is the tendency to identify the self with the nation.[7] In other words, people high in honor ideology seem to fuse their individual identities with that of the collective honor circle—in this case, the nation as a whole. Second, and following somewhat from the first, people high in honor ideology tend to take threats to the nation's honor as personal threats.[8] To threaten, exploit, offend, or defile the collective is to threaten, exploit, offend, or defile *them* as individuals. Thus, honor-oriented people appear to do what Andrew Jackson did—connecting their identity and their personal honor with the identity and honor of the collective honor

---

7. To capture this, we modified four identity items from Luhtanen and Crocker's (1992) collective self-esteem scale. An example item is: "In general, belonging to my national group is an important part of my self-image."

8. Example items capturing this tendency were: "I take it personally when others 'bad-mouth' my country" and "I am offended if other people have little or no respect for my country."

circle. Psychologically, the two are one, each an integral part of a whole.

Bill Swann, a social psychologist at The University of Texas, has recently identified this tendency, which he calls "identity fusion," as one of the key factors in people's willingness to die for their group (Swann et al., 2014). Identity fusion is what Swann describes as "a visceral sense of oneness with a group" (p. 913), something that is deeply imbedded within the person's psyche and that draws on an emotional reservoir that goes beyond rational or utilitarian thinking. Swann and colleagues note that the group can be as broad as the nation as a whole, but it is more common with smaller groups, such as families, teams, or friends. Furthermore, he and his collaborators have discovered that the reason identity fusion seems to occur is that the individual casts a psychological net around the broader group and pulls the net tightly around them. In doing this, the individual comes to feel that the larger group is like a family. And there is no one we would be willing to die for more than we would for family.

This thinking by fused individuals sounds familiar, doesn't it? Isn't this the type of phenomenon we see often in the military? Indeed, what is the single most common label that soldiers who have fought together tend to give one another? "These are my brothers." Perhaps this is also why military units frequently get the same tattoo, as a physical mark of their shared identity. They might not look alike or sound alike or have the same family name, but they can create symbols of a shared identity through tattoos. They can also do so through developing a common language flowing from their shared experiences, using nicknames for one another that outsiders don't know (and couldn't possibly understand—not without going through what the group has gone through together).

Such identity-fused groups display an extreme willingness to sacrifice their lives for one another, a willingness that is evident in survey studies as well as in the behavior of actual group members. Recall, for example, the study I described back in Chapter 5 on soldiers who received the CMH during World War II. This medal, which is given to soldiers who display acts of uncommon bravery and self-sacrifice—often, the ultimate sacrifice—appears to have been given more frequently to soldiers from honor states than to soldiers from nonhonor states. This pattern fits well with what we see among people who endorse the honor code. They tend to see their group's honor as their own. They fuse their personal identities with the identities of their honor circle (such as their country or their fellow soldiers). They take offenses to their honor circle as offenses to their own honor, and they act according to the dictates of the honor syndrome, which means responding, when necessary, with violence, and being willing to give their lives for the welfare of the honor circle.

Together, these data also help to explain why Army recruitment rates are significantly higher in honor states than they are in non-honor states (Brown et al., 2014a)—a fact that predates the Civil War.[9] Although geographic factors might account for any such differences in recruitment into the Navy or the Air Force (it's hard to have a meaningful Naval presence in Kansas, for instance), the Army can be everywhere, so it makes the best test case for comparing the willingness of young men and women in honor-oriented regions of the country to serve their nation in a manner that could lead to their death. If you need to raise an army, people with a strong honor orientation make great recruits.

This Means War!

Allan Dafoe, a political scientist at Yale University, and Devin Caughey from the Massachusetts Institute of Technology, have taken the link between honor and sacrifice one step further to argue something that seems consistent with all the data I have described, but that also seems rather difficult to prove—namely, that an honor-based concern for reputation has actually motivated some U.S. Presidents to engage in military actions more readily than other Presidents. In particular, Dafoe and Caughey have argued that Presidents from Southern states, those characterized by heightened concerns for honor, are especially likely to engage the nation's armed forces abroad. Furthermore, they have claimed that once a President decides to use military force, he is more

---

9. For a similar discussion of the military-mindedness of Southern states going back to before the Civil War, see Fischer (1989).

likely to stay the course and keep those militarily forces engaged for longer if that President is from an honor state in the South (Dafoe and Caughey, 2013).

Because of this tendency to stay the course, Dafoe says, the United States is more prone to win these military engagements when a Southerner is President. These are dramatic claims, to say the least. Is there any evidence to back them up?

According to Dafoe and Caughey (2013), there is. The notion that a concern for honor is a motive for going to war is not a new one. Philosophers from Thucydides to Hobbs have said as much, noting that leaders not only wish to expand their honor through the glory of conquest and expansion, but also they may strive to defend their honor from assaults and deter would-be aggressors by establishing their reputations for rock-solid resolve during conflict. These motives make sense, and they fit well with historical anecdotes and the claims made by kings throughout history. They also fit well with the logic of personal honor defense described back in Chapters 1 and 2. Being known as a country that is willing and ready to defend its interests with military force might deter other nations from risking war by encroaching on its lands, attacking its ships at sea, or incarcerating diplomats or businesspeople from its country who are operating within other nations' borders. As President Teddy Roosevelt famously said, "Speak softly and carry a big stick." And, I might add, make sure that people see the stick and believe you are ready to use it.

Of course, the fact that rulers have cited honor (their own or their nation's) as the motive for military actions doesn't actually mean that honor *truly* compels them. That could just be self-serving propaganda, after all. Proving that a concern for reputation and status *really* motivates military actions, especially in the modern era, is a tricky matter. Dafoe and Caughey took a bold step toward doing just that, however.

These researchers analyzed the tenures of 11 Southern and 25 non-Southern U.S. presidents (between the years 1816 and 2001), comparing them across three dimensions: (1) whether serious international disputes that involved at least a threat of force ended up involving the *actual use* of U.S. military forces, (2) *how long* military engagements lasted when they did occur, and (3) the likelihood that a military engagement would end in victory for the

United States. Dafoe and Caughey (2013) suggest that Southern Presidents who have been steeped in a culture of honor are more likely to have strong reputational concerns, particularly concerns about their (and the United States') reputation for "resolve" in the face of conflicts—that is, a reputation for not backing down when conflicts escalate, and for being willing to make good on one's threats.

As I noted earlier, this type of concern parallels nicely the type of individual concern with reputation that is the hallmark of honor cultures. In addition, the notion that honor cultures tend to arise in lawless environments, where there is no strong state or reliable system of law enforcement to protect people's interests and punish those who break the rules, bears a striking resemblance to the nature of international relations. Despite the existence of the United Nations, there is no true governing body capable of enforcing international laws and mediating with force and surety among nations. Thus, international disputes mirror in important ways the sorts of disputes typical of honor cultures. In such conflicts, reputation for resolve is key to effective deterrence, and perhaps to success as well.

Dafoe and Caughey's analysis (2013) is amazing, both for its sophistication and its conclusions. Their results show that Southern Presidents are *twice as likely* as non-Southern Presidents to use military force in international disputes. When force is used, it tends to last *twice as long* under Southern Presidents. And, perhaps most striking of all, when military forces are engaged, the conflict is *three times more likely* to end in victory for the United States under a Southerner. These differences hold up, according to Dafoe and Caughey, even controlling for differences across time, the relative status of the United States among the nations of the world, the President's political party, whether the President had personally served in the military, how well or poorly the economy was faring at the time he took office, and how much time had passed since the last time the United States was engaged in a military conflict, among a host of other such variables.

Dafoe and Caughey (2013) note, however, that these differences stand in contrast to another finding—specifically, that Southern and non-Southern Presidents are equally likely to encounter serious international disputes during their terms in office. Thus, it is not the case that Southern Presidents *create* more conflicts. However, when a serious conflict arises, Southern Presidents behave in very different ways compared with non-Southern Presidents, with very different results. As President George W. Bush said to the U.S. Congress after invading Iraq, "For diplomacy to be effective, words must be credible. And no one can now doubt the word of America" (Bush, 2004).

This sentiment does not appear to be limited to U.S. Presidents, either. Dov Cohen has analyzed voting records of members of the U.S. Congress in the two years before the first Gulf War in 1991 (Cohen, 1996). He found five proposals in the House of Representatives and five proposals in the Senate that were defense related (for instance, funding bills for the U.S. military, and the vote to authorize the use of military force in the Gulf War). Cohen found that members of the House and Senate who came from honor states were substantially more likely than members from nonhonor states to vote "hawkishly"—that is, in a pro-military manner, supporting not just greater spending on the U.S. military, but also supporting military intervention in the Gulf. Honor-oriented leaders might not always provoke military conflicts, but when such conflicts begin, they tend to go "all out" to fight them.

Terrorism

My bedroom in the apartment that my family lived in for a time overlooked the Oklahoma City Bombing Memorial. The Memorial is absolutely beautiful at night, so bright that even 18 stories above it, my bedroom was almost light enough to read a book in the dead of night. Rows of chairs with glass bases—one chair for each of the 168 victims who died in the bombing—are illuminated from within, standing vigil next to a shallow reflection pool. On either end of the pool is a large, wall-like gate with the times 9:01 and 9:03 emblazoned on separate ends to bookmark the time the bomb exploded. These gates are reflected on the smooth surface of the shallow pool between them.

On the morning of April 19, 1995, Timothy McVeigh—an American from Arizona and veteran of the first Gulf War—parked a van filled with explosives next to the Alfred P. Murrah Federal Building on NW 5th Street in the heart of downtown Oklahoma City. At 9:02 a.m., he detonated his homemade bomb, completely blowing out a large portion of the federal building as he did so. It was an act of domestic terrorism, the worst in American history. McVeigh was angry at the federal government for a variety of reasons, not least of which was the government's raid two years earlier on a compound in Waco, Texas, where a cult had entrenched itself, armed to the teeth and ready to resist any government intrusions. When the Bureau of Alcohol, Tobacco, and Firearms attempted to serve a search warrant on the compound, a standoff ensued that ended with the deaths of most of the people inside. McVeigh saw this and other such events as indications of federal tyranny, and he believed himself to be standing up for his fellow Americans and the cause of liberty in committing his atrocity.

Although McVeigh's assault on the Murrah building was the worst such attack in American history, it certainly does not stand alone. Every year people plan and execute domestic terrorist attacks in the United States, although few capture the sort of attention that McVeigh's did, for obvious reasons. Many of these attacks are thwarted by authorities, and those that aren't often result in little loss of life. Even if they fail to make the headlines, though, these events are tracked by federal agencies. Before the attacks of 9/11, the primary agency keeping track of these attacks was the Federal Bureau of Investigation (FBI), and it gave a public report of these attacks (both prevented and completed) to the U.S. Congress each year. Those event summaries are thus readily available for citizens to view.

Realizing this, Collin Barnes and I decided several years ago to examine the prevalence of these domestic attacks as a function of geographic differences in honor orientation (Brown and Barnes, unpublished data). We reasoned that if honor-oriented people feel a sense of fusion with their honor circles (such as their families, teams, communities, and even nations), and if honor-oriented people exhibit excessive risk-taking, hypervigilence and hyperaggressive responses to honor threats, along with a greater willingness to sacrifice themselves, if necessary, for the good of their honor circles, then perhaps these acts of domestic terrorism might be more common in honor states compared with nonhonor states. When we examined the FBI reports to Congress from the years 1996 to 2005, what we found mirrored almost exactly what we saw with regional patterns of school violence. The similarity between the regional patterns of school violence and domestic terrorist incidents was actually uncanny. Just more than 77% of the 102 domestic terrorism cases reported by the FBI during this time occurred in honor states—an occurrence rate that remained significantly elevated even after we controlled for a host of statewide differences (such as rurality, religiosity, and economic factors), as we had in other regional studies.[10]

By now, this remarkable finding shouldn't be terribly surprising, even if it is somewhat frightening. Anyone who has paid attention to international terrorist incidents during the past two decades can see the evidence of honor ideology at work in these incidents. The rhetoric of honor surrounds these international terrorist attacks, whether they occur in Europe, in Africa, or Asia. Osama bin Laden himself, mastermind of 9/11 and other attacks against Americans, was as honor oriented as they come. According to one recent biography of the Saudi–born terrorist, bin Laden infused everything he did with an eye toward defending what he saw as his own honor and that of his people (broadly construed). His honor circle encompassed all faithful Muslims, but especially those suffering from what he perceived as the "imperialism and decadence" of Western or Jewish powers.

As Michael Scheuer (2011) writes of bin Laden:

Even Osama's recreational activities had a hard, often dangerous edge to them. From his youngest days, he preferred volleyball, soccer, swimming, hunting, and other strenuous outdoor activities. . . . A boyhood friend also said that during summer vacations, Osama greatly enjoyed mountain climbing in a range on the Syria–Turkey border,

---

10. These data and analyses have not been published previously, but the incident data are available from reports downloadable from the U.S. Federal Bureau of Investigation at http://www.fbi.gov/stats-services/publications. For our analyses, we excluded any cases in which a foreign group is believed by the FBI to have been responsible, including those from Puerto Rico (groups pursuing the independence of Puerto Rico periodically set off bombs, especially in New York City, to protest what they view as imperialistic domination by America). A chi-square test comparing the frequencies of these incidents across honor states and nonhonor states was highly significant: chi square = 30.7, $p < .001$.

where, according to his sister, he could be found "climbing mountains too rugged for any human being" (p. 36).

Scheuer goes on to describe how bin Laden enjoyed racing cars at dangerous speeds through the desert to see how fast they were capable of going. Bin Laden, he notes, "came to believe that a Spartan, rural life made society stronger, better able to resist threats; that it preserved man's martial spirit; and that it equipped him to renew decaying urban societies" (Scheuer, 2011, p. 37).

Despite growing up the son of a wealthy Muslim father with many wives (and 53 children!) more than a century apart from Davy Crockett, not to mention worlds away, the similarities between these men are more than trivial. Both were known to be intensely stubborn when they settled on a plan of action, both behaved excessively whenever it came to promoting their masculine image, and both took threats to their honor very seriously. One became a frontier hero, at least in legend if not in fact; the other became an international terrorist. But both men were intensely interested in how the world viewed them. Both men, it seems, were ruled thoroughly by the obligations of the honor syndrome.

An Honorable Death

The honor circle undoubtedly begins with the family. As we saw in Chapter 6, honor concerns appear to motivate a unique pattern of baby-naming practices, creating a subtle social signal that reveals the connection between honor norms and patriarchal attitudes, even among well-educated people. From ancient times to the modern era, the family-based honor circle included an extended kinship network of grandparents, aunts and uncles, cousins, and so on.

In contemporary America, with its emphasis on individualism and mobility, this kinship network has been replaced in part with other types of groups. These alternative groups can include sports teams and sports fan networks, as well as military groups. The honor circle can even extend to the broad, abstract concept of the nation. But as we've seen, a sense of "family" still seems to undergird the spirit of unity that binds honor-oriented people to their nonkin groups, breeding a sense of loyalty and commitment that can even promote the willingness to die for the honor circle. Considering the inclination of honor-oriented leaders to engage in military actions against other nations, this willingness to make the ultimate sacrifice makes for a formidable pairing.

These group dynamics are kind of remarkable given the extremely individualistic nature of American culture, as discussed previously. Other cultures around the world that are much more collectivistic have retained much stronger honor dynamics related to family than we tend to see in the United States, as we will explore in Chapter 8. However, before we leave the American family, it is worth considering whether there are any additional family honor phenomena that we can discover in the United States.

A few years ago, I was eating lunch with my parents. They had flown from the heart of Dixie to visit their grandsons (I've given up the illusion that they make this long trek to see *me*, and I'm okay with that). Their return flight was in a few hours, so we had traveled half the distance to the airport and had stopped for a bite to eat so that they wouldn't be stuck with airport food. I was, as usual, talking to them about honor cultures, when my father asked me an interesting question: "Are there more or fewer nursing homes in honor cultures than elsewhere?"

I had no answer. I hadn't even considered the matter, or anything related to it, before that moment. I could make a case for *more* nursing homes to exist in honor cultures, all else being equal, as a manifestation of people's desire to provide care to their aging parents. Providing such care could be an expression of their honor values. With more reflection, however, I realized that the opposite might be even more likely, although for exactly the same reason. What I mean by that is that there might be *fewer* nursing homes in honor-oriented places *because* people are honor bound to provide care for their aging parents. If they do so in their own home, this would reduce the need for nursing homes.

I had seen this very dynamic myself. My parents had brought their own aging parents into their home when they could no longer care for themselves. First was my father's mother (whose husband had died of a stroke several years before), who had broken her hip—an injury that is all too common among the elderly and that can sometimes precipitate their demise. Later, after she had passed away, my parents moved my mother's father into their home, after he experienced a debilitating stroke.

I had also witnessed the transmission of this norm for caring for the previous generation when my wife's sister and her new husband brought *both* of my in-laws into their home to help care for them. I had spoken with my brother-in-law privately while they were still contemplating this decision. "Don't do it," I told him. "You're newlyweds. You haven't even been married for a year. This will be hard. This will be terrible. It's not something you have to do. No one expects you to."

But he didn't listen to my warnings, despite my playing the psychologist card at one point—an unsportsmanlike move, perhaps, given my lack of professional expertise on the matter, but I figured it was for his own good. It didn't seem to matter that no one expected him to do it. This was something that he expected of himself. He had lived with his own grandmother for a time as a child when she moved in with *his* parents so they could care for her. He had seen this practice modeled, and so it seemed only natural to him that he and his new wife would take in *her* parents when their health needs required more care and attention than they could provide for one another. He never said it was a matter of honor, but he didn't have to.

So, do honor states have more people living in nursing homes or fewer? The answer, it turns out, is fewer. Of course, that might just be because older people in honor states are more prone to live on their own in their twilight years, refusing assistance despite their needs. But this does not appear to be the case. In fact, fewer people 65 years old or older live alone in honor states than in nonhonor states, according to data available from the U.S. Census Bureau (www.census.gov).[11]

---

11. Specifically, my analysis of the Census data shows that an average of 5.2% of the over-65 crowd across all nonhonor states lived in a nursing home in the year 2000 compared with an average of 4.1% across all honor states. That doesn't seem like a big difference, but it is statistically significant. Likewise, 26.9% of this same age group lives alone in nonhonor states compared with 26.0% in honor states, also a small but statistically significant difference. These analyses control for the percent of each state's population living in a rural area, the percentage of each state that is white (non-Hispanic), and each state's level of economic deprivation (all of these control variables are available online from the U.S. Census Bureau (www.census.com).

These patterns are not iron-clad evidence for the notion that people living in honor states are more likely to care for their aging parents in their own homes, but they are, at least, consistent with this possibility. And that seems great, doesn't it? Here we have one of just a handful of examples discussed so far in this book of a *positive* feature of the honor code. It *is* good, isn't it?

I think it is, but it might actually have a dark side to it as well. Remember the key predictors of suicide risk discussed in Chapter 4? According to suicide researcher Thomas Joiner, a sense of social disconnection and a sense of being a burden on loved ones seem to be the key motivational factors for committing suicide. When combined with the ability to harm the self, which is acquired over time through small experiences that build up one's psychological tolerance for pain and self-injury, these motivations can turn into actual suicide attempts.

Now, consider in particular the feeling of being a burden on loved ones who have taken you into their home. If you are an elderly man in an honor culture, the psychological pain of this sense of burdensomeness might be particularly difficult to bear. Older men often have trouble feeling useful and needed because they are typically barred from many childcare opportunities in which older women might engage. This may be because of social expectations and the opportunities that other people afford them or because of personal avoidance of those opportunities resulting from those same social expectations (or the result of their *prior avoidance* of childcare, which can leave them without the basic skills needed to be effective caregivers).

As I've noted, the impact of feeling like a burden can be enhanced by the ideology of honor. When that feeling is combined with the practical difficulties men face in finding purpose and social value in their old age, being cared for by their children or grandchildren might end up adding insult to injury. In effect, having to be cared for by others might actually *enhance their sense of burdensomeness*, the pain of which is magnified by the ideology of honor, leading to a substantially greater risk of suicide in older men living in honor cultures.

This is precisely the pattern we see when we look at age trends in suicide death rates for honor states and nonhonor states. As shown in Figure 7.1, suicide death rates among men (specifically

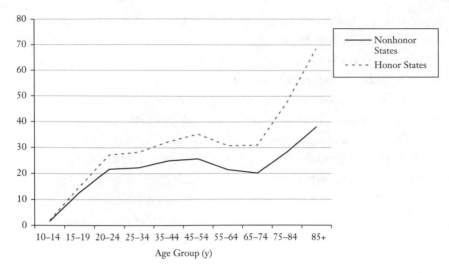

Figure 7.1 Suicide death rates (per 100,000) among white men as a function of age and state honor status, 1999 to 2010.

white men, in this figure) increase with age until the late 40s, after which they decrease somewhat until the late 60s. However, suicide death rates increase again in the 70s, which is just after the point of retirement for most American men. As shown in Figure 7.1, this increase is *profoundly greater* for men living in honor states. It seems there is more than one form of sacrifice for the sake of the honor circle, only this one doesn't end in a medal.[12]

Discussion Questions

1. If honor ideology binds individuals more tightly to their groups, and that bond of loyalty is fierce enough to motivate them to sacrifice their lives for their groups, how do you think honor-oriented people might respond to

---

12. Age-related trends for white women follow a very different pattern. Specifically, among women the curve is much less steep, and it tapers off much earlier. During the early 50s, it begins to turn downward, and it stays on this downward trajectory through the 80s. Thus, there is no evidence of an upturn in later life as we see among white men, either for women living in honor states or for women living in nonhonor states.

those who violate this loyalty norm? Have you ever seen such a dynamic at work in a group?

2. What are some other ways that honor might enhance loyalty to groups besides motivating people to sacrifice their life?
3. How well do you think cultivating a "reputation for resolve" works for leaders involved in international conflicts? How have you seen that dynamic play out in the Middle East or elsewhere with Presidents George W. Bush and Barack Obama, or with other world leaders?

For Further Reading

Barnes, C. D., R. P. Brown, M. Carvallo, J. Lenes, and J. Bosson. 2014. My country, my self: Honor, identity, and defensive responses to national threats. *Self & Identity* 13:638–662.

Cohen, D. 1996. Law, social policy, and violence: The impact of regional cultures. *Journal of Personality and Social Psychology* 70:961–978.

Swann, W. B., Jr., M. D. Buhrmester, A. Gomez, J. Jetten, B. Bastian, A. Vázquez, A. Ariyanto, T. Besta, O. Christ, L. Cui, G. Finchilescu, R. González, N. Goto, M. Hornsey, S. Sharma, H. Susianto, and A. Zhang. 2014. What makes a group worth dying for? Identity fusion fosters perception of familial ties, promoting self-sacrifice. *Journal of Personality and Social Psychology* 106:912–926.

CHAPTER EIGHT

A Most Honorable Place

"JAMILA! JAMILA!" EXCLAIMED the young boys who clamored around her, pressing close for her attention. Her wide smile lit up the throng of Afghani boys in this poor, rural village. Lashkar was a community of roughly 1000 people located on a wide plateau in the mountains of southeast Afghanistan in Paktika Province.[1] Paktika is one of 34 provinces that divide this country of 30 million people, and it sits right on the border with Pakistan's North and South Waziristan. With its rugged terrain offering safe passage to scores of Taliban fighters crossing back and forth from Afghanistan to Pakistan, this region was among the most dangerous parts of the country.

Jamila was the Afghani nickname of Julia, a representative from the U.S. State Department serving as the civilian leader of the Provincial Reconstruction Team in Paktika. She came from a family of diplomats, having a father, mother, and step-mother who served as representatives for the United States around the world. Julia's previous posts with the State Department included

---

1. The name of this town has been changed to protect the people living there from any possibility of reprisals, a possibility made all the more likely by the withdrawal of U.S. forces from Afghanistan. For similar reasons, I have changed the name of the U.S. State Department official, at her request.

Chile, Israel, and Algeria. This was her most challenging assignment to date.

Being surrounded by villagers like this made her military security detail nervous. Their job was to be nervous, though, so she didn't mind. Dressed in her gray cargo pants and thin black jacket over a longer pink shirt that fell a foot or so below her waist, topped off by a thick Kevlar vest, she stood out in more ways than one in this crowd. A head taller than the biggest of the boys, she also wore a bright pink headscarf, which loosely cradled the red curls framing her fair, freckled face. It's hard to imagine a starker contrast with her surroundings. That contrast made her an easy target for a sniper, so her detail had good reason to be nervous. Nervous and vigilant.

Here, at least, in this tiny village, they had learned to relax *a little*. The main threats to her safety did not seem to be from within the town. It was the perimeter that represented the greatest probability of danger, and there the soldiers were anything but relaxed. It was their job to spot a sniper, whose own job was to avoid being spotted before he hit his target.

"Jamila! Jamila!" the boys continued to chant, as she honed in on familiar faces and asked them about their studies in school. The few who were learning English practically screeched with delight when she would change from speaking Pashtu, one of the two official languages of Afghanistan, to English. Eager to show what they were learning, some tried to reply to her questions in English as well, before reverting back to Pashtu. She was a welcome novelty in Lashkar, a place where the surprising or unfamiliar more often than not would bring suffering or even death. In this land torn for more than three decades by civil wars and foreign invasions, life was chaos. Life was uncertainty. Surprises were generally unwelcome. But Jamila, Julia, was an exception.

It was now around noon on this bright October day. High up in the mountains, the air was crisp and cool and dry, so the warm rays of the sun overhead would be comforting for anyone not wearing a Kevlar vest. The military prep team had arrived about an hour earlier to secure the village before her arrival. She was there, after all, not to laugh with young boys, but to speak to the old men, the tribal elders, whose help she needed.

Her role in Afghanistan was a complicated one. *Everything in this country is complicated for an outsider*, she thought. Nothing was simple. Nothing was just as it seemed to be. *A man who smiles and speaks politely might still try to kill you*, she remind herself. *Never assume that you fully understand a person here, much less a conflict* between *people*. Her job was in part to help mediate social conflicts, bringing together men whose strife represented a threat to security. She needed the tribal elders in villages like this one to confide in her and to tell her who was at war with whom, and what kind of peace offering could be made to help bring the parties together. In this way, she would build trust and goodwill, which would be needed in full measure for the other part of her job: convincing people not to assist or join the Taliban.

Learning Pashtu, she found, was one of the greatest tools she had acquired. Her facility with languages had served her well in her many posts with the State Department. She could converse with relative ease in Spanish, French, Hebrew, and now Pashtu. Speaking their language, without the aid of an interpreter, communicated respect to these tribal elders. This show of respect meant everything to them, for they were Pashtun men. Pashtun men have a code that they live—and die—by: Pashtunwali (literally, "the way of the Pashtun").

The people of Afghanistan maintain strong ethnic and tribal identities. As members of the largest tribe, comprising about 40% of the population, the Pashtun were, for a long time, the equivalent of Afghanistan's highest social caste (former Afghan President Hamid Karzai is Pashtun). Pashtuns themselves are organized into smaller tribal affiliations, with subtribes, clans, and *kahols* underneath them. A *kahol* is a social unit comprising multiple families that trace back to a common male ancestor, six or more generations into the past. The *kahol* is arguably the most important unit of social life because it organizes and influences a person's daily experiences and key life events, from business and commerce to friendships and marriage. Like many societies in this part of the world, the Pashtun people were originally nomadic herders, but their nomadic lifestyle had been replaced by a more stable agricultural lifestyle several centuries ago for most Pashtuns. Despite this fundamental shift, in many parts of Afghanistan, little else has changed in the social organization and social values of the Pashtun people during the past millennium.

This consistency is arguably a result of the power of Pashtunwali. This code of ideals is at the extreme end of the honor syndrome. Afghanistan might thus be considered the ultimate example of an honor culture among the nations of the world. The preeminent values in Pashtunwali include bravery, respect for elders, tenacity, loyalty, being true to your word, reciprocity, hospitality, revenge, and the willingness to defend one's honor—which is tied intimately and inextricably to the honor of one's family, *kahol*, clan, and tribe—with aggression. An honorable Pashtun man will die or kill for honor. That's his code.

Pashtun families are patrilineal to an extreme, and this emphasis on male lineage is reflected in the value placed on men and women, boys and girls. For instance, monetary penalties for crimes (which are typically paid to avoid the instigation of a blood feud—hence, such payments are known as "blood money") are paid in units related to the price paid for a bride, which is a locally determined norm known as a *khun*. Different crimes come with different penalties. Injuries resulting in the loss of an ear are to be compensated at ½ *khun*, and those resulting in the loss of a thumb or all four fingers on a single hand are to be compensated at 1 *khun*. If a man is murdered, this most serious of crimes is to be compensated at 1 to 2 *khun* (depending on whether it was accidental or premeditated), if the offender and his family wish to avoid a blood feud with the victim's family. However, if a woman is murdered, the blood money required as compensation is only ½ *khun*. Thus, the value of a woman's life is equivalent to the value of a man's ear.

Into this world marched Julia, her bright blue eyes and gleaming smile disarming the fierce men she encountered in villages like Lashkar. Remarkably, her being a woman proved to be one of her greatest assets—a paradox of grand proportions. Life in Afghanistan was, indeed, complex. Afghanis were overly used to foreign men, some well-meaning, many bumbling, and some simply greedy and looking for an opportunity to exploit. But a foreign *woman*, especially one with authority, was something new, something interesting. Julia found on more than one occasion that she had become the poster child of Afghani self-help messages. "See this foreign woman, here to help us? She leaves her home, her family, to work for our good. What are *you* doing to help Afghanistan?" village elders asked of their young men. Many in Paktika called her "sister Jamila," a term of affection that few Americans could claim. "I would give my blood for you," a tribal leader had once told her. Abdullah, the Afghan political expert who traveled with her wherever she went, remarked almost in awe that he had never heard a Pashtun say this to a non-Pashtun. Clearly, she was making an impression here.

The *shura*, a gathering of the tribal elders and the rest of the men of Lashkar (including the boys of the village), lasted several hours into the afternoon. The men and boys were seated on the ground, with benches brought out for their American and Afghan guests. Several elders spoke, and Julia spoke as well, highlighting the value of U.S.–Afghan cooperation and the importance of Afghans themselves working to build a positive future while resisting the pull of the insurgents. She had done this many times, and she had become comfortable delivering the message. It was a message she believed in, so she could deliver it with passion. When she spoke of the pain and suffering that so many in Afghanistan had experienced throughout the years, her grief was genuine, and its truth shone through. Her honesty and courage demanded attention from these men, and that attention was followed by a strange respect they would show to no woman of their own people. Indeed, in all her visits to this village, she had never once met a woman or girl. When the Blackhawk helicopters arrived, all females turned into smoke, disappearing into the shadows of Lashkar's mud huts.

The *shura* ended around 3:00 p.m., and the guests wanted to be sure to leave in time to arrive back at their camp before dark. It wasn't safe to be out after dark. Not in Paktika.

As the crowd began to disperse, an older man in a yellow turban approached Julia. Motioning subtly for her to follow, he turned and began to stroll causally away from the town center. Julia made eye contact with the three soldiers escorting her and quietly told them to follow. She let the yellow-turbaned man continue on his way for several more seconds before she began to follow, saying goodbye to people as she went. Trying to keep an eye on the man without appearing to follow him, she almost didn't see the tribal elder before it was too late. This elder was one of the few men she had encountered in Lashkar who always seemed a bit displeased at her presence. Had she bumped into him, as she nearly did, it could have been disastrous. Men, as a rule, do not make physical contact with women who are not in their families. A slight pivot on her left foot saved her from this disgrace, and she was able to continue on.

The man with the yellow turban led her and her security team out from the center of town down a small, rocky path toward a low hill dotted with scraggly trees. He walked very slowly, so it took little time for Julia to catch up to him. He said nothing as they walked together up the rocky trail. Soon, they rounded a bend, and as they did so, she was surprised to see another man, this one with a soft white hat that looked like a short fez, staring at her. Behind him were four more men. She quickly assessed their ages as something more than 40, but she knew how hard it was to guess people's ages in this harsh land. Most people, she had found, were younger than they looked. They nodded almost imperceptibly at the man in the yellow turban, and he nodded back.

A knot quickly formed in Julia's stomach. Had she just been led into a trap? Her security team had already reacted, pulling up on either side of her, one spinning around so that his back was to her, scanning the path behind them. Someone—was it one of her people?—cocked a gun near her. It took a moment for her brain to register the sound of the M-9's slide, but once she did, she realized that it had, indeed, been one of the soldiers in her security detail. The men in front of them remained still, their eyes fixed not on Julia and her escorts, but on the surrounding hills and the path behind them. The situation had the potential to be threatening, but these men were not quite playing the part she would expect of a squad of hitmen. They didn't even appear to be armed.

As Julia and her team, armed with M-4s and M-9s, drew closer, she recognized one of these men. She couldn't remember his name, but he had stood with his hand on the shoulder of a young boy who had greeted her by name when she arrived that day. What surprised her then, and what she now remembered, was that the boy had not used her Afghan name, but her *American* name. She had quickly realized that he was reading it off her vest, which she found remarkable. Most people in Paktika couldn't read in Pashtu, much less in English. The man—she guessed it was the boy's father—caught her eye now, and although he did not smile, the expression on his face somehow put her at ease.

Realizing that she had been holding her breath for the past 10 seconds, she let it out slowly, not wanting to appear as tense as she felt. She hated to appear weak or afraid, either in front of these Afghani men or in front of her security team.

"Keep going," she instructed her escorts in English.

As they made another slight turn in the path, the man in the yellow turban appeared once again, this time only about 10 ft away. He was standing with a group of five other men, these looking older and more weathered than the five they had just passed moments before. One of them had something in his hands. She couldn't quite see what it was, but he seemed nervous. That made *her* nervous.

Pashtunwali is really *normative* law, insofar as it encompasses the system of social expectations and values that govern everyday life for the Pashtuns, as well as many non-Pashtuns, in Afghanistan. But what about the "real" law? What about the formal set of laws, penalties for law breaking, and systems of law enforcement in this country? How do these modern codes of conduct and contemporary institutions differ from the ancient code of Pashtunwali?

After American military forces and their coalition partners ousted the Taliban from power in 2002, dramatic social changes in Afghanistan seemed to be taking place. Schools for girls were reopened or built (although finding educated women to teach in them proved to be a serious challenge), and an international press for the inclusion of women in the new Afghan Parliament resulted in a meaningful number of women becoming members of the new government. The Afghanistan Independent Human Rights Commission (the AIHRC) was formed to consult with and assist government agencies with understanding and reforming human rights problems in the country, particularly with regard to women and children. With the passage of the Elimination of Violence Against Women law (often known by the acronym EVAW) in 2009, an important step in this healing process seemed to have been taken.

Unfortunately, the hope for a new Afghanistan remains little more than a fantasy for most women living in this country, and the passage of a few laws at the national level is unlikely to do much to usher in a new way of life. Recently, an amendment to the criminal code was passed by the Afghan Parliament that forbade relatives of an accused person from testifying against him or her in a court of law. Unlike the protection from being coerced into testifying against one's spouse that is part of the American justice system, this change to the Afghan legal code would mean that family members who witnessed the abuse of a young girl or woman by her husband, brothers, or father could not testify against the perpetrator, no matter how severe the abuse. Nor could a wife testify against her husband, even if he had tried to kill her.

To make matters even worse, women who have fled abusive husbands have often found no protection from the police or courts. In fact, when women flee from abusive husbands who have accused them of marital unfaithfulness, these women are frequently charged with "moral crimes" by the very justice system whose protections they sought, according to the AIHRC (Saramad and Sultani, 2013). Indeed, the majority of women in prison are behind bars for just such moral crimes. The best estimates to date are that nearly 90% of Afghan women experience some form of physical or sexual abuse during their lifetime, most often at the hands of family members or spouses (Baldry et al., 2013). This may well be the highest such rate of any nation in the world.

A recent study highlights one of the most basic challenges facing the pursuit of social change in the protection of women's rights in this country. The study was conducted by a group of social scientists from Italy led by psychologist Anna Costanza Baldry, and it focused on the attitudes and intentions of Afghani police officers (Baldry et al., 2013). For their study, the researchers presented a situation to more than 100 police officers (only a few of whom were female) that the researchers had adapted from an actual police file involving a family dispute. In this situation, police had been called by the mother of a young woman who, she said, was being severely beaten by the young woman's husband. The mother said she was afraid for her daughter's life, and she asked the police to intervene. On arriving at the victim's home, the police found the young woman in tears, bloodied and bruised by her attacker. The husband told the police to leave; this was a family matter and did not concern them.

Interviewing the young woman in private, the police heard her story. Her husband had become furious, she said, when she came home later than she normally did. He yelled at her for dishonoring him, claimed that she was having an affair, and started beating her with his fists. He even threw a chair at her and threatened to kill her.

All the police officers in the study read this description. Every detail was exactly the same for everyone, and the details matched what had really happened in the original case file. But, at this point in the study, the researchers varied what officers read next. Some officers read that the young woman admitted to being unfaithful to her husband, whereas other officers read no admission of infidelity. Last, the officers in the study were asked to rate the severity of this family dispute, how they felt about the legitimacy of a man beating or wanting to kill his wife for being unfaithful, and how they themselves would respond if they encountered this situation as officers. Would they arrest the alleged perpetrator? Would they encourage the victim to file a formal complaint? Would they gather additional evidence needed to prosecute the husband?

The results of this study were striking on multiple levels. Police officers who read that the victim had admitted to having an affair with another man reported more favorable attitudes toward wife beating and indicated they would be less willing to intervene in the situation compared with police officers who did not read an admission of infidelity. This pattern of results confirmed what Baldry and colleagues (2013) expected: an admission of unfaithfulness caused a significant change in police officers' attitudes about intimate partner violence and their intentions to do anything about it, despite the law (which, at that time, specified up to two years imprisonment for husbands who kill their wives for adultery—the same prison term specified for women convicted of committing adultery, incidentally). But what might be even more appalling than the ease with which violence against women is justified is the fact that, even in the absence of an admission of infidelity by the victim, police in this study were not particularly likely to indicate an intention of intervening. Specifically, on a 9-point scale, where 1 meant "not at all likely" and 9 meant "absolutely likely," the average intention to intervene by police was just a little more than 3.0! And that average only went *down* for officers who read her admission of infidelity.

Faced with such meager prospects of help from police, and worried they might even be put in jail on charges of immoral behavior if they come forward, why would any Afghan woman ever bother to report her husband's abuse? Few ever do.

Gender-Bending in Afghan Culture

Imagine how people would respond if a girl in your child's kindergarten class came to school dressed as a boy, with a boy's name, and joined in with the boys during recess rather than with the girls. Perhaps in kindergarten it might be viewed as a cute little oddity or a phase. "She's such a little tomboy. Her mother should take pictures of her playing baseball with all those boys. They will make great blackmail photos for her wedding rehearsal dinner, won't they?" Despite changing cultural norms, after a couple of years of this, eyebrows might start to be raised and some would eventually complain to the teacher or the school principal. "It's just not *right*," they would argue. Appeals to nature and to all that is holy would soon follow, and, at some point, someone might get sued. That's often how we handle these sorts of things in the United States, unfortunately.

Imagine, then, if a girl living in Afghanistan tried to pull off this sort of gender-bending experiment. In Afghanistan, honor killings are promoted as a means of protecting family honor when an unmarried woman is seen in public with a male who is not a family member. Girl clothing is radically distinct from boy clothing, and the distinctions go far beyond color. Boys can wear blue jeans. Girls wear dresses at home and burqas outside the home. Boys have short hair and girls have long hair. A girl who got caught trying to pass as a boy would surely suffer the most terrible of fates. Right?

Everything I know about honor cultures tells me this would be true. It turns out, however, that everything I know is wrong, at least in this matter. In fact, on occasion, particularly in families full of girls with no sons, young girls can live double lives as boys.

Azita Rafaat became a member of the Afghan Parliament after the Taliban were deposed by American forces in 2002, one of only

68 women at the time to take this post in the new government. Like other women in Parliament, however, Azita Rafaat could run for office only with the permission of her husband, Ezatullah Rafaat, which was given grudgingly. Azita's income, after all, could vastly improve the family's economic situation, but her working outside the home could also stain the family's reputation. It was a difficult choice for Ezatullah to make, but Azita was used to difficult choices being made on her behalf. She had, after all, been a top student growing up in Kabul, with dreams of a medical career until her father decided she was going to marry her cousin, a farmer who already had one wife. His first wife had proved to be something of a disappointment, having failed to produce a son for him. Consequently, he sought a second wife, and like many Afghani men, he did so within the confines of his extended family.

Unfortunately for Ezatullah, his second wife was no more successful than his first at giving him a much-prized son. As it turns out, biology actually works the same way in Afghanistan as it does in the rest of the world, and it is the husband who determines the sex of a child, not the wife. Like his first wife, Azita bore him only girls (the first two were twins, whose birth caused her mother-in-law to burst into tears). Azita felt like a failure. The family felt like a failure. Until one day, Azita and Ezatullah decided to turn their six-year-old daughter, Manoush, into their six-year-old son, Mehran.

As a boy, Mehran could go outside and play. He could escort his sisters to the market. He could even work outside the home. He enjoyed freedoms and opportunities as Mehran that he couldn't even dream of as Manoush. One day, when his body started changing and he could no longer be a man-about-town without risking his family's honor, he would have to revert to being Manoush. But until that day came, he would wear his jeans and necktie with the rest of the boys. Until that day came, his half-life would feel whole. When he made the transition back to being a girl, he would have the help of his mother, Azita, who would guide him through those turbulent waters with the voice of experience, for she, too, had once run wild through the streets of Kabul in jeans and a necktie. Just as no one had complained or lobbied or threatened to sue when she exchanged her dresses for pants, no one seemed to mind that her daughter, Manoush, had become her son, Mehran.

This transformation, in a meaningful way, had probably enabled her husband to grant permission for Azita to run for Parliament. With a son, he could lift his head up in Afghan society. With a son, he was a real man, and the threat to his honor of having a working wife was neutralized. So, for now, he would allow Azita to serve Afghanistan as a member of Parliament (Nordberg, 2010).

This gender-bending practice seems surprising from a culture that puts so many constraints on girls and women. It can be hard to understand how a society that places such a high value on masculinity would permit females to pass as males, even during childhood. Perhaps by understanding the incredible value of sons in this society, though, we can begin to understand how such a surprising practice might evolve within Afghan culture. And, to be clear, the practice of passing off girls as boys is not terribly common (although exactly how common it really is cannot be determined, because it is not something that people talk about openly for fear of damaging someone's reputation—a taboo act in an honor culture, with potentially serious repercussions).

What may be even more common than this practice of temporary gender switching is something to which, until recently, Westerners were oblivious: in Dari (the second official language of Afghanistan), it is called *bacha baz*, which means "boy player."[2] It is, essentially, pedophilia, but on a more socially approved and massive scale than pedophilia in any Western nation. Unlike the comparatively innocuous practice of gender switching, the practice of *bacha baz* amounts to the serial rape of young boys by older men. In Western countries, having a beautiful woman on a man's arm (or one on each arm) is often considered a sign of masculine prestige. Women have always been seen as a man's reward for achieving high social status. But in segments of Afghan society, in part because of an understanding of Islamic law that paints women as being unclean, many men have difficulty viewing women with sexual desire. Lust is supplanted by disgust through the power of social conditioning. The result is an insidious perversion of normal sexual desire in some adult men, leading to this abhorrent practice of pedophilia (similar to an ancient practice among

---

2. A story on this practice that first brought it to my attention was reported by Stanford journalism professor Joel Brinkley (2010) for the *San Francisco Chronicle*.

high-status men in the Roman Empire). The scantily clad, big-breasted blonde of Western culture is replaced by boys with bells on their toes, sometimes known as "dancing boys."[3]

Is This Just Islam Gone Wild?

When I talk to people, formally or informally, about honor cultures, I often get asked whether all this "honor culture business" is really just a manifestation of Islam (sometimes formulated as "radical Islam," but more, I think, from a sense of political correctness than from a sense of what "radical" and "nonradical" Islam might look like). In short, people ask, have social scientists who study the honor syndrome simply rediscovered religion?

This question surfaced recently when I was talking with a friend of mine about the terrorist attacks at the satirical French magazine *Charlie Hebdo*. The two men who stormed the Paris offices of *Charlie Hebdo* on January 7, 2015, yelled the customary "God is great!" slogan, so common to Islamic terrorists, before they opened fire with automatic rifles on the staff of the magazine, killing 11 people before escaping into the French countryside. The men were, apparently, fed up with the magazine's publication of cartoons that depicted Muhammad (itself a sin in Islam) and insulted the fundamentalist sects of their faith. Surely, this and other such attacks are really about religion and not just about a cultural syndrome that crosses religious and geographic boundaries.

This seems like a reasonable and plausible connection to make. Islam is the honor syndrome wrapped in sacred garb, it might seem. I myself once assumed this to be at least partially true, as I, like many Westerners, had no shortage of anecdotes I could draw on in which the insult–revenge cycle characteristic of the honor syndrome was enacted by self-proclaimed defenders of the Muslim faith. Simply pondering how the cultural ideology of honor might be linked to Islamic fundamentalism, one can easily see how the two might be

---

3. There is an allusion to this practice in Khaled Hosseini's bestselling book, *The Kite Runner*, although the example is clouded by the fact that the man responsible is the villain of the story (Hosseini, 2003).

intimately connected. Honor cultures, after all, tend to spring up in places where poverty is widespread and long term, which is typical of societies with herding (rather than agricultural) economies. Islam sprung up in the Middle East within just such a herding ecology. Honor cultures also develop where law enforcement is weak and unreliable, which has long been true of the Middle East and places where Islam has spread, such as North Africa. Furthermore, Islamic fundamentalists always seem to be angry about insults to Islam posed by Western culture, and hypersensitivity to insult is the *sine qua non* of honor culture. Three for three. Case closed.

Attractive as this reasoning seems, the connection between Islam and honor ideology is not so straightforward. Some have assumed a similar association between honor and Christianity in the United States. This assumption follows, in no small part, from the fact that honor states in America are most prevalent in the South and West, and the South is the heart of the so-called Bible Belt. A simple examination of the percentage of people who report attending church frequently shows that, as you might expect, people in honor states are more likely to be churchgoers compared to people in nonhonor states. Religious people are honor-oriented people, whether they are Islamic or Christian.

It turns out, though, that this is flawed reasoning. To be clear, consideration of geographic overlaps between religious regions or nations and honor-oriented regions or nations is a fine start to testing the possibility of a connection, but it's not enough.[4] The next step in testing for a connection between honor ideology and religiosity is to examine this link among individuals, and when my collaborators and I have done this, what we typically find is an association that's just about zero. As in no association. Zilch. Nada. Nuthin'.[5] Thus, what might seem to be a reasonable

---

4. This problem is an example of what is known as the *ecological fallacy*

5. Technically, this utter lack of association only holds when we look at religiosity and the *masculine* dimension of the honor code. When we examine the *feminine* dimension, which focuses on the importance of loyalty and sexual purity, there is, in fact, a small association between honor ideology and religiosity. That modest degree of overlap makes sense in light of the typical exhortation to sexual restraint common to most religions. Nonetheless, even this relationship is small, and the most prominent element of the honor syndrome is not this feminine dimension, but the masculine one, I would argue.

connection between Christianity and honor ideology, supported indirectly through a regional overlap between honor-oriented states and Bible-oriented states, turns out, on closer inspection, to be a statistical ghost.

The same sort of presumed association between honor ideology and Islam might also turn out to be a ghost. Yes, the Quran uses language typical of honor cultures, and yes, some of the most extreme honor cultures in the world are Islamic nations. We also know that some of the worst and most extreme examples of honor-related behavior can be found in Islamic cultures, as presented in this chapter in painful detail. These things are all true. However, the question at hand is whether these examples of honor-related behaviors are really about *religious devotion* per se.

A recent study that I discovered suggests to me that the answer is *no*. This study, conducted by a pair of criminologists from Cambridge University, Manuel Eisner and Lana Ghuneim, examined the attitudes of about 800 Jordanian teens toward honor killings (Eisner and Ghuneim, 2013). There are several remarkable findings from this study, but the one most relevant here is that the teens' religiosity levels had no relation to their attitudes toward honor killings, nor did the teens' categorical religious affiliation (specifically, whether the teens identified themselves as Muslim or non-Muslim). Thus, kids who were Islamic and very religious were not any more favorable toward honor killings than less religious non-Muslim kids. Strikingly, some 40% of boys and about 20% of girls reported favorable attitudes toward the idea of honor killings, so there was lots of room for religiosity to play a role (not to mention a big social problem for the nation of Jordan!). But religion didn't seem to matter much, just as we found in our assessments of personal religiosity and honor ideology in the United States.[6]

Is religion in general, or Islam in particular, *irrelevant* when it comes to honor-related violence, such as the recent attacks in Europe? Again,

---

6. James Bowman (2006) has discussed at length the thesis that religion has actually contributed substantially to the decline of the honor code in Western cultures. His argument is that religion and honor are value systems that vie for people's ultimate devotion (one is reminded of the biblical insight that a person cannot serve two masters). Is reputation your god or is Someone else? If your reputation might suffer if you follow a religious mandate to love your neighbor as yourself, to return good for evil, or to forgive those who persecute you, which path do you choose?

I think the answer is *no*. Religion is not irrelevant. Rather, I think that religion gives people a sense of collective identity that then provides the framework for their sense of "us" versus "them." Their religious identity tells them who the good guys are and who the bad guys are. But religion also provides what I call "symbols of sensitivity." These symbols tell people which insults should be most offensive and which insults rise to the level of deserving and justifying the righteous indignation that fuels dramatic acts of violent retribution. Such acts are not really driven by love for God, love for Muhammad, or love for Jesus. They are driven by love for self, for one's reputation, and for the collective honor of a group with which a terrorist identifies. When that group is threatened, either directly or symbolically, the individual feels threatened, and that feeling of threat can lead to violence in those who embrace the ideology of honor.

Nujood

The Great Hall of the courthouse in Sana'a was packed with people—mostly men, with a scattering of women milling about, covered head to toe in their heavy, dark robes. Among the shadows near the walls, a tiny black figure darted, occasionally wandering out into a cluster of women, only to scurry back to the shadows after mere moments. As the figure stood framed by the night of an old woman's skirts, all you could see was her bright eyes. At some point, she gathered her courage and hurried over to an old man in a beard sitting authoritatively at a large table. All faces turned toward her as her voice rang out in the Great Hall, clear and defiant. "I want a divorce!" she exclaimed.

I've read about more instances of women being abused—beaten, mutilated, raped, or killed—than I care to ponder, but one of these instances stands out to me, not for its extremity, although it is extreme, but rather for the herculean courage of the young woman in coming forward and insisting on justice. What is especially remarkable about her is that she isn't really a young woman at all. She's a 10-year-old girl named Nujood Ali.

In her autobiography, *I Am Nujood, Age 10 and Divorced* (Ali and Minoui, 2010), she describes her life of poverty and suffering. She was born into a typical family in the nation of Yemen, at the tip of the Arabian Peninsula, and she lived in an extended household comprising one father, his mother and two wives, 10 siblings, and five half-siblings (more were grown and lived elsewhere). Nujood's own mother, Shoya, had been given in marriage to Ali Mohammad al-Ahdel when she was only 16, and he took a second wife four years later, a distant cousin named Dowla. Nujood was born in the tiny, rural village of Khardji, but following the rape of her older sister (at the age of 13—she was forced to marry her rapist after the attack), the family moved to the larger city of Sana'a, the capital of Yemen.

The culture of Yemen is very similar to that of Afghanistan. Both nations suffer high rates of poverty and illiteracy. Both nations have experienced multiple civil wars in recent decades as well as many foreign invasions throughout the centuries. The people of both countries are almost entirely Muslim (99% or more) and live primarily in small villages or towns rather than in cities. Everyday life in both Yemen and Afghanistan is ruled by tribal systems of law and custom similar to Pashtunwali, described earlier. And in both nations, women enjoy few civil rights or freedoms other than those that might occasionally be granted them by their fathers or husbands. Consequently, the plight of women in both countries is among the worst of any place in the world.

Into such a world little Nujood was born, and after approximately 10 years of life (no one is completely sure exactly how old she is; birth records in rural villages are rare), she was given in marriage to a man three times her age. He beat her, raped her, and terrorized her, and he was joined in his terrorizing by his mother, who lived in the same house. She was appalled at Nujood's reluctance to serve him sexually and in all other ways, and she let her displeasure be known to Nujood every day. It was not Nujood's place to withhold herself from her new husband. It was not her place to complain. It was her duty to obey. Her disobedience was dishonoring to her husband and, by extension, his family.

But Nujood had the courage, at the tender age of 10, to disobey. She had the courage to complain to her parents, and when they refused to hear her pleas for succor, she sought redress in the courts of Sana'a. There, she finally found relief, after lucking upon a sympathetic judge and securing the passionate patronage of a women's rights attorney who took up her cause and fought for her. The legal age of marriage for girls in Yemen, after all, is 15, despite the Yemeni proverb, "To guarantee a happy marriage, marry a nine-year-old girl" (Ali and Minoui, 2010, p. 74). Although it is not uncommon for girls to be married younger than 15, the age of 10 is considered, by most, to be inappropriately young. Ten is, at least, too young to defend in a public court of law, even by those who might feel inclined to wink at such a practice.

Nujood's courage in rejecting the social mandates of her honor culture won her freedom from her husband, who was jailed for a short time after her divorce was granted. Her family, of course, was embarrassed by her behavior (not her husband's) and the stain it brought to the family name, but this was something Nujood could live with. She could live with just about anything, she decided, short of living with *him*. Sadly, Nujood's story is an exception in this part of the world, where such abuse is frequently covered up in the name of protecting people's honor, their *sharaf*. Some people might disapprove of a man who marries such a young girl, or who beats her, as Nujood's husband did, but they would be just as likely, if not *more* likely, to disapprove of a person who got involved in someone else's personal business and caused them public disgrace. After all, the value of a woman's life is equivalent to a man's ear, so cases like Nujood's often go ignored, and victims are forced to suffer in silence and shame. Lacking hope for any reprieve, some even resort to suicide, either out of protest or simply as a means of escape.

It's worth noting that these extreme examples of gender-based violence and attitudes toward the subjugation of women that uphold these behaviors as normative might feel outlandish to many Westerners. However, reflecting back on Chapter 3, we can see that they are mere extensions of the sorts of attitudes and behaviors that exist even among well-educated Americans, among whom the endorsement of honor ideology goes hand in hand with the sexual objectification of women as well as attitudes supportive of men's greater social power. These attitudes appear to translate into higher rates of rape and domestic homicide in more honor-oriented regions of the United States. Thus, although Nujood's story might strike many people as horrific—a sentiment that I share—it is not wholly different from what we see in a less extreme honor culture. It's different primarily as a matter of degree, not kind.

I focused this chapter mainly on the culture of Afghanistan, and in many ways I think that Afghanistan represents the most extreme honor culture in the world. It certainly seems extreme, doesn't it? Some if its practices feel exotic and barbaric to Westerners, who cannot fathom how people live under such a code of behavior, ruled by the fear of dishonor for themselves and their families. But this code of behavior, extreme though it may be, is not unique to Afghanistan, Yemen, or the other nations of South Central Asia. If we were to think of Afghanistan's extreme honor culture as a great mountain—so high that the air is hard to breathe at the top—then as we traveled west from this nation, we would descend only a few hundred feet as we passed through Iran, Iraq, Jordan, Syria, and Turkey. If we dipped southward through the Arabian Peninsula and continued west onto the continent of Africa, through Egypt, Libya, Tunisia, Algeria, and Morocco, we would lose a few hundred feet more if we stayed to the north, along the coast of the Mediterranean. Traveling southward we would descend farther still, as we would if we were to travel north to the continent of Europe, through Portugal and Spain, Italy, Greece, and Bulgaria. Those European countries that ring the Mediterranean would still be part of the mountainside, although the mountain here gets much steeper and our descent would pick up speed rapidly, with only modest plateaus of honor culture rising in Poland to the northeast and Scotland to the far northwest.

If we were to travel eastward down the mountain from Afghanistan's peak, we would find little relief in Pakistan, but as we continued east the descent would get steeper into India, China, Mongolia, and the other "face cultures" of southeast Asia, such as Laos and Thailand to the south, or the Koreas and Japan to the north. The mountain would plateau farther north in Russia, then fall off rapidly in an almost sheer cliff down to sea level at Finland, Sweden, and Norway.

The colonial histories of the Americas help us to understand why social scientists identify many of the countries of Central and South America as honor-oriented countries—think of these countries as smaller mountain chains in the shadow of the great mountain far to the east. Because Spain and Portugal were the dominant colonizers in Central and South America during the 16th, 17th, and 18th centuries, the cultural legacies of these Mediterranean nations remain rooted in the social landscapes of the southern hemisphere of the Americas. The subsequent histories of immigration to and migration within these countries, along with the United States and Canada to the north, add the peaks and valleys to this mountain chain.[7]

The point of this geological metaphor is that the honor syndrome affects many cultures all around the world to varying degrees and is mixed in with other factors that influence social life, from economics to religion. Thus, when we look at a culture like Afghanistan's and we consider some of its more extreme practices that reflect its Pashtun code of honor, we should think of these practices as differences of *degree*, not of *kind*, from what we experience in less honor-bound societies. In the United States, we do not accept the idea that women who dress immodestly in public should be stoned. That would be barbaric. And yet, white men in southern and western states in America kill their romantic partners, or former partners, at significantly higher rates compared to white men in northern states, and they show a similar pattern with rape. Likewise, American male college students who personally endorse the ideology of honor tend to objectify women sexually, as I discussed in Chapter 3.

Although these patterns of thought and behavior might seem less extreme than overt honor killings or the related treatment of women in countries such as Afghanistan, they really aren't all that far removed, are they? I don't imagine the victims of domestic abuse in the United States see these behaviors as being particularly different. Violence in the service of honor is violence, no matter how it gets labeled or where it occurs. As the saying goes, you can put lipstick on a pig, but it's still a pig.

---

7. This loose metaphorical approach to describing international patterns of honor orientation has an empirical basis in a recent study that my colleagues and I conducted (Brown et al., under review) in which we used the power imbalance between men and women in politics and business to serve as a proxy for a country's adherence to the honor code. The beauty of this simple approach is that it depends on the choices societies make, rather than what people are willing or able to report on an attitude survey. This gender-power scoring system has proved capable of predicting such things as national investments in the military and lack of investment in mental health care, consistent with some of the findings reported already in this book for the more honor-oriented states in the United States.

As Julia and her security detail approached the small band of tribal elders on the path ahead of them, one of them began to draw in the dirt with a stick. As she drew closer, she saw that he was drawing a map of the main road over the mountains into Lashkar. These elders, like the five sentinels behind them on the path who were watching the surrounding hills and blocking anyone who might approach from the village below, were unarmed. They had arranged this meeting at great personal risk to tell Julia about a cluster of improvised explosive devices they knew had been planted on the road between Lashkar and a nearby Afghan army base.[8] Had her team headed to that base from Lashkar, they would surely have detonated this cluster, drawn in the dirt in the shape of a butterfly. How ironic, she thought to herself, that something from nature of such beauty would symbolize something so ugly in the hands of people.

As soon as they had told her about the butterfly bomb and she had thanked them for sharing this life-saving information, risking their own lives in the process, the meeting was over. The old men seemed relieved, and one even smiled at her. She was their Jamila. Although she was a foreigner, she was their adopted little sister. She felt, in that moment, a wave of gratitude for these men and the hospitality they were showing her. Hospitality, in Pashtunwali, is not just about giving a guest to your home the choicest piece of meat at your table. It is about honoring a guest, and even protecting a guest from harm. Even a guest who is an enemy might receive protection from a Pashtun man of honor. How much more so their Jamila? She knew that some of these men might abuse their wives when they got home that night. Who knew what happened behind the closed doors of the homes into which she had never been invited in Lashkar? They might engage in a whole host of unpalatable behaviors that made her stomach churn when she considered them, but today they had offered her a gift that could cost them dearly if the wrong person learned what they had told her. Today they had treated her as an honored guest, a person worthy of respect. And she could work with that.

---

8. Earlier that day, a small band of insurgents had come through Lashkar and warned the villagers not to travel on that road because of what they had planted there.

Discussion Questions

1. This chapter briefly touched on the empirical association, or lack of association, between honor ideology and religion (see also note 6). Do you agree with the argument that religion and honor ideology are inherently opposed to one another?

2. What are some ways that social scientists could rank or otherwise measure the honor orientations of nations around the world? What are some of the pros and cons of the different approaches that social scientists might use to do so?

3. What are some other ways you could imagine honor ideology influencing gender identity—the beliefs about what it means to be a man or a woman—as well as gender roles and expectations within a society? What other cultural factors do you think might come into play that might mitigate or enhance these ideological influences?

For Further Reading

Baldry, A. C., S. Pagliaro, and C. Porcaro. 2013. The rule of law at time of masculine honor: Afghan police attitudes and intimate partner violence. *Group Processes and Intergroup Relations* 16:363–374.

Eisner, M., and L. Ghuneim. 2013. Honor killing attitudes amongst adolescents in Amman, Jordan. *Aggressive Behavior* 39:405–417.

CHAPTER NINE

Embracing Honor

ESTHER WAS AN UNUSUAL QUEEN.

In fact, Esther wasn't even her real name. Her real name was Hadassah. It was a Jewish name, meaning "Myrtle." The myrtle tree grew throughout her homeland of Israel and it was renowned for the beauty of its aromatic flowers and its fragrant oils, which were used in perfumes. Remarkably, the beauty of the myrtle tree was accompanied by an unusual hardiness, for it was capable of growing even in poor, rocky soil. Esther, Hadassah, was well named.

Like her namesake, she was beautiful and hardy. Despite being an orphan, raised by her much older cousin, Mordecai, and his wife, and despite being a member of a Jewish community living in exile far from their homeland, deep in the heart of the Persian Empire, she seemed to be thriving. She was smart. And she was a survivor.

These were qualities that would come to serve her well after she was made queen under rather unusual circumstances. The year was 483 BC, and Xerxes, the King of Persia, was planning his grand strategy for conquering the Greeks, taking up the mantle of war from his late father, Darius I. Darius had planned to attack Athens, but he was distracted by a revolt in Egypt and had died before he could carry out his invasion of the Greek city state.

Xerxes, oldest son of Atossa, daughter of the Persian hero Cyrus the Great, then succeeded his father to the throne of the largest empire in the world—an empire that ranged from India all the way to Ethiopia. He was a man of royal blood, a man of immense power and authority. He was also a man who took his honor very seriously.

As such, he decided that his great military planning sessions would be accompanied by an exhibition of his riches. You might think that a king who was planning to attack an enemy in a far-away land would begin tightening his belt, perhaps levying a new tax on his people to fatten the royal coffers before what would surely be an expensive campaign. But not Xerxes. His grand exhibition lasted for 180 days, at the end of which Xerxes invited the entire capital city of Susa to bathe in the glory of his largesse at a banquet that lasted an entire week.

Now, when I say he invited the entire city of Susa to the party, what I really mean is that he invited all of the *men* of Susa to the party. The only women typically invited to such events were prostitutes. Thus, the Queen of Persia, Vashti, decided to throw her own party for the women of the palace. There's no reason to assume that Vashti's party was seen as competition for Xerxes. After all, Vashti herself wasn't invited to the king's little soirée, nor would she likely have wanted to be. She wasn't a whore, after all. She was a queen.

That might be why, on the seventh day of Xerxes's party, under the influence of a great deal of wine and the pressure to end a great party with something big, the king decided to do something outrageous. He decided to summon Queen Vashti to the party wearing her crown—some scholars suggest this meant she would be wearing *only* her crown. Imagine how insulted she must have felt, regardless of whether she was expected to wear clothes to the party. Simply to show up and be paraded in front of all of these drunken men would have been a great stain on her reputation. So, as a woman of dignity, she did the only thing she could to preserve her honor. She refused the invitation.

Seething with rage and humiliation (and a lot of alcohol—never a good combination), King Xerxes called upon his legal advisors for their input on what should be done with Vashti for disobeying his command to appear at his party. Memucan, one of his advisors, proclaimed that Vashti had transgressed not only against King Xerxes, but against *all men* of the empire, "For the queen's conduct will become known to all the women, causing them to look with contempt on their husbands by saying, 'King Xerxes commanded Queen Vashti to be brought in to his presence, but she did not come.' And this day, the ladies of Persia and Media who have heard of the queen's conduct will speak in the same way to all of the king's princes, and there will be plenty of contempt and anger" (Esther 1:17–18; New American Standard Version). This threat to the king's honor was a threat to all men in the empire, and it could not be ignored.

So Xerxes issued a royal decree that Vashti would never again be allowed into his presence. She would be replaced as queen by another, a woman more worthy of the crown in which she refused to appear at his party.

This royal drama is what set the stage for Hadassah, the little orphaned Jewess, to become queen of the Persian Empire. Several years after his infamous party, Xerxes succeeded in putting down rebellions in Egypt and Babylon, and he had even taken the Greek city of Athens after defeating the armies of Leonidas at Thermopylae (at great cost). However, his victories would prove short-lived and he would eventually be defeated by the Greeks in 480 BC at the Battle of Salamis. To add insult to injury, the Babylonians were making trouble again while he was away, so Xerxes was forced to return home to avoid a full-blown rebellion in the heart of his empire. His expensive campaign would thus end without the great triumph he had sought so desperately.

What does a king do in the face of such a blow to his pride? Well, among other things, he sleeps with a lot of women, and Xerxes had no shortage of women in his harem to stroke his pride. But his return home reminded him that he no longer had a queen, for he had deposed the beautiful Vashti before he had left for battle. Thus it was that he began to look for a replacement queen. Xerxes ordered that all the most beautiful virgins in Susa and the surrounding provinces be "gathered" (a nice way of saying "kidnapped") to the royal palace under the care of Hegai, the royal eunuch. During that time, they would enjoy the greatest spa package in the world, replete with fancy meals, beauty treatments, and luxurious baths in myrrh. At the end of their year of grooming, they would be summoned, one at a time, to the king's chambers for a night of frolicking (a nice way of saying that Xerxes would rape them and send them away to live out the remainder of their youth in his harem). Keeping in mind that women married very young in the ancient world, these virginal girls were probably in their early teens when Xerxes stole them from their families to be deflowered at his leisure, until he found one worthy of becoming his queen. This is how he spent his days recovering from his defeat by the Greeks.

Little Hadassah entered Xerxes's palace under a false name, the Persian name Esther. Her cousin and guardian, Mordecai, had instructed her not to reveal her nationality, perhaps fearing that doing so would reduce the odds of her being chosen by the king. A man of his fine pedigree surely wouldn't stoop to take a Jewish girl as his bride, would he? Probably not, although he would certainly stoop to have sex with her, effectively ending her chances of ever becoming the bride of a nice young Jewish man. An unmarried woman who was not a virgin was the lowest of the low in the ancient world. She would have no social standing, no worth, and no protection. She would most likely end up a prostitute. Mordecai would not let that happen, not if he could help it.

So Mordecai sent her off with sage counsel to hide her identity, and he visited the palace regularly to check on her, probably continuing to advise her and groom her for her big night. Perhaps his advice led to her finding favor in the eyes of Hegai, the eunuch, who then gave her special treatment and her own set of attendants until she was finally summoned by the king. It's unclear why, but the grooming and advice seem to have paid off. Esther was chosen. She would not be relegated to the king's harem. She would become queen.

In a Disney movie, the story might end there. The little orphan girl becomes a princess and lives happily ever after. However, the tale of Esther did not end with her coronation. Her drama continued when, years later, a plot was hatched by Haman the Agagite to incite a genocide of the Jews. His plot was largely a response to feeling insulted by Esther's cousin Mordecai, who refused to bow down to him in public. This insult could not go unpunished, so Haman plotted for a way not only to humiliate Mordecai, but also to exact revenge on all of Mordecai's people. It would be up to

Esther to seek the favor and pardon of Xerxes, but royal protocol forbade anyone, least of all a woman, from initiating an audience with the king. To violate this protocol meant death for the presumptuous transgressor.

Thus, the tale of Esther is a tale of honor from start to finish. Honor-bound people perceive honor threats, and honor-bound people react to those threats, often with what appears to be excessive aggression (most people would include genocide in the category of "excessive aggression"). Esther's story is not at all unique, either in the Bible or among other ancient texts. The first recorded song in the Bible is the song of Lamech, a descendant of Cain's (who murdered his brother, Abel). Lamech proclaims in his song the virtues of vengeance, announcing he has already killed two men for insulting him, and he would avenge a threat to his honor 77 times over. Lamech was the first gangsta' rapper.[1] The Bible, likewise, is not unique among ancient texts in displaying tales of honor. Virtually every ancient story involves honor, from *The Iliad* to *Gilgamesh*. The story of human civilizations throughout history is the story of people bound by the honor syndrome.

Honor, Now and Then

The honor syndrome is not just about ancient civilizations and ancient codes of conduct as this book has described. The honor syndrome remains an important part of social life for many people around the world, from Afghanistan to Alabama to Algeria. Consider, for instance, one of my favorite examples of honor on display at the World Cup in 2006. The incident, now somewhat famous, involved Algerian–born French soccer star Zinedine Zidane head-butting an Italian opponent, Marco Materazzi, in the chest.[2] From most people, a head-butt to the chest would

---

1. Contrast Lamech's proclamation with Jesus's words to Peter in Matthew 18—in response to the question, "How many times must I forgive my neighbor?" Jesus replies, "Seventy-seven times." I don't think this number was picked at random from the number line. I think it was a reference to Lamech.
2. I know, I know, Zidane is not a "soccer star"; he's a "footballer." But he really isn't. Football is a different sport (see Chapter 7).

not amount to much, but from Zidane it was a stunner, knocking Materazzi to the ground. What provoked the assault that led to Zindane being ejected from the game? Was it a racial slur, as many speculated in the days that followed? Did Materazzi call Zidane a terrorist or something equally obnoxious? No and no. It turns out, Materazzi insulted Zidane's sister. For someone like Zidane, steeped in the honor culture of his parents' homeland of Algeria, such an insult is greater than a racial slur, and it cannot be ignored—even if *not* ignoring it means getting ejected from the final game of the World Cup, and the last game of your career. Even if it means your team loses that final game (which they did). Stained honor must be cleansed.

Asked about whether he would be willing to apologize to Materazzi almost four years later, Zidane's response was classic honor syndrome: "Never. It would be to dishonor me. . . . I'd rather die."

Several years after this event at the World Cup, another honor-wrapped incident occurred that would lead to the deaths of more than 30 people. It was January 13, 2012, and the cruise ship *Costa Concordia* was sailing near the coastline of the Tuscan island of Giglio. Too near the coastline, it turns out. The ship hit a reef, took on water, and turned over on its side that night, forcing the evacuation of its 4252 passengers and crew, resulting in the sinking of the largest passenger ship in history.[3]

The reason the *Costa Concordia* was sailing so close to the shore was that its captain, Francesco Schettino, decided to perform what is known as a "near-shore salute." This was not the first time Schettino had done this kind of maneuver, which creates an impressive spectacle for people on shore, especially at night. Records indicate he had done this several times before, including August of the previous year. But this time was different. Perhaps he was more distracted than usual by the presence of his new girlfriend, Domnica Cermortan, who later admitted that she was on the bridge with him when the ship struck the reef. I can only

---

3. The *Costa Concordia* was 952 ft long, with a tonnage of 114,147 GRT and a capacity of more than 4800 crew and passengers. In comparison, the RMS *Titanic* was 882 ft long, with a tonnage of 46,328 GRT and a capacity of approximately 3500 crew and passengers.

imagine that his commentary to the young woman as he initiated the dangerous maneuver went something like, "This is a very risky thing to do, of course, but what's life without a little danger? I live for danger." That's why he was the captain of a cruise ship.

To make matters worse, Schettino failed to stick around when the evacuation began. There were around 300 passengers still onboard the cruise ship when he claims he lost his balance and "fell" into a lifeboat, which took him safely to shore. On arrival there, he was berated by the commander of the local port authority, Gregorio De Falco, and was ordered to get back to the ship until the rest of the passengers were safe. His lawyer would later argue at trial that De Falco's harsh tone and stern words had damaged Italy's reputation more so than Schettino's inept sailing, and that exonerating Schettino would go a long way toward restoring Italy's poor image in the eyes of the world. The logic of this argument is not nearly as interesting to me as the simple fact that *Italy's reputation* would ever be brought up during Schettino's trial as part of any kind of legal argument. Italy is, not surprisingly, a Mediterranean honor culture.[4] In February 2015, Schettino was convicted of manslaughter and sentenced to 16 years in prison. We can all pray that Italy's reputation may yet be restored one day.

In social science research, we have a saying: "*Data* is not the plural of *anecdote*." In other words, citing a bunch of anecdotes does not mean you have data. It means you have found a bunch of examples that fit the story you are trying to tell, and that isn't what social science research is all about. So, let's consider some data on the dynamics of honor in the world beyond the United States, more structured and systematic than the simple cases I have described so far. Considering the claimed roots of the American South's honor ideology described back in Chapter 1, let's go back to Scotland to see what social residue the honor syndrome might have left there.

In addition to being one of the primary historical sources of honor ideology in the United States, Scotland makes a fantastic place to examine contemporary honor dynamics outside America because it shares a language, government, and legal system with

---

4. For a classic anthropological study of several Mediterranean honor cultures, see J. G. Peristiany's (1966) edited volume, *Honour and shame: The values of Mediterranean society.*

its southern neighbors, England and Wales. These commonalities allow us to compare Scotland with England and Wales with greater confidence than if we were comparing countries with different languages, different definitions of legal concepts such as homicide, and different social norms with respect to things such as reporting a death as a suicide. For all these reasons, the quality and comparability of the data across these regions of Great Britain are excellent.

In Chapters 2, 4, and 5, I discussed some of the research on honor dynamics in the United States that has revealed reliably elevated rates of argument-related homicide, accidental death (as a proxy for excessive risk-taking), and suicide in the more honor-oriented states in the South and West compared with the North. With the modest exception of suicide, which is still somewhat socially stigmatized (although not nearly as severely in North America as it is in other parts of the world), these causes of death are relatively straightforward. If a medical examiner or coroner determines a person died from a gunshot wound that was not self-inflicted, for instance, he or she typically rules the death a homicide and records the cause of death accordingly. If it is later determined the gun went off accidentally, the cause of death is amended to reflect the apparent facts of the case. Such cause-of-death statistics thus make a nice source of data for honor-related phenomena, although they do not incorporate such features as perceived motives or the relationships among victims and their murderers in the way that police data might. As a result, cause-of-death statistics don't tell us as much as we might want to know, but they can still give us a reliable and broad picture of the reasons that people in a particular location seem to be dying.

Let's take a look at how modern-day Scotland compares with England and Wales, and Northern Ireland along these three key dimensions (homicide, accidents, and suicide).[5] As shown in Table 9.1, modern-day Scotland stands out among these three regions in each and every one of these honor-linked causes of death. This

---

5. These data were taken from the World Health Organization's online death statistics repository (see http://www.who.int/healthinfo/mortality_data/en/), back before they stopped reporting these statistics separately for Scotland, England, and Wales. I have no idea why this change was made, but I consider it most unfortunate.

Table 9.1 RATES (PER 100,000) OF HOMICIDE, SUICIDE, AND ACCIDENTAL DEATHS (A PROXY FOR EXCESSIVE RISK-TAKING) IN SCOTLAND, ENGLAND/WALES, AND NORTHERN IRELAND.

VARIABLE	SCOTLAND	ENGLAND/ WALES	NORTHERN IRELAND
Homicide			
Men	3.5	0.5	2.8
Women	0.7	0.2	0.9
Suicide			
Men	18.5	10.1	15.4
Women	5.6	2.9	3.6
Accidents			
Men	31.3	24.7	32.1
Women	25.1	18.7	19.5

Data cover the years 1999 to 2006.

pattern is somewhat remarkable insofar as the data in Table 9.1 lack the nuance available in prior analyses of honor-related behaviors in the United States, such as whether a homicide is argument related and whether offenders live in small towns or large metropolitan areas. Adding these sorts of qualifiers enhances the picture of honor-based violence and death considerably. Yet, even without these nuances, the picture is clear enough. Modern-day Scotland retains an apparent vestige of its honor-oriented past relative to the rest of Great Britain, just as the American South and West do.

It is also noteworthy that Northern Ireland is more similar to Scotland than it is to England and Wales on almost every indicator (particularly among men; among women, Northern Ireland is sometimes more like Scotland and sometimes more like England/ Wales). Recall from Chapter 1 that Northern Ireland is where King James encouraged southern Scots to settle (the "Ulster Plantation") during the first part of the 17th century as part of his grand scheme to help control the Irish, ever a source of trouble for English monarchs. It was because of the massive immigration of Scots to Northern Ireland that these immigrants became known as the "Scotch-Irish" when they eventually arrived in America. And although we might attribute the elevated rates of homicide in

Northern Ireland to the ongoing cultural strife between Protestants and Catholics there, homicide rates in Northern Ireland are actually slightly *lower* than they are in Scotland, and this notion of quasi-religious conflict would not go far in explaining the elevated rates of suicide or accidental deaths that we also see there. These patterns, I argue, are better explained by the ideological legacy of honor brought to this part of Ireland by the Scots of the 17th century.

Returning to the Roots of the Honor Syndrome

When I hear the word *lawlessness*, I almost always think of the American Wild West, particularly during the frontier days of the 1880s. It wasn't as if no one on the Western frontier had ever heard of a law before, nor was it that they all thought most laws or social norms were stupid. What made the Western frontier wild—lawless—was that enforcement of the law was so terribly difficult. There might well have been an adequate ratio of law keepers (sheriffs, marshals, magistrates, and so on) to citizens, although this is debatable. However, even if this ratio had been reasonably high, there was simply too much land for the available law enforcement officers to, well, enforce. Another way of thinking about this is that the ratio of law keepers to citizens might have been fine, but the number of law keepers per square mile was far too low. In a population-dense city, the problems tend to be the reverse, with too low a ratio of law keepers to citizens.

This was the world of people like Wyatt Earp, discussed back in Chapter 2. Earp was hardly better than the cowboys he tried to wrangle for much of his life. Not only had he been arrested more than once himself, including one time for being a horse thief, but much of his adult life was spent running card games that were little better than con jobs. In fact, he even was involved in organizing a boxing match that turned out to have been "fixed." He certainly was not the great lawman he appears to be in the movies about his life. Perhaps the most remarkable thing that Earp ever achieved was to rewrite his own story and recast himself as a hero of the Wild West, which he did by socializing with reporters and movie producers during the early days of what would become Hollywood.[6]

The West of Earp's era was lawless not because there weren't any actual laws, but because everyone knew that enforcement of the law was spotty at best. When people believe that other people in their community are flouting the rules and getting away with it—in other words, when people believe that the rule of law is weak—this perception sets the stage for a downward spiral of anti-social behaviors, as I described back in Chapter 1.

This sense of lawlessness helps to create the social building blocks for honor cultures. Several recent studies by different groups of social scientists have made this link clear. In one, researchers measured college students' retrospective reports of how much violence they experienced in their home growing up, how much crime they witnessed or heard about in their neighborhood, and how effective the police seemed to be in their communities (Pedersen et al., 2014). All three of these retrospective reports were associated with how high these college students scored on a measure of honor-related beliefs and values.

In another recent study (Simons et al., 2012), a separate group of researchers took this type of approach even further, this time gathering information from young people about their current living conditions, and adding two important features: evidence of aggression and delinquency by these adolescents, and multiple genetic markers the researchers had reason to believe were linked to what you might think of as "socialization sensitivity." What I mean by *socialization sensitivity* is the tendency of a person to conform to his or her social environment, picking up social norms and habits of thinking and acting from others, for good or for ill. The researchers believed that kids who had more of these genetic markers for socialization sensitivity would be more prone to exhibit aggression and delinquency, but *only* if they *also* lived in dangerous, lawless neighborhoods. More important, the researchers argued that kids with these genetic markers for socialization sensitivity who lived in *safe* neighborhoods replete with social cues for lawfulness (in other words, fewer "broken windows," as described in Chapter 1)

---

6. Earp died before the first movie about his "life" (or the fictionalized version of his life that he had concocted) made it to the big screen in 1929.

would actually be the *least* aggressive and delinquent of all the kids in the study.

That is exactly what the researchers found. Kids high in socialization sensitivity (as assessed through specific genetic biomarkers) exhibited especially high levels of aggression and delinquency (including gang-related delinquency) if they were surrounded by cues of lawlessness, but kids with this same socialization sensitivity showed especially low levels of aggression and delinquency if they grew up surrounded by cues of lawfulness. Furthermore, the researchers showed that the link between socialization sensitivity and aggressive delinquency among the kids who lived in lawless neighborhoods could be explained through the kids' endorsement of honor ideology![7]

This is the first study I know of to link the honor syndrome to both genetics and lawless environments—and it blew my mind. The genetic markers the researchers examined in this study had been shown previously to relate to sensitivity to environmental cues (mostly negative ones, such as growing up in abusive homes), but these researchers took those prior studies to a different level entirely. Their study, as far as I have been able to determine, is solid, and their conclusions appear to be valid. It's a truly remarkable finding.

Do you have to live in a violent home or in a violent neighborhood to absorb the ideology of honor, though? Do you have to be socialized in the frontier world of Wyatt Earp or the mean streets of modern-day, inner-city Atlanta to pick up the values of the honor syndrome? Not at all.

Consider how many different ways we might get bathed in the ideology of honor in our daily lives as we grow up. If you've ever sat quietly and listened unobtrusively to young boys playing basketball or just about any other competitive game, you will likely hear little pieces of honor ideology falling from their lips as they exhort one another to "man up!" If someone fails to "man up,"

---

7. In statistical terms, this analysis is what is known as a *mediation analysis* (see Chapter 2). The mediator in this case is endorsement of the tenets of the honor syndrome, and the mediation analysis attempts to determine whether a potential mediator can explain or account statistically for the association between two other variables—in this case, socialization sensitivity and aggressive delinquency.

he gets verbally (and perhaps physically) pounced on by the others and insulted in ways designed to inculcate the value system of the honor syndrome. The insults are likely to go straight to the vitals, designed to emasculate their victims. The taunting boys might start off light, such as simply calling him a girl, followed by crass terms for female body parts, such as pussy, then going right into the homosexual slurs, such as queer or faggot. These sorts of insults are designed to attack the core of a boy's masculinity, and they are powerful for that very reason (it might be worth noting that the most powerful insults for girls tend to indicate their lack of sexual modesty, such as slut and whore, rather than their lack of bravery or toughness).

A study on reactions to insults found just this pattern (Saucier et al., 2014). Researchers at Kansas State University led by Donald Saucier asked men about the insults they experienced that they found most offensive and that caused them to get into physical fights. Men in these studies consistently indicated that homosexual and feminine insults were the most provocative and insulting. About *half* the men in one study indicated they had actually gotten into at least one fight in their lives over an insult, and of these the most common types of insults that had instigated a fight were ones falling into the homosexual or feminine categories. Call a young man a little girl and he might feel compelled to prove that he isn't. More important, the men in this study who were most offended by these insults and most likely to report reacting aggressively to them were men who scored high on a measure of honor ideology.

This ritual gets played out on basketball courts, sports fields, and living room floors (also known as wrestling rings) everywhere, but especially in places where the honor syndrome rules. Boys are socialized to fear such threats to their masculinity from a fairly young age and to do what they can to preempt them by displays of social proof. It's far better to prevent such an insult from ever occurring than to be forced to react to one after the fact. When the suggestion has been made public that he does not, in fact, have a penis, a young man knows that he has an uphill battle ahead of him to undermine that claim. The burden of proof is on him, not on his accuser.

Boys don't have to learn to fear this ritual just from first-hand experience. They can also learn it by observing others go through it, regardless of whether they take part in the taunting liturgy themselves. They can also learn it even more indirectly through popular songs and movies. You don't have to be a country music devotee to know how common honor themes are in country music. It's interesting to ponder when the last time was that a noncountry pop song delved into the issue of domestic abuse, for instance. Can you think of *any* pop songs during the past 20 years that have done so? But even people who don't listen to a great deal of country music may know of more than one such song in the country genre, sung not by obscure artists, but by the top country music performers of the day—from Martina McBride and the Dixie Chicks to Carrie Underwood and Miranda Lambert. I don't believe this is a coincidence. People sing about what they know and what they've seen in life. Likewise, the songs that achieve great popularity are those that resonate with the experiences of listeners.

We don't have to single out country music for evidence of honor themes. You can find them in the most popular films in Hollywood just as easily. I recently did just that with my colleague Jennifer Barnes, a developmental psychologist (Barnes and Brown, under review). We had our research assistants examine the movie trailers from the 100 top-grossing films of all time at the U.S. box office (as of March 2013). These films spanned multiple genres, including romance, science fiction, drama, comedy, adventure, horror, animation, and fantasy. The trailers from these films were watched and then coded for the presence of seven honor-related themes, such as revenge for an insult or attack, reputation, justification for violence, or even an explicit reference to honor.

The results were striking. On average, the movie trailers for the 100 highest grossing films of all time contained four of the seven possible honor themes. Although a *mere* 29% of the movie trailers contained an explicit reference to revenge, 81% referenced an insult or other transgression, and 71% referenced reputation. Forty-four percent of the trailers depicted violence as being morally justified, and 52% mentioned honor or an honor code explicitly. None of these movies was a western, incidentally.

It seems that from the playground to the movie theater, we can experience the socializing forces of the honor syndrome. You might wonder, though, about how deeply these honor messages sink into our psyches. In many of the studies I've mentioned throughout this book, participants completed some sort of questionnaire about their honor-related beliefs and values. Such questionnaires are a staple of psychological research, as well as of social science research more broadly. If you want to know what people think or feel, one of the simplest ways to find out is just to ask them.

There are important limits, though, on what people can (or will) tell you when you just ask them outright. For one, people sometimes don't want you to know what they think or feel, or how they have behaved in the past, or how they believe they would respond in the future. Some reluctance to tell the truth, the whole truth, and nothing but the truth is typical in socially sensitive domains, such as violence or mental health, but it can even be seen in more innocuous domains. Anytime people worry about what a confession might reveal about them, the value of a simple questionnaire will be limited.

Another limitation to asking people about their thoughts and feelings occurs as a result of something more subtle than their worrying over what other people might think. Sometimes people are *unable* to tell you what they think or feel because they don't entirely know. This might seem like a strange or even arrogant thing to claim. After all, who knows our innermost thoughts and feelings better than we do? My guess is the answer is no one. But not always. Human beings are great at making up narratives that they tell themselves and others to make sense or to create coherence out of their lives. We make sense out of senseless things that happen to us. We create meaningful stories out of events that have little inherent meaning. The process of meaning-making can be healthy and beneficial, but it can also be little more than a convenient fiction.

Because of this fictional veneer that our overt answers to overt questions can reflect, psychologists have worked hard to come up with clever ways to peer underneath the conscious stories that people tell in an attempt to determine whether there might be some other stories they're unable to tell. Although Freud and his followers first popularized the idea that the unconscious mind was alive with activity beyond what could be discerned by mere introspection, their approaches to uncovering the details of this activity were not very good—sometimes little more than their own fictional narratives, for which they usually charged a hefty price.

During the past few decades, however, social scientists have worked hard to come up with more reliable and valid methods for peering beneath the conscious veneer, and they have come up with a handful of useful tools for doing so. One such approach involves presenting people with pictures, such as a picture of a face or a weapon, but doing so at extremely short intervals—so short, in fact, the conscious mind is unable to perceive them. The unconscious mind, though, works much more quickly, registering pictures and even words at remarkable speeds. Although it can't perform complex mathematical calculations, predict stocks, or invent new apps, the unconscious mind is very good at a few things, including recognizing stimuli with strong personal relevance. The intensity of this unconscious processing is so great, in fact, that the emotional associations unconsciously energized by one stimulus can actually "bleed over" onto another stimulus.

My colleagues and I took advantage of this fact to explore how deeply the honor syndrome can sink into the depths of the unconscious mind (Imura et al., 2014). In our study, we modified a clever procedure created by social psychologist Keith Payne, now at the University of North Carolina at Chapel Hill. This procedure, called the *affect misattribution procedure* (or AMP), involves presenting people with words they are told to ignore. "Don't let the words distract you or otherwise influence you," people are told. The words appear briefly (150 msec), but long enough for people to register them consciously and be aware of their meaning. Rather than responding to these words, though, people are told to pay attention to the picture that appears in the same spot in which the words previously appeared. This picture is actually a Chinese pictograph, and it, too, appears only briefly on the computer screen. What people are asked to do is simply report how pleasant they felt the Chinese pictograph was.

The logic of the AMP is that as long as people are able to read English words, they won't be able to resist processing the meaning of the words that first appear on the screen, even when they are told to ignore them. They can't resist because reading is automatic, at least for literate adults. But the *meaning* of the words is partially idiosyncratic, varying from one person to the next, especially when it comes to something such as how a person feels about a concept invoked by the word.

Consider, for instance, the word *tough*. If you are a chef, this word might have a seriously negative connotation. *I hope no one eats my roasted duck and calls it "tough,"* you might think. If you are a student, you might likewise have negative associations with the word *tough*—as in, *That exam was really tough* or *That professor is good, but she's really tough; I can only take one class from her in a single semester.*

What if the ideology of honor has dripped slowly into the depths of your unconscious mind? How, then, would you feel about the word *tough*? Would it have a negative association or a positive one? To test this idea, Mikiko Imura, Melissa Burkley, and I presented people with seven honor-relevant words (such as *honor*, *strength*, *tough*, and *brave*) and seven dishonor-relevant words (such as *insulted*, *weakness*, *coward*, and *shame*) using Keith Payne's AMP. People saw these words, along with a bunch of neutral words, very briefly, but were told to ignore them and to concentrate instead on the pictographs that followed them. As in the standard AMP, they were supposed to report whether they felt the pictographs were pleasant or unpleasant, using the + and - keys on the keyboard to register their impressions.

What we found was that people, on average, were indeed unable to resist the pull of the honor and dishonor words, although they had been told to ignore and not be influenced by them. In a sense, being able to ignore these words probably felt like a challenge, a competition of sorts. But no matter. Reading, as they say, is fundamental, and like thousands of research participants before them, our participants were influenced by the words they were supposed to ignore. Because of this influence, the pictographs that appeared after honor-related words somehow felt more pleasant than the pictographs that were shown after neutral words, which in turn felt more pleasant than the pictographs that followed the dishonor-related words.

Furthermore, people's scores on this "honor AMP" test were modestly but significantly correlated with their scores on a standard, explicit measure of their honor ideology endorsement on a scale they had completed several weeks beforehand. People who scored high on the explicit measure tended to score high on the implicit measure. Perhaps even more interesting, though, was that at the end of the study, we gave our research participants a surprise memory test for all the words they had seen—the ones we told them to ignore. Overall, people's memories for these words were not very good, consistent with our instructions to pay no attention to them. People, on average, could recall fewer than four of the 21 words they had seen. We found, nonetheless, that people's incidental memories for the honor and dishonor words, independent of their memories for the neutral words, were predicted by how they scored on *both* the explicit honor ideology scale *and* by how they scored on the honor AMP. Both their conscious and unconscious honor orientations mattered, in other words. These orientations affected how much they attended to honor-related stimuli in their environment, even if they weren't aware of actually attending to them.

This study shows that honor ideology can sink deeply into people's psyches, below the conscious level into the unconscious realms beneath. Although there was a modest connection between people's scores on the conscious and unconscious honor measures, this connection was weak enough that there were people in our study who consciously rejected the honor code—overtly disagreeing with statements such as "A man has the right to act with physical aggression toward another man who calls him a coward"—but who nonetheless responded more favorably than other people to words such as *honor* and *respect*, and less favorably to words such as *dishonor* and *insulted*. The honor syndrome is, it seems, a deep well within the human psyche. It resides within one of the most fundamental dimensions of our identities—our definitions of manhood and womanhood—and its image can be seen in the deepest recesses of our unconscious minds.

Conclusion: How, Then, Shall We Live?

In early fall 2011, I got an e-mail from the public affairs office at my university. The e-mail was just a friendly "heads-up" about an online column criticizing me for some research my graduate students and I had just published on excessive risk-taking and honor ideology in the United States. I had done several interviews about this research already, and there were a number of online posts swirling around the bowl of the Internet. When I got the e-mail from the public affairs office alerting me to this particular online column, I lost no time clicking my way to the website of my accuser. My accuser, it turned out, was an author, online columnist, and self-styled Southern comedian named Lucy Adams. Ms. Adams had apparently read something she found online about our research and she did not appear to care much for it. After very briefly summarizing our studies, she wrote in her column:

> As we mark the 10-year anniversary of 9/11, I take issue with him and his findings and his railroading of the Culture of Honor. Brown, cloistered within the walls of academia, has a lot to learn. The Culture of Honor is so much more than defending one's reputation. It is willingness to take a stand for one's convictions. It is holding high expectations for the conduct of others. It is protecting the weak, rescuing the stranded and opening a door for a lady. . . . It's the reason why firefighters and police ran into the burning, disintegrating Twin Towers when everyone else ran out, risking their own lives to save others. . . . And it's why professors get to sit in their air-conditioned offices surrounded by dusty books, thinking up dusty thoughts, and impugn the very thing that ensures their opportunity to do that. I expect my three sons, in whatever they choose to do and wherever they choose to go, to hold fast to their values, to give aid and assistance to those less fortunate than themselves, and to never ever be afraid to step up and defend what they hold dear. Doing what's right always involves risk, but it's the cultured, honorable thing to do. (Adams, 2011)

Because I had some time to kill, and maybe more than a little motivation, I decided to respond to Ms. Adams in an e-mail. Noting first my own upbringing in the honor culture of the American South, I expressed my dismay at the fact that she had impugned my reputation in such a personal and public way without apparently having read our article. I then went on to describe what I and other social scientists had discovered about the dynamics of honor cultures during the previous two decades—including elevated rates of argument-related homicide among men, rape and domestic assault, divorce, drunk driving, suicide, school shootings, and extreme militant responses to terrorist threats. Although perhaps one could "spin" the last of these in a positive manner (I would not), the rest are most definitely not honorable, I noted in my response to Ms. Adams.[8] These behaviors are, nonetheless, consequences of a cultural ideology that places defense of reputation (especially for men) among the highest virtues, and that is arguably the central feature of cultures of honor, whether in the Southern United States, the Lowlands of Scotland, or the Middle East (all places where honor ideology prevails). I went on to note one of my favorite elements of the Southern honor culture in the United States, and one of the reasons I would rather live there than anywhere else—the norm of politeness. However, as I noted:

> There is a dark side to this politeness, as it seems to be a rather thin veneer of virtue on top of a bubbling cauldron of macho wrath. Thus, a Southern male is more prone to overlook a minor social trespass than a Northern male is, but once a certain threshold is reached, the Southerner overcompensates and goes ballistic. That's the response that leads to the elevated rates of argument-based homicides that researchers have noted time after time.

I did mention some other positive elements to honor culture we have found, some of which have been described in this book and some of which have yet to see the light of day, sitting in a file drawer in my dusty office, waiting for an interested graduate student to pull them out. Perhaps someone will get interested enough to pursue these findings with additional studies so that we can be more confident of what we have before we try to run off and publish them. We'll see. I ended my e-mail to Ms. Adams with the following:

> As a social scientist, I go where the data take me, whether it's to pleasant or unpleasant places. Behaviors associated with honor ideologies are more frequently of the latter type, it seems, your protestations notwithstanding. I am sorry if the data offend you (they make me sad, more than anything else, as these are MY people I am studying). I only hope that you, like me, will not let this offense translate into closed-mindedness, but will take the facts as they are (not how we want them to be) and learn from them . . . . It is the job of academics like me, surrounded by our "dusty old books," to discover reality, using evidence and systematic analysis, rather than relying on

---

8. Lucy Adams, http://mirror.august.com/stories/2011/09/15/opi_627578.shtml. Accessed September 15, 2011.

anecdotes viewed through the lens of cultural ideologies. That's the job I'm paid to do, whether or not I always like what I find. But on one point that you made, I think we can agree: I do, indeed, have a lot to learn. (Personal Communication, September 10, 2011)

Reading back over my little diatribe, I am a little embarrassed at how pompous some of it sounds, even to me. This critic had sounded off about something she didn't know much about, and I let her have it. It felt good, too. Ironically, both her response to my research and my response to her criticisms were examples of *exactly* what social scientists have pointed out about honor cultures. We honor-oriented folks get our panties in a twist rather easily when we feel that we, or our people, have been insulted. And we simply cannot let that sort of thing stand. We *must* respond.

In the end, I think she felt badly that she had written such an overly personal criticism about my research, and she was good enough to allow me to post a response on her website. I don't know if anyone ever read my comments, but I was impressed by her openness to my rejoinder. So, separated by more than a thousand miles of Southern country, we hugged it out and went our separate ways.

Typically, that's not how conflict goes among honor-oriented people. Had she been a man, and had we lived in the same town, I'm not sure how it would have ended. The lives lost throughout human history in the maintenance and defense of honor—individually or collectively—cannot be counted with confidence, but I will put my own estimate in the millions (hey, it's my book, right?). Add to that the dollars spent adjudicating honor-based crimes and bolstering our military arsenals, and the emotional suffering experienced as a result of violence, abuse, or shame, and you've got a whale of a debt to pay by this idea we call honor.

What, then, is the alternative? When I have spoken to groups of students or community members about the research covered in this book, I sometimes get push-back along the lines of Ms. Adams's criticism, followed by some version of the question, "So, are you saying that we should chuck the honor code altogether and replace it with dishonor?"

Of course, that's not at all what I am saying. Claiming that we must choose between an honor culture and a dishonor culture is a false dichotomy of the highest order. That's not the choice we face.

Social scientists who study culture have identified honor cultures as one type of human society. Another type is the face culture, such as those in Southeast Asia (similar to honor cultures in some respects, but different in others). Yet another type of culture is the dignity culture, and this type is well worth considering as an alternative to honor culture. In an honor culture, respect and social worth must be earned. Because they must be earned, they can be lost by failing to live up to the high standards of the honor code. When lost, they might be impossible to regain. In a dignity culture, however, social worth is assumed by default. People in a dignity culture are more likely to grant respect to others simply by virtue of their being human. That doesn't mean that everyone is equally respected or respectable. Reputations can be enhanced in a dignity culture, just as reputations can be damaged in a dignity culture. But the battle for social worth is not fought every day with the same ferocity as it is in a typical honor culture, because it doesn't have to be. Dignity is *assumed*, whereas honor is *earned*.

Throughout this book I have talked about honor research in the United States and used the regional classifications of honor states and nonhonor states. However, I could have substituted the term *dignity states* for nonhonor states. In studies on honor orientations in America, some social scientists have done exactly that, characterizing the approach to social worth prevalent throughout the North, from Maine to the Dakotas, as the approach common to dignity cultures. When we recognize the existence and viability of this dignity approach to social worth, we at least have a cultural alternative to consider in lieu of the honor syndrome. This alternative, at least within the United States, is associated with lower rates of honor-related homicide, excessive risk-taking, suicide, and all the other social pathologies described in this book (although, to be fair, it is also associated with less politeness, and a weaker emphasis on positive reciprocity and loyalty, among other things).

Now, let's say that when we weigh the pros and cons of these different approaches to human worth, after careful thought we decide to embrace the cultural approach of the honor syndrome. Even then, we still face a fundamental choice about definitions. *What do we think it means to be a person of honor?* What do we think honor *ought* to look like? Is it about showing how tough you are or how brave and strong you are, if you are a man? If you are a woman, is it about showing how loyal and chaste you are (no matter how much your husband might beat you)? We have been, and are being, programmed by our culture to think in certain ways about what "real men" and "good women" look like. Human beings are sociocultural sponges, learning from those around them about how social value can be attained. We learn this better than we learn anything else, even language. We are programmed from birth to death by the names our parents give to us before we take our first breath, by the messages we hear on the radio and in movies, by the slurs that are thrown at us on the playground, and by the status we receive, and sometimes lose, as we grow into adulthood.

Our cultural programming comes handed down to us from ancient days even before Esther became queen of Persia. This cultural legacy is passed from one generation to the next, through overt and obvious channels and through implicit and subtle ones. So, the question is, will we be passive receptacles of this programming? Will we receive it, take it in, let it become part of us, molding and shaping us into the image of the honorable man or woman that someone, somewhere, a long time ago decided "worked" well for them? Or will we use those wonderful brains we've been given to step back and consider what and who we really want to be?

In a sense, this was what Lucy Adams might have been trying to do. I took issue with her defense of honor culture, however, because her assertions about what honor culture "is really about" reflected an ideal that did not comport with reality. That's an important difference. What honor culture appears to be is not what we might want it to be. What it *is* does not fit its name. We can talk about protecting the weak, standing up for what is right, and so on, but there is so little evidence that these behaviors are particularly characteristic of honor cultures. Rather, cultures that dictate that a person's worth depends on the extent to which he or she lives up to the code of the honor syndrome are cultures that produce shame, hypervigilence to insult, and gross overreactions when honor threats are perceived. The firefighters and police officers who ran into the Twin Towers on 9/11 didn't do it because they were steeped in the mandates of the honor code. They did it because they were brave. They did it because they had compassion for the people stuck in those buildings. They did it because it was their job. As much as some of us might want to credit the honor syndrome for such acts, there just isn't much evidence in support of doing so.[9]

There is, in my opinion, a massive disconnect between the rhetoric and the reality of the honor syndrome. The rhetoric of honor was expressed quite well by Ms. Adams in her response to our research on honor and risk-taking. I think you could make a good case for this view of honor culture being summed up perfectly by the fictional hero Captain America. Captain America is superhumanly strong, unbelievably brave, intensely loyal, and polite almost to a fault. I think Lucy Adams had an image in her mind of Captain American when she described what she thought honor cultures are really about. But Captain American is a myth. The reality is what has been described throughout this book, which paints a much less generous picture of the honor syndrome than any defender of honor culture will ever acknowledge (although there are, as I've noted, some bright spots in this picture). This disconnect, ironically, is likely a consequence of the dynamics of the honor syndrome itself. In an honor culture, we don't talk about things that bring shame to others, unless those others are our enemies. So, even if we all know that our neighbor or coworker is beating his wife, we don't talk about it. Even if we know an unusual number of people who have committed suicide, we don't talk about it. But talking about it is a prerequisite to change. Just as with self-change, cultural change demands first that we engage in honest self-reflection and admit we have a problem. It demands that we engage with the reality of our lives, not just with the comfortable fiction that we, and others, attempt to sell.

The second step to cultural change might be even more difficult, though. If we can acknowledge the chasm between our

---

9. For the record, I did investigate this very phenomenon after Ms. Adams suggested it, examining the number of firefighters per capita who had died in the line of duty during the prior decade. I found no evidence of a higher rate of deaths among firefighters living in honor states compared with those living in nonhonor states. This is precisely what we *would* expect to see if firefighters from honor states were exhibiting excessive courage and a greater willingness to sacrifice themselves because of the mandates of the honor syndrome (unless they were simultaneously more skilled than firefighters from nonhonor states). It seems that people who run into burning buildings for a living are just generally brave folks, whatever their cultural backgrounds.

reality and our ideals, then we still have to figure out how to deflate the power of the honor syndrome. One viable possibility, I think, has been expressed beautifully by Princeton philosopher Kwame Anthony Appiah in his book *The Honor Code: How Moral Revolutions Happen* (Appiah, 2010). Appiah notes the role of cultural honor systems throughout history in different parts of the world in creating or perpetuating immoral social practices, from Western dueling to Eastern foot binding. He also notes, though, that in case after case, these practices were upended when enough people began to mock them.[10] Mockery, after all, is the enemy of respect, and respect is the basis of worth in an honor culture.

A great example of this sort of mockery can be seen in a set of public service ads produced by the state of Minnesota a few years ago. The series was called "Mr. Machismo," and each ad featured something stupid that men sometimes do in service of their macho self-concepts, ending with a plea not to be "that guy." These sorts of ads won't do much to stop men from wanting to be seen as brave and daring, but they might plant the seeds of subversion that could, one day, undermine some of the power of the honor syndrome.

I have to admit, this has been true for me. As a child of the American South, I grew up stewed in the cauldron of honor that was the legacy of my Scotch-Irish forebears and the people who settled the South centuries ago. Catching myself telling my sons to "man up" and realizing in those moments that my dominant concern is not really with the virtues of courage or social responsibility, but with the dangers of reputation damage that accrues to boys who fail to live up to the mandates of the honor code, I am learning to stop and modify my orientation. I don't exhort my sons to display cowardice when I turn away from the honor code, but instead encourage them to exhibit real virtues that don't have to do with defending their (or my) reputation. Blowing your top when someone cuts you off in traffic, for example, and calling your

10. Appiah (2010) also suggests that the widespread adoption of certain practices, such as dueling, that had previously been normative only among social elites, diminished the high status of these practices. When they became common among the commoners, they lost their appeal among the well-to-do, which made enforcement of laws against them much easier, leading to their relatively quick demise.

response brave or "standing up for what's right" does not actually make it a brave or courageous act. That's not what real bravery is. That's not what *real* men do, I tell them.

For instance, my wife's mother spent her life as a nurse, and in that role she saw countless cases of severe head trauma among people riding motorcycles without helmets. So, when my kids were very young, as we would drive around town or across the country, my wife and I would mock people we encountered who were riding helmetless. "That guy is really foolish," we would point out. It wasn't long before this came to be something of a family game of "see who can find foolish people on the road first." My sons will no doubt do some foolish things of their own as they grow to be men, just like their father and his father before him, but riding a motorcycle without a helmet is probably not going to be one of them. They know they would be mocked, not admired, for doing this.

Consistent with Appiah's thesis, I try to remember to mock instances of behavior deriving from the honor syndrome, in others or in myself, in front of my sons. My goal in doing this is that they will not adopt unquestioningly the habits of thinking, feeling, and behaving that are the legacy of this cultural system. I want them to grow up to be men of true honor, who define human worth in ways that transcend the shallow, reputation-oriented ideals of the honor syndrome. As I pursue these goals in raising my sons, I suspect I am reforming my own psyche almost as much as I am shaping theirs.

Discussion Questions

1. As you consider the scope of history and what you've read in this book, do you think the honor syndrome has done more harm or more good for humanity? Why?

2. What do you think might be some ways to change the honor syndrome from the inside? What sorts of persuasive appeals might be made, and how should they be made, to reduce the power of some of the pressures inherent in honor cultures?

3. What good things might be lost if we were somehow able to undermine all honor cultures in the world? Can you imagine ways of weaving these good things into the fabric of society apart from the motivational forces of the honor syndrome?

For Further Reading

Appiah, K. A. 2010. *The honor code: How moral revolutions happen*. New York: W. W. Norton.

Imura, M., M. Burkley, and R. P. Brown. 2014. Honor to the core: Measuring implicit honor ideology endorsement. *Personality and Individual Differences* 59:27–31.

Simons, R. L., M. K. Lei, E. A. Stewart, S. R. H. Beach, G. H. Brody, R. A. Philibert, and F. X. Gibbons. 2012. Social adversity, genetic variation, street code, and aggression: A genetically informed model of violent behavior. *Youth Violence and Juvenile Justice* 10:3–24.

Scales Measuring Endorsement of Honor Ideology

S EVERAL DIFFERENT SCALES TO capture the extent to which people embrace or reject the ideology of honor have been developed and tested during the past few years. Two such measures presented below are the Honor Ideology for Manhood (or HIM) scale (Barnes et al., 2012) and the Honor Ideology for Womanhood (or HIW) scale (Barnes et al., 2014). Each scale captures what some researchers believe to be the most central and common features of honor ideology for men and women around the world. For copyright reasons, I have included only portions of these scales in this appendix.

Note: On the HIM (as well as the HIW and the Honor Concerns [HC] scales), respondents indicate the extent to which they agree or disagree with each statement using a scale ranging from 1 (disagree strongly) to 9 (agree strongly). The complete scales include more items than are shown here.

Example Items from the 16-Item HIM Scale

1. A man has the right to act with physical aggression toward another man who calls him an insulting name.
2. A real man doesn't let other people push him around.

3. A man has the right to act with physical aggression toward another man who slanders his family.
4. A real man never lets himself be a "door mat" to other people.
5. A man has the right to act with physical aggression toward another man who openly flirts with his wife.
6. A real man will never back down from a fight.

Example Items from the 12-Item HIW Scale

1. A respectable woman knows that what she does reflects on her family name.
2. A good woman is loyal to her family members, even when they have behaved badly.
3. A good woman stands by her man at all times.
4. A respectable woman avoids any behavior that might bring shame on her family.
5. A good woman never flirts with a man who is not her husband or boyfriend.
6. A respectable woman never wants to be known as being sexually permissive.

Another approach to measuring honor ideology was taken by IJzerman and colleagues (IJzerman, vanDijk, & Gallucci, 2007). Their Honor Concerns (or HC) scale includes nine items, five of which are presented here. These items are less abstractly ideological than items from the HIM or the HIW, taking more of a personal approach to measuring honor ideology endorsement. In my lab, we typically administer the HC scale with a 9-point response scale just like that for the HIM and HIW (where 1 = strongly disagree and 9 = strongly agree). We have found that scores on all three of these scales correlate strongly. Furthermore, using a statistical technique called *factor analysis*, we have also seen that there is a "common core" to these three scales (e.g., Barnes et al., 2014).

Example Items from the 9-Item HC Scale

1. My honor depends on the appreciation and respect that others have for me.
2. I could not have respect for myself if I did not have any honor.

3. I think that a public humiliation would be one of the situations that would violate my honor the most.
4. I think that honor is one of the most important things that I have as a human being.
5. It is my duty to be constantly prepared to defend the honor of my family.

APPENDIX B

Analyses of Penalties in Football for Personal Fouls and Unsportsmanlike Conduct

USING DATA COMPILED FROM schools' reports of their football team rosters (which indicated the state from which each player hailed), the following multiple regression analysis predicts the average number of penalties each team received per game for personal fouls and unsportsmanlike conduct (averaged across the 2011–2012 and 2012–2013 football seasons) from a host of variables related to each school or the state where each school is located (Table B1). The key predictor variable in the analysis is the percentage of each team's roster in 2011 from an honor state in the U.S. South or West—a variable labeled "Honor Roster." This analysis includes the teams from the three U.S. military academies. Excluding these three teams does not change the results in any meaningful way, however.

Control variables in this analysis include the following:

1. Whether the school is public or private (coded as 0 for public, 1 for private)
2. The percentage of the state's population living in a rural area (according to the 2010 U.S. Census)

Table B1. MULTIPLE REGRESSION ANALYSIS OF AVERAGE PENALTIES EARNED PER GAME FOR PERSONAL FOULS AND UNSPORTSMANLIKE CONDUCT

PREDICTOR VARIABLE	B	SE	T-TEST	P VALUE
Honor roster	.460	0.161	2.86	.005
Rurality	−.020	0.004	−4.48	.000
Economic deprivation	.149	0.088	1.70	.091
Temperature	−.017	0.007	−2.39	.019
Public/private	−.405	0.126	−3.21	.002
Win (%)	−.273	0.265	−1.03	.305

SE = standard error.

3. An economic deprivation variable composed of standardized indices of the poverty rate, the unemployment rate, and median income (reverse-scored before combining with poverty and unemployment)
4. The mean temperature from September through November of the city (or nearest city) in which each school is located
5. Each team's percentage of wins across the 2005 to 2011 seasons (as an index of the team's competitiveness)

For those of you who don't read statistical tables like this for a living, what this analysis shows is that, holding constant variables such as state rurality, economic deprivation, temperature, and so on, the percentage of a team's roster that hailed from an honor state in 2011 was capable of predicting—beyond chance levels—the number of "dirty penalties" that team received across the 2011 to 2012 and 2012 to 2013 football seasons.

What all this means is that teams with more players from honor states subsequently earned more penalties for personal fouls and unsportsmanlike conduct. This analysis and its results support rather nicely the more general findings reported in Chapter 7 that the games with the most such dirty penalties were most likely to be games in which at least one team from an honor state was playing. But this team-level analysis goes much further in making this point because teams are not homogeneous with respect to the origins of their players. Not all players on a team located in an honor state are *from* an honor state, just as not all players on a team located in a nonhonor state are *from* a nonhonor state. This team-level analysis thus gives us more confidence that something cultural underlies these dirty penalties, rather than something incidental.

References

Ali, N., and D. Minoui. 2010. *I am Nujood, age 10 and divorced*. New York: Broadway Books.

Appiah, K. A. 2010. *The honor Code: How moral revolutions happen*. New York: W. W. Norton.

Archer, J. 2000. Sex differences in physical aggression toward partners: A meta-analytic review. *Psychological Bulletin* 126:651–680.

Baldry, A. C., S. Pagliaro, and C. Porcaro. 2013. The rule of law at time of masculine honor: Afghan police attitudes and intimate partner violence. *Group Processes and Intergroup Relations* 16:363–374.

Barnes, C. D., R. P. Brown, M. Carvallo, J. Lenes, and J. Bosson. 2014. My country, my self: Honor, identity, and defensive responses to national threats. *Self & Identity* 13:638–662.

Barnes, C. D., R. P. Brown, and L. L. Osterman. 2012. Don't tread on me: Masculine honor ideology in the U.S. and militant responses to terrorism. *Personality and Social Psychology Bulletin* 38:1018–1029.

Barnes, C. D., R. P. Brown, and M. Tamborski. 2012. Living dangerously: Culture of honor, risk-taking, and the non-randomness of "accidental" deaths. *Social Psychological and Personality Science* 3:100–107.

Bowman, J. 2006. *Honor: A history*. New York: Encounter Books.

Braga, A. A., and B. J. Bond. 2008. Policing and disorder hot spots: A randomized controlled trial. *Criminology: An International Journal* 46:577–607.

Brinkley, J. 2010. Afghanistan's dirty little secret. *The San Francisco Chronicle*, August 29, p. E-8.

Brown, R. P., M. Carvallo, and M. Imura. 2014a. Naming patterns reveal cultural values: Patronyms, matronyms, and the culture of honor. *Personality and Social Psychology Bulletin* 40:250–262.

Brown, R. P., M. Imura, and L. Mayeux. 2014b. Honor and the stigma of mental healthcare. *Personality and Social Psychology Bulletin* 40:1119–1131.

Brown, R. P., M. Imura, and L. L. Osterman. 2014c. Gun culture: Mapping a peculiar preference for guns in the commission of suicide. *Basic and Applied Social Psychology* 36: 164–175.

Brown, R. P., L. L. Osterman, and C. D. Barnes. 2009. School violence and the culture of honor. *Psychological Science* 20:1400–1405.

Bush, G. W. 2004. Address before a joint session of the Congress on the State of the Union. January, 20, 2004. http://www.presidency.ucsb.edu/ws/index.php?pid=29646 (accessed July 12, 2013).

Cheng, C., and M. Hoekstra. 2012. *Does strengthening self-defense law deter crime or escalate violence? Evidence from the Castle doctrine.* Working Paper. Department of Economics, Texas A&M University: Bryan-College Station.

Cohen, D. 1996. Law, social policy, and violence: The impact of regional cultures. *Journal of Personality and Social Psychology* 70:961–978.

Cohen, D., and R. E. Nisbett. 1994. Self-protection and the culture of honor: Explaining southern violence. *Personality and Social Psychology Bulletin* 20:551–567.

Cohen, D., R. E. Nisbett, B. F. Bowdle, and N. Schwarz. 1996. Insult, aggression, and the southern culture of honor: An "experimental ethnography." *Journal of Personality and Social Psychology* 70:945–960.

Cohen, D., J. A. Vandello, S. Puente, and A. K. Rantilla. 1999. "When you call me that, smile!": How norms for politeness, interaction styles, and aggression work together in southern culture. *Social Psychology Quarterly* 62:257–275.

Dafoe, A., and D. Caughey. 2013. *Honor and war: Southern US presidents and the effects of concern for reputation.* http://dx.doi.org/10.2139/ssrn.2343466 (accessed May 29, 2014).

Daly, M., and M. Wilson. 1988. *Homicide.* Hawthorne, NY: Aldine de Gruyter.

Eisner, M. 2001. Modernization, self-control and lethal violence. *British Journal of Criminology* 41:618–638.

Eisner, M., and L. Ghuneim. 2013. Honor killing attitudes amongst adolescents in Amman, Jordan. *Aggressive Behavior* 39:405–417.

Fischer, D. H. 1989. *Albion's seed: Four British folkways in America.* New York: Oxford University Press.

Gal, D., and J. Wilkie. 2010. Real men don't eat quiche: Regulation of gender-expressive choices by men. *Social Psychological and Personality Science* 1:291–301.

Gebauer, J. E., M. R. Leary, and W. Neberich. 2012. Unfortunate first names: Effects of name-based relational devaluation and interpersonal neglect. *Social Psychological and Personality Science* 3:590–596.

Guinn, J. 2011. *The last gunfight: The real story of the shootout at the O.K. Corral—and how it changed the American West.* New York: Simon & Schuster.

Hoitt, J. B. 1890. *Excellent quotations for home and school selected for the use of teachers and pupils.* Boston, MA: Lee and Shepard Publishers.

Hosseini, K. 2003. *The kite runner.* New York: Riverhead Books.

IJzerman, H., W. W. van Dijk, and M. Gallucci. 2007. A bumpy train ride: A field experiment on insult, honor, and emotional reactions. *Emotions,* 7:869–875.

Imura, M., M. Burkely, and R. P. Brown. 2014. Honor to the core: Measuring implicit honor ideology endorsement. *Personality and Individual Differences* 59:27–31.

Joiner, T. 2005. *Why people die by suicide*. Cambridge, MA: Harvard University Press.

Keizer, K., S. Lindenberg, and L. Steg. 2008. The spreading of disorder. *Science* 322:1681–1685.

Kelly, M. H. 1999. Regional naming patterns and the culture of honor. *Names* 47:3–20.

Leary, M. R., R. M. Kowalski, L. Smith, and S. Phillips. 2003. Teasing, rejection, and violence: Case studies of the school shootings. *Aggressive Behavior* 29:202–214.

Lee, M. R., W. B. Bankston, T. C. Hayes, and S. A. Thomas. 2007. Revisiting the Southern culture of violence. *Sociological Quarterly* 48:253–275.

Leyburn, J. G. 1962. *The Scotch-Irish: A social history*. Chapel Hill, NC: University of North Carolina Press.

Lieberson, S., and F. B. Lynn. 2003. Popularity as a taste: An application to the naming process. *Onoma* 38:235–276.

Luhtanen, R., and J. Crocker. 1992. A collective self-esteem scale: Self-evaluation of one's social identity. *Personality and Social Psychology Bulletin* 18:302–318.

Mark, T. L., D. L. Shern, J. E. Bagalman, and Z. Cao. 2007. *Ranking America's mental health: An analysis of depression across the states*. Washington, DC: Mental Health America.

McClellan, C., and E. Tekin. 2012. *Stand your ground laws and homicides*. National Bureau of Economic Research no. 18187. June.

Newman, K. S., C. Fox, W. Roth, J. Mehta, and D. Harding. 2005. *Rampage: The social roots of school shootings*. New York: Basic Books.

Newport, F. 2011. *Americans prefer boys to girls, just as they did in 1941*. http://www.gallup.com/poll/148187/Americans-Prefer-Boys-Girls-1941.aspx?utm_source (accessed June 30, 2011).

Nisbett, R. E., G. Polly, and S. Lang. 1995. Homicide and U. S. regional culture. In *Interpersonal violent behavior: Social and cultural aspects*, ed. B. Ruback and N. Weiner, 135–151. New York: Springer.

Nordberg, J. 2010. "Where boys are prized, girls live the part." *The New York Times*. September 20, p. A-1.

Osterman, L. L., and R. P. Brown. 2011. Culture of honor and violence against the self. *Personality and Social Psychology Bulletin* 37:1611–1623.

Patton, L. 2013. "Why are Texans such dirty, dirty football plaers?" http://www.lewpblog.com/2013/09/20/why-are-texans-such-dirty-dirty-football-players/ (accessed June 20, 2014).

Pedersen, E. J., D. E. Forster, and M. E. McCullough. 2014. Life history, code of honor, and emotional responses to inequality in an economic game. *Emotion* 14:920–929.

Peristiany, J. G. 1966. *Honour and shame: The values of Mediterranean society*. Chicago, IL: The University of Chicago Press.

Rice, O. K. 1982. *The Hatfields and the McCoys*. Lexington, KY: University Press of Kentucky.

Saramad, M. H., and L. Sultani. 2013. *Violence against women in Afghanistan*. Report to the Afghanistan Independent Human Rights Commission: Kabul, Afghanistan.

Saucier, D. A., D. F. Till, S. S. Miller, C. J. O'Dea, and E. Andres. 2014. Slurs against masculinity: Masculine honor beliefs and men's reactions to slurs. *Language Sciences* 52: 108–120.

Scheuer, M. 2011. *Osama Bin Laden*. New York: Oxford University Press, 36–37.

Simons, R. L., M. K. Lei, E. A. Stewart, S. R. H. Beach, G. H. Brody, R. A. Philibert, and F. X. Gibbons. 2012. Social adversity, genetic variation, street code, and aggression: A genetically informed model of violent behavior. *Youth Violence and Juvenile Justice* 10:3–24.

Stewart, G. R. 1979. *American given names*. New York: Oxford University Press.

Swann, W. B., Jr., M. D. Buhrmester, A. Gomez, J. Jetten, B. Bastian, A. Vázquez, A. Ariyanto, T. Besta, O. Christ, L. Cui, G. Finchilescu, R. González, N. Goto, M. Hornsey, S. Sharma, H. Susianto, and A. Zhang. 2014. What makes a group worth dying for? Identity fusion fosters perception of familial ties, promoting self-sacrifice. *Journal of Personality and Social Psychology* 106:912–926.

Tamborski, M., and R. P. Brown. 2011. *Validation of a continuous measure of the culture of honor in the U.S.* Poster presented at the annual meeting of the Society for Personality and Social Psychology, San Antonio, TX, January 27–29, 2011.

Timmerman, T. A. 2007. "It was a thought pitch": Personal, situational, and target influences on hit-by-pitch events across time. *Journal of Applied Psychology* 92:876–884.

Tjaden, P., and N. Thoennes. 2000. *Extent, nature, and consequences of intimate partner violence: Findings from the national violence against women survey*. Washington, D.C.: U.S. Department of Justice, National Institute of Justice, NCJ 181867.

Vandello, J. A., J. K. Bosson, D. Cohen, R. M. Burnaford, and J. R. Weaver. 2008. Precarious manhood. *Journal of Personality and Social Psychology* 95:1325–1339.

Vandello, J. A., and D. Cohen. 1999. Patterns of individualism and collectivism across the United States. *Journal of Personality and Social Psychology* 77:279–292.

Vandello, J. A., and D. Cohen. 2003. Male honor and female fidelity: Implicit cultural scripts that perpetuate domestic violence. *Journal of Personality and Social Psychology* 84:997–1010.

Vandello, J. A., D. Cohen, R. Grandon, and R. Franiuk. 2009. Stand by your man: Indirect prescriptions for honorable violence and feminine loyalty in Canada, Chile, and the United States. *Journal of Cross-Cultural Psychology* 40:81–104.

Varnum, M. E. W., and S. Kitayama. 2011. What's in a name? Popular names are less common on frontiers. *Psychological Science* 22:176–183.

Wallis, M. 2011. *David Crockett: Lion of the West*. New York: W. W. Norton.

Weber, E. U., A. Blais, and N. E. Betz. 2002. A domain-specific risk-attitude scale: Measuring risk perceptions and risk behaviors. *Journal of Behavioral Decision Making* 15:263–290.

Wyatt-Brown, B. 1986. *Honor and violence in the old South*. New York: Oxford University Press, 14.

Index

The entries for "*n*" and "*t*" indicate an *n* for notes and a *t* for tables.

accidental deaths
Barnes, Tamborski, and Brown study on, 81–84, 84*t*
CDC on, 82
in England, Scotland, Wales, 170–71, 171*t*
health professional shortage area and, 83
International Classification of Diseases on, 82n1
regional differences, 82–83
UPDF and, 83
whites and, 83–84, 84*t*
Adams, Lucy, 180–83, 182n8, 185, 186
affect misattribution procedure (AMP)
Imura, Burkley, and Brown study on honor-relevant words and, 179–80
in unconscious mind, 178–80
Afghanistan
AIHRC in, 147, 148
EVAW law in, 147
Lashkar, 141, 142, 144, 161
tribal systems of law, 157
women in, 148–49, 157
Afghanistan culture, 148–49
extreme honor culture in, 159
gender-bending in, 150–53, 153n2
Julia, as State Department diplomat and, 141–47, 141n1, 161
Pashtun tribe, 143–47, 160, 161

Afghanistan Independent Human Rights Commission (AIHRC), 147, 148
Afghan Parliament, Rafaat in, 150–51
aggression
delinquency and, 173–74
football, in intergroup context, 120
higher testosterone levels and, 31
honor cultures promotion of, 51
North, South, West U.S., response to insults by, xi, 31–32, 183
physical, insults to men and, 175–76
social dynamics of, 23
socialization sensitivity and, 173–74
aggressive masculinity
behavioral displays of, 31–32
to defend women's reputations, 51
aging parents care, 135
in honor states, 136–37, 136n11
AIHRC. *See* Afghanistan Independent Human Rights Commission
Aikman, Troy, 86–87
Alabama-Auburn football rivalry, 114, 115, 116, 116n2, 117
Alamo, Crockett, D., at, 3, 93
Albion's Seed (Fischer), 59
Ali, Nujood, 156–58
America. *See* United States
American Wild West, lawlessness in, 172–73
AMP. *See* affect misattribution procedure

antidepressant medications, 69–70, 71
anti-immigration attitudes, 125–27
Appiah, Kwame Anthony,
   187–88, 187n10
argument-based homicide, in U.S.,
   54–55, 170
   Nisbett and colleagues on, 27–28
   in nonhonor states, 28
   small-town effect on, 29–30, 30n4
   in South, 30n4, 182
Arizona Territory, 19–20
Army recruitment rates, 91, 91n7, 128
ATF. *See* Bureau of Alcohol, Tobacco,
   and Firearms
authoritarianism
   anti-immigrant attitudes, 125–27
   Barnes and colleagues study
      on, 125–26
   honor ideology link to, 125–26
   stereotype tendency of, 124–25

Baldry, Anna Costanza, 148–50
Barnes, Collin, xii
   accidental deaths study, 81–84, 84t
   authoritarianism study, 125–26
   CMHs for acts of valor study, 90–92
   domestic terrorism study, 132–33
   honor roster, team penalties
      study, 119–20
   intergroup conflict response
      study, 122–23
   school violence study, 34–35
Barnes, Jennifer, 176
BCS. *See* Bowl Championship Series
Behan, Johnny, 21
Behavioral Risk Factor Surveillance
   System, of CDC, 67n3
beliefs and values, 57
   honor syndrome and, xiv–xv,
      24–26, 58–59
   men emotional vulnerabilities and,
      50–51, 75, 78–79, 81–82
   on naming, 95–98, 107–10, 185
   penal code and, 37–40
   of Scotch-Irish, 13–15, 14n6, 24, 29
betrayal, as violence motivator, 4,
   28, 121
bin Laden, Osama, 16, 133–34
biological measure, of femininity, 50
blacks. *See* nonwhites
Bomb Arson Tracking System, of
   ATF, 35
Borland, Chris, 87

Bowdle, Brian, 31–33
Bowl Championship Series (BCS), 114
   penalties per game in, 117–18, 118t
Braveheart film, 5–6
broken window effect, 9, 173
   Giuliani use to combat crime, 9n3
   Groningen city, study of, 7–8
   lawlessness cues and, 7
burdensomeness feeling, for suicide, 65
   depression and, 64
   honor culture and, 66, 137
Bureau of Alcohol, Tobacco, and
   Firearms (ATF), Bomb Arson
   Tracking System, 35
Burkley, Melissa, 179–80
Bush, George W., 15, 16, 131
business names, violent images in, 109–10

Cagle, Chris, 81
Canada, domestic violence
   response in, 54
Carvallo, Mauricio, 104–8
castle doctrine, 38
Caughey, Devin, 128–30
CDC. *See* Center for Disease Control
   and Prevention
Center for Disease Control and
   Prevention (CDC)
   on accidental deaths, 82
   Behavioral Risk Factor Surveillance
      System of, 67n3
   on gun ownership, 67n3
   on suicide rates, 68
Cermortan, Domnica, 168–69
Charlie Hebdo terrorist attack, 153
children
   honor-related naming practices, xiii,
      95–98, 106n2, 107–10, 185
   parental support of aggression, for
      honor threats, 35n7
   parents' seeking mental health ser-
      vices for, 75
   retaliatory violence of, in honor
      states, 34–35
   unusual names for, in individualistic
      culture, 101
Chile, domestic violence
   response in, 54
Clanton, Billy, 19, 21
Clanton, Ike, 19–21
Clinton, Bill, 91
CMH. *See* Congressional Medal
   of Honor

Cohen, Dov, xi
  conflict escalation study, 32–34
  gun control legislation, 38
  on homicides, in honor states, 37–38
  insults by stranger study, 31–33
  on paradox of politeness, 34
  women's perceived faithfulness and
      men's honor study, 52–53
collective honor. *See also* honor circle
  in football, 114–20
  personal honor connected to, 66, 114,
      120, 121, 123, 126–27, 126n8
  in religiosity, 156
collective self-esteem scale, of Luhtanen
      and Crocker, 126n7
collectivistic culture, 66, 68, 74, 100, 135
concussion scandal, of NFL, 85
  Aikman on, 86–87
  Borland on, 87
conflict escalation study, by Cohen and
      colleagues, 32–34
Congressional Medal of Honor (CMH),
      for acts of valor
  Barnes, Dodd, and Brown study
      on, 90–92
  identity fusion and, 127–28
cortisol level, in stress, xii, 31
Costa Concordia sinking, 168–69, 168n3
country music, honor themes in, 176
Couric, Katie, 113
Couvillon, Marty, 117, 119–20
cowardice, masculinity and, 49
crime
  FBI statistics, on relationship vio-
      lence, 54–55, 55n3
  minimalist approach to reduce, 9n3
  moral, of women in Afghanistan, 148
Crocker, J., 126n7
Crockett, Davy, 19, 121, 134
  at Alamo, 3, 93
  debt of, 2–3
  Scotch-Irish background, 5, 15, 16
  Wallis on, 3, 93
Crockett, John, 2
cultural change
  honest self-reflection for, 186
  honor syndrome power deflated
      for, 187

Dafoe, Allan, 128–30
Daly, Martin, 56n5
Darius I, 163
De Falco, Gregorio, 169

defense-related violence, 39–40
delinquency, aggression and, 173–74
Department of Justice, U.S., on domes-
      tic violence, 46
depression
  antidepressant prescriptions and,
      69–70, 71
  burdensomeness feeling and, 64
  Osterman and Brown, on levels
      of, 69–70
  SAMHSA data on, 70
  seeking mental health services for,
      70, 71, 73
dignity cultures
  honor culture transitioned into, xiv
  reputation in, 184
dignity states, nonhonor states as, 184
disconnectedness, suicide and, 64–65,
      66, 137
disorder conditions, in Groningen
      study, 7–9
Dodd, Kevin, 120n4
  CMHs for acts of valor study, 90–92
  on honor roster, team penalties
      and, 119–20
domestic homicide
  rate, in relationship violence, 55–56,
      55t, 57
  whites' rates of, 55, 55t, 56
domestic terrorism
  Barnes and Brown study on, 132–33
  FBT data on, 133, 133n10
domestic violence, xiii, 43–47, 160
  Chileans and Canadians
      response to, 54
  honor states tolerance of, 52–53
  nonhonor states attitude toward, 53
  social scripts for male, 53–54
  social stigmatization of woman
      leaving, 53
  stalking, 46, 56
  U.S. Department of Justice on, 46
  victims of, 47, 47n1, 51
  woman's infidelity and, 51,
      56n5, 148–50

Earp, Morgan, 19, 21
Earp, Virgil, 19
Earp, Wyatt, 19–21, 172–73, 173n6
ecological fallacy, 154n4
Edward the Long Shanks of England
      (king), 5
Eisner, Manuel, 155

Elimination of Violence Against
    Women (EVAW) law, 147
emotional vulnerabilities, of men, 50–
    51, 75, 78–79, 81–82
England, 5, 12
    accidental deaths, homicides, suicides
        in, 170–71, 171t
    name concentration in, 102
    Scottish Lowlands invasion, 6
Equal Rights Amendment, honor states
    and, 59
Esther (queen), 163–67, 185
EVAW. See Elimination of Violence
    Against Women

face culture, in Southeast Asia, 184
faithfulness of women, men's honor
    link to, 54
    Vandello and Cohen study, 52–53
    women's response to physical
        altercation, 52–53
Federal Bureau of Investigation (FBI)
    crime statistics on relationship vio-
        lence, 54–55, 55n3
    domestic terrorism data, 133, 133n10
felony homicides, 28–29
femininity
    biological measure of, 50
    honor culture definition of, 51
film, honor themes in, 5–6, 176–77
firefighters, honor syndrome and, 181,
    185–86, 186n9
Fischer, David H., 13, 59
    on patronym system, of
        Scotch-Irish, 104
    on Scotch-Irish clans, 13, 103–4
football, 134
    aggression, in intergroup
        context, 120
    Alabama-Auburn rivalry, 114, 115, 116,
        116n2, 117
    Barnes, Brown, and Dodd study, on
        honor roster in, 119–20
    Couvillon statistics on, 117, 119–20
    Patton, L., data on, 117–18, 118t
    penalties in, 117–20, 118t, 195–97, 196t
    team honor connection to personal
        honor, 114–20
Freud, Sigmund, 177–78

Gallup Poll, on parents' gender
    preference, 108
game of chicken, xii, 32, 92–93

gender
    -based violence, in Yemen, 157–58
    parents preference of, 108
gender-bending, in Afghanistan
    girls doubling as boys, 150
    pedophilia, 152–53, 153n2
    Rafaat daughter raised as
        son, 151–52
genetics, lawlessness environments
    and, 173–74
Ghuneim, Lana, 155
Giuliani, Rudy, 9n3
good woman, in honor culture, 51, 66,
    185, 192
Gosling, Ryan, 48
Graham, James (Earl of
    Montrose), 98–99
Great Britain. See England
Groningen study
    on broken window effect, 7–8
    order and disorder conditions
        in, 7–9
group. See also intergroup conflict
    extreme acts, in service of, 114
    individual identity fusion
        with, 127–28
gun control legislation, in honor
    states, 38
gun ownership, 38, 67, 67n3

Hatfield, Anderson "Devil Anse," 4, 15
Hatfield, Floyd, 4
health professional shortage area
    accidental deaths and, 83
    suicide and, 68
height advantage, in Presidential
    elections, 88–89, 88n2
Hispanics/Latinos
    collectivistic culture of, 100
    gun ownership, 38
    honor culture of, 29n3
Holiday, Doc, 19
homicide. See also argument-based
        homicide; domestic homicide
    Daly and Wilson, on jealousy
        and, 56n5
    for defense, in honor states, 37–38
    in England, Scotland, and Wales,
        170–71, 171t
    felony, 28–29
    Northern Ireland rates of, 171–72
    stand-your-ground laws and, 39
    whites and nonwhites rates of, 29

Honor and shame: The values of Mediterranean society (Peristiany), 169n4
honor circle. *See also* collective honor
  of bin Laden, 133–34
  in football, 114–20, 118*t*, 134, 195–97, 196*t*
  identity fusion in, 127–28, 128n9
  kinship network, 14, 15, 134–38, 136n11
  patriots and, 15, 120–28, 126n8
  Presidential military action, 128–31, 134
  terrorism, xiii, 113–14, 131–34, 153, 181, 185–86
The Honor Code: How Moral Revolutions Happen (Appiah), 187
Honor Concerns (HC) scale, 191–93
honor culture, xv, 9, 75, 78, 137, 169
honor dynamics, of Scotland, 169–70
honor ideology
  measure, 84
  naming preferences associated with, 103
  in U.S., nation understanding through, xiv, 16
Honor Ideology for Manhood (HIM) scale, 191–92
Honor Ideology for Womanhood (HIW) scale, 191–92
honor killings, Islam, 155
honor-oriented countries, 159–60, 160n7
honor-related characteristics, Tamborski and Brown on, 26
honor roster, in football, 119–20
honor states, 154, 184. *See also* South, U.S.; West, U.S.
  aging parents care in, 136–37, 136n11
  antidepressant medications use less in, 71
  argument-based homicides in, 28
  Army recruitment rates, 128
  attitude toward women, 59
  businesses with violent names, 109–10
  depression levels higher in, 71
  domestic violence tolerance, 52–53
  felony homicides in, 28–29
  football game penalties in, 117–19, 118*t*, 195–97, 196*t*
  gun control legislation in, 38
  gun ownership in, 38, 67

law and, 37–40
less matronym use in, 107
listing of, 25*t*
mental health services investment and, 74–75, 74*t*
patronyms use in, 107
people over 65 living alone in, 136, 136n11
rape rates in, 55–56, 55n4, 55*t*
reputation and defense of self, property, family emphasis, 27
response to honor threats, 27, 29
school violence, 34–35
soldiers acts of valor, 90–91
stand-your-ground laws in, 39–40
suicide rates higher in, 68, 69, 69*t*, 71
town names with violent words, 108
variation within, 26–27
honor themes
  in country music, 176
  in film, 5–6, 176–77
honor threats
  honor states response to, 27, 29
  parental support of children's aggression from, 35n7
  reputation and, 27
Hosseini, Khaled, 153n3
Houston, Sam, 15, 121
hypersensitivity, to insults, xi, 183

I Am Nujood, Age 10 and Divorced (Ali and Minoui), 156–57
identity fusion
  CMH recipients and, 127–28
  of individual with group, 127–28
  in military, 127, 128n9
  symbols of shared identity, 127
  willingness to die for group, 127–28
Imura, Mikiko
  gun ownership study, 38
  honor-relevant words study, 179–80
  patriarchal baby-naming system study, 104–8
  on suicide methods, 72–73
individual identity fusion, with group, 127–28
individualistic culture, 135
  name influenced from, 99–101, 103
  of U.S., 100
  voluntary settlement hypothesis for, 100–101
infidelity, domestic violence and, 51, 56n5, 148–50

instincts, suicide and callousness
  to, 65–66
insults
  absence of, Southern males response
    to, 32, 32n5
  film reference to, 176
  hypersensitivity to, xi, 183
  male aggression over homosexual and
    feminine, 175–76
  about masculinity, 175
  North, South, West U.S., aggressive
    response to, xi, 31–32, 183
  Saucier study on reaction
    to, 175–76
  by stranger, 31–33
intergroup conflict
  Barnes, Osterman, and Brown study
    on, 122–23
  stranger-danger scenarios, 123
intergroup context, 120n5
  football aggression and, 120
International Classification of
    Diseases, 82n1
international conflicts, Presidential
    military action and, 129–30
international terrorism, 16, 133–34
interrogation techniques, severe, 123
intimate partner violence. *See* domestic
    violence
Ireland
  James I plan to subdue, 12
  migration from Scottish Lowlands,
    12, 171
Islam, 152
  Charlie Hebdo terrorist attack, 153
  Eisner and Ghuneim study on honor
    killings, 155
  fundamentalism, 153–54

Jackson, Andrew, 15, 120–21
James I of England (king), 12, 171
James VI of Scotland (king)
  becoming James I of England, 12
  tree planting laws by, 12n5
Japan, *seppuku* ritual in, 73
jealousy, 51
  Daly and Wilson, on homicide
    and, 56n5
Joiner, Thomas, 63–67
Jolie, Angelina, 50
Julia, State Department diplomat, in
    Afghanistan, 141–47, 141n1, 161

Kelly, Michael, 108–10
kinship network, 134–38
  aging parents care, 135–37, 136n11
  nursing homes and honor culture, 135
  older men burdensomeness, 137
  of Scotch-Irish, 14, 15
The Kite Runner (Hosseini), 153n3

Lambert, Miranda, 176
Lamech, 167, 167n1
Lars and the Real Girl, 48
Lashkar, Afghanistan, 141, 142, 144, 161
Lauer, Matt, 113
law, honor and
  castle doctrine, 39
  Cohen on, 37–38
  gun control legislation, in honor
    states, 38
  gun ownership, 38
  homicide, in honor states, 37–38
  honor states more permissive gun
    laws, 39–40
  sentence reduction, in honor
    states, 37–38
  stand-your-ground laws, 39–40
lawfulness, 173–74
lawlessness
  in American Wild West, 172–73
  broken window effect and, 7
  cues, 7–8
  genetics and, honor syndrome
    link, 173–74
  socialization sensitivity and, 173–74
legacy naming, 106n2
legends
  Crockett, 2–3, 5, 15–16, 19, 93,
    121, 134
  Earp, W., 19–21, 172–73, 173n6
Leonidas at Thermopylae, 165
Leyburn, James, 9n4
Lieberson, Stanley, 102, 103
lineage, 95–111
  individualistic culture and, 99–101,
    103, 135
  namesaking and, 105–7, 106n2, 106t
  names and, 99–110, 101n1
  Prince George of Cambridge, 95–96
location, school shootings influenced by,
    xii, xiii, 35–36
Lowland Scotland. *See* Scottish
    Lowlands
loyalty reputation, of women, 11, 51, 185

Luhtanen, R., 126n7
Lynn, Freda, 102, 103

Martin, Trayvon, 38–39
masculinity, 33, 48
  aggressive, behavioral displays
    of, 31–32
  cowardice and weakness
    perception, 49
  honor culture definition of, 51
  insults about, 175
  Lars and the Real Girl, 48
  rites of passage, 49
  social measure of, 49, 50–51,
    80–81, 184–85
  virility, 58
mastectomy, 50
Materazzi, Marco, 167–68
matronym, 104–8
  Carvallo, Imura, and Brown study
    on, 105
  honor states less use of, 107
McBride, Martina, 176
McClellan, Chandler, 39
McCoy, Randall, 4–5, 15, 16
McLaury, Frank, 19, 21
McLaury, Tom, 19, 21
McVeigh, Timothy, 131–32
meaning-making process, 177
mediation analysis, 174n7
  on patriarchal attitudes, 107–8
Mediterranean honor cultures,
    169, 169n4
men. *See also* masculinity;
    Southern males
  emotional vulnerabilities of, 50–51,
    75, 78–79, 81–82
  honor link of, to women's
    faithfulness, 52–54
  insults to, physical aggression
    and, 175–76
  patronyms and, 103–8
  real man, 47–51, 58, 66, 81–82, 152,
    185, 191–92
  suicide, of older, 137–38, 138f
mental health services, xiii, 76–77
  depression, seeking help for,
    70, 71, 73
  honor states reluctance to invest in,
    74–75, 74t
  nonhonor states and, 74–75, 74t
metropolitan areas, suicide rates in, 69,
    69n5, 69t

military
  CMH, for acts of valor,
    90–91, 127–28
  identity fusion in, 127, 128n9
  Presidential action, 128–31, 134
minimalist approach, to reduce
    crime, 9n3
Minnesota, namesaking scores in, 106,
    106n2, 106t
Minoui, D., 156–57
mockery, of honor syndrome
    behavior, 187–88
Mordecai, 163, 166

names
  businesses with violent, 109–10
  Carvallo, Imura, and Brown on
    patriarchal system for, 104–8
  individualistic culture influence on,
    99–101, 103
  Lieberson and Lynn, on trend toward
    unique, 102, 103
  random selection of, 99
  social rejection, for unusual,
    101, 101n1
  of towns, Kelly on, 108–10
  uncommon spelling of
    common, 101
  unusual, by parents for
    children, 101
namesaking, regional differences in,
    105–7, 106n2, 106t
naming, xiii
  beliefs, values influence on, 95–98,
    107–10, 185
  legacy, 106n2
  of Prince George of
    Cambridge, 95–96
National Football League (NFL)
    concussion scandal, 85–87
national identity, Scotch-Irish lack
    of, 14–15
National Survey on Drug Use and
    Health, of SAMHSA, 70
NFL. *See* National Football League
9/11. *See* World Trade Center
    terrorist attack
Nisbett, Richard, xi
  on argument-based homicide, in
    U.S., 27–28
  honor culture systematic study
    by, 27–29
  insults, by stranger study, 31–33

nonhonor states. *See also* North, U.S.
   argument-based homicides in, 28
   as dignity states, 184
   felony homicides in, 28–29
   gun ownership in, 38
   mental health services investment,
      74–75, 74*t*
   in North, U.S., 25, 25*t*
   rape rates in, 55–56, 55n4, 55*t*
   soldier acts of valor, 92
   suicide rates in, 68, 69, 69*t*, 71
   thoughts on women, in domestic
      violence, 53
   variation within, 26–27
nonmetropolitan areas, suicide rates in,
      69, 69n5, 69*t*
nonwhites, 91
   accidental deaths and, 84
   homicide rates, 29
   rape rates, 55n4
   suicide rates of, 68, 69, 69*t*
North, U.S.
   insult response, xi, 31–32, 183
   nonhonor states in, 25, 25*t*
North Carolina, namesaking scores,
      106, 106n2, 106*t*
Northern Ireland, 5, 13, 15, 103
   homicide rates in, 171–72
   Scotch-Irish immigration
      to, 12, 171
nursing homes, honor culture
      and, 135

Obama, Barack, 88n3
O.K. Corral, gunfight at, 19–21
Oklahoma City bombing, 131–32
Oklahoma horn honking and traffic
      rage, 22–23
one-upmanship, violence from, 29–30
order conditions, in Groningen
      study, 7–9
Osterman, Lindsey, xii, 68
   on depression levels and
      antidepressant
      medication, 69–70
   gun ownership study, 38
   honor culture and suicide
      study, 66–67
   intergroup conflict response
      study, 122–23
   school bombings study, 35
   school violence study, 34–35
   on suicide methods, 72–73

pain tolerance, suicide and, 65, 71
Paktika Province, Provincial
      Reconstruction Team in, 141
paradox of politeness, 34
parents
   care of aging, 135–37, 136n11
   Gallup on gender preference by, 108
   nonmental health doctors for
      children, 75–76
   support for children's aggression,
      from honor threats, 35n7
   unusual names for children, in indi-
      vidualistic culture, 101
Pashtun tribe, in Afghanistan, 143–47,
      160, 161
Pashtunwali law, 147
patriarchs
   Brown, Carvallo, and Imura on baby-
      naming and, 104–8
   of Scotch-Irish, 103–4
patriots, in honor circle, 120–28
   Jackson and, 15, 120–21
   personal identity fused with collec-
      tive, 126–27, 126n8
patronyms, 103
   Brown, Carvallo, and Imura study
      on, 104–8
   honor-oriented men patriarchal
      attitudes, 108
   honor states use of, 107
   Scotch-Irish and, 104, 111
Patton, George, 15
Patton, Lew, 117–18, 118*t*
Payne, Keith, 178–80
pedophilia, 152–53, 153n2
penal code, beliefs and values for, 37–40
penalties, in football, 117–18, 118*t*
   analyses of, 195–97, 196*t*
   Brown, Barnes, and Dodd on, 119–20
Peristiany, J. G., 169n4
personal honor, collective honor con-
      nected to, 66, 114, 120, 121, 123,
      126–27, 126n8
physical and sexual abuse, of
      Afghanistan women, 148–50
police, honor syndrome and, 181,
      185–86, 186n9
politeness norms, 182
   of Southern males, in absence of
      insults, 32, 34, 40
Presidential elections
   height advantage, 88–89, 88n2
   Obama as 43rd President, 88n3

risk-taking behavior for
   leadership, 87–90
Scotch-Irish background of, 88–89,
   88n4, 89n5
Presidential military action, 134
   Bush and, 131
   Dafoe and Caughey on, 128–30
   in international conflicts, Presidents
      from Southern states
      and, 129–30
Prince George of Cambridge, 95–96
Provincial Reconstruction Team, in
   Paktika, 141
provocation, violence triggered by, 63
psychological research, limits to, 177
purity reputation, of women, 11, 51, 185

Rafaat, Azita, 150–52
rape
   data, in relationship violence, 55, 55t
   honor and nonhonor states rates of,
      55–56, 55n4, 55t
   whites rates of, 55, 55n4, 55t
real man, in honor culture, 47–51, 58,
   66, 81–82, 152, 185, 191–92
relationship violence
   domestic homicide rate data, 55–56,
      55t, 57
   FBI data on, 54–55, 55n3
   honor ideology promotion of, 54–55
   rape rate data, 55, 55t
religiosity
   collective identity, 156
   honor ideology connection to, 153–
      56, 154n4, 155n6
   symbols of sensitivity in, 156
reputation
   in dignity culture, 184
   film reference to, 176
   in honor culture, xi–xii, xiv, 10–11
   honor threats and, 27
   women's loyalty and purity, 11, 51, 185
   Wyatt-Brown on, xii
retaliatory violence, of children
   and adolescents in honor
   states, 34–35
revenge, xii, 144, 153–54, 176
risk-taking behavior, xiii, 79–94
   accidental deaths, 81–84, 82n1, 84t,
      170–71, 171t
   CMH to soldiers, for acts of
      valor, 90–92
   NFL concussion scandal and, 85–87

positive aspects of, 90
Presidential elections and, 87–90,
   88n2, 88n3, 88n4, 89n5
rites of passage, masculinity and, 49
Roosevelt, Teddy, 129
rule of law, 7, 24

SAMHSA. See Substance Abuse
   and Mental Health Services
   Administration
Saucier, Donald, 175–76
scales, of honor ideology endorsement
   HC, 191–93
   HIM, 191–92
   HIW, 191–92
Schettino, Francesco, 168–69
Scheuer, Michael, 133–34
school bombings
   ATF Bomb Arson Tracking
      System on, 35
   Osterman and Brown study on, 35
school shootings
   in honor states, 34–35
   location influence on, xii, xiii, 35–36
   time of year influence on, xii, 35–37,
      36n8, 37t
school violence, 133
   Brown, Osterman, and Barnes study
      of, 34–35
   school shootings, in honor
      states, 34–35
Schwarz, Norbert, 31–33
Scotch-Irish, 14n6, 26, 27
   attitude toward women, 59
   beliefs and values, 13–15,
      14n6, 24, 29
   clans, Fischer on, 13, 103–4
   honor culture norms of, 109
   immigration to Northern Ireland,
      12, 171
   kinship loyalties of, 14, 15
   national identity and, 14–15
   patriarchs of, 103–4
   patronyms normative pattern of, 111
   patronym system, Fischer on, 104
   South and West, U.S., honor code of,
      14, 16, 24, 29
   U.S. immigration by, 11–16, 24
Scotch-Irish background
   of Crockett and McCoy, 5, 15, 16
   of Jackson, 120–21
   in Presidential elections, 88–89,
      88n4, 89n5

Scotland, 5–11
  accidental deaths, homicides, suicide
    in, 170–71, 171*t*
  honor dynamics of, 169–70
  U.S. migration from, 11–16, 24
Scottish Lowlands, 7, 9n4, 10, 12
  England invasion of, 6
  honor culture developed in, 9
self-destructive behavior, 65, 67, 71
sensitivity
  hypersensitivity, to insults, xi, 183
  socialization, 173–74
  symbols of, in religiosity, 156
seppuku ritual, in Japan, 73
sexual abuse. *See* physical and
    sexual abuse
sexual objectification, of women, xiii,
    57–59, 158, 160
shame, honor culture and, 73
small-town effect, on argument-based
    homicides, 29–30, 30n4
social dynamics, of aggression, 23
social expectations, for defense-related
    violence, 39–40
socialization sensitivity, aggression
    and, 173–74
social measure, of masculinity, 49, 50–
    51, 80–81, 184–85
social rejection, for unusual names,
    101, 101n1
social script, 24
social stigmatization, of woman leaving
    domestic violence, 53
soldier acts of valor, CMHs for, 90–92
South, U.S.
  aggressive response to insult, xi,
    31–32, 183
  argument-based homicide rate,
    30n4, 182
  businesses with violent names, 109–10
  higher namesaking scores, 105–6
  as honor states, xiii–xiv, 24–25, 25*t*
  Presidents from, military action
    and, 129–30
  Scotch-Irish honor code, 14,
    16, 24, 29
Southeast Asia face culture, 184
Southern males
  physiological signs of stress, 31
  politeness norms of, 32, 34, 40
  response to absence of insults,
    32, 32n5
stalking, 46, 56

stand-your-ground laws
  homicide rate increase, by white
    males after, 39
  in honor states, 39–40
  McClellan and Tekin study on, 39
Stanton, Bill, 4
State Department diplomat, Julia as,
    141–42, 141n1
stereotype tendency, of
    authoritarianism, 124–25
stranger-danger scenarios, 123
stress, physiological signs of
  cortisol level increase, xii, 31
  testosterone levels, higher, 31
Substance Abuse and Mental Health
    Services Administration
    (SAMHSA)
  National Survey on Drug Use and
    Health, 70
  on parents' seeking mental health
    services for children, 75
suicide, xiii, 61–62, 68n4, 77–78
  burdensomeness feeling, 64, 65,
    66, 137
  callousness to instincts, 65–66
  CDC on rates of, 68
  depression levels, Osterman and
    Brown on, 69–70
  disconnectedness, 64–65, 66, 137
  in England and Wales, 170–71, 171*t*
  gun ownership and, 67
  gun use for, 72–73
  health professional shortage area
    and, 68
  honor culture and, Osterman and
    Brown on, 66–67
  Imura, Osterman and Brown on
    methods of, 72–73
  Joiner on, 63–67, 137
  methods used, 71–73
  of older men, 137–38, 138*f*
  of older women, 138n12
  rates of, 68, 69, 69n5, 69*t*, 71
  in Scotland, 170–71, 171*t*
  self-destructive behavior and pain
    tolerance, 65, 71
Swann, Bill, 127–28
symbols of sensitivity, in religiosity, 156
systematic studies, 27, 27n2

Tamborski, Michael
  accidental deaths study, 81–84, 84*t*
  on honor-related characteristics, 26

Tekin, Erdal, 39
terrorism, xiii, 133–34
  Charlie Hebdo attack, 153
  Oklahoma City bombing, 131–32
  World Trade Center attack, 113–14,
    181, 185–86
testosterone levels, higher for
    aggression, 31
time of year, school shootings influ-
    enced by, xii, 35–37, 36n8, 37*t*
Timmerman, T. A., 120n5
Today Show, 113
tolerance
  of domestic violence, in honor
    states, 52–53
  pain, suicide and, 65, 71
Tourette syndrome (TS), 76–77
town names, Kelly on, 108–10
traffic rage, Oklahoma horn honking
    and, 22–23
tribal systems of law, in Afghanistan and
    Yemen, 157
TS. *See* Tourette syndrome

Ulster Plantation, 12–13
Ulster Scots. *See* Scotch-Irish
unconscious mind, xiii
  Freud on, 177–78
  honor syndrome and, 178–80
  Imura, Burkley, and Brown on
    honor-relevant words
    and, 179–80
  Payne AMP procedure, 178–80
United States (U.S.), xiv, 46. *See also*
    North, U.S.; South, U.S.;
    West, U.S.
  argument-based homicide in, 27–30,
    30n4, 54–55, 170, 182
  cause-of-death statistics in, 170
  geography of honor in, 24–26, 25*t*
  individualistic culture of, 100
  name concentration in, 102
  rule of law in, 24
  Scotch-Irish immigration to,
    11–16, 24
unknown, pervasive death factor
    (UPDF), accidental deaths
    and, 83
Updyke, Harvey, Jr., 116, 116n3
U.S. *See* United States

Vandello, S., 52–53
Vashti (queen of Persia), 164–65

violence, 19–41. *See also* domestic
    violence; relationship violence;
    school violence
  betrayal as motivator of, 4, 28, 121
  business names images of, 109–10
  defense-related, 39–40
  Earp, W., and, 19–20
  justified, in film, 176
  one-upmanship effect on, 29–30
  provocation triggering, 63
  retaliatory, of children and adoles-
    cents in honor states, 34–35
voluntary settlement hypothesis, for
    individualist culture, 100–101

Wales
  accidental deaths, homicides, suicides
    in, 170–71, 171*t*
  honor dynamics in, 170
Wallace, William, 6
Wallis, Michael, 3, 93
war
  defense proposals, by honor state
    Congress members, 131
  honor as motive for, 128–29
  international, Presidents from
    Southern states and, 129–30
  Presidential military action and, xiii,
    128–31, 134
weakness, masculinity and, 49
West, U.S.
  aggressive response to insult, xi,
    31–32, 183
  businesses with violent
    names, 109–10
  higher namesaking scores, 105–6
  as honor states, xiii, 24–25, 25*t*
  Scotch-Irish honor code, 14,
    16, 24, 29
  voluntary settlement hypothesis and,
    100–101
whites
  accidental deaths and, 83–84, 84*t*
  homicide rates, 29
  rape and domestic homicide rates, 55,
    55*t*, 56
  suicide rates, 68, 69, 69*t*
Wilson, Margo, 56n5
women. *See also* domestic violence;
    matronym
  accidental death, of white, 84, 84*t*
  in Afghanistan, 144 (*See also*
    gender-bending)

women (*Cont.*)
    Baldry study on police and
      domestic violence, 148–50
    education and government
      inclusion for, 147–48
    few civil rights of, 157
    infidelity and, 148–50
    moral crimes of, 148
    physical and sexual abuse of, 148–50
    Rafaat, 150–52
   aggressive masculinity to defend
    reputations of, 51
   honor states and Scotch-Irish attitude
    toward, 59
   loyalty and purity reputation, 11, 51, 185
   sexual objectification of, xiii, 57–59,
    158, 160
   suicide, of older, 138n12
The Wonderful World of Disney, Crockett,
   D., on, 2
World Health Organization, death
   statistics repository of, 170n5

World Trade Center terrorist
   attack, 113–14
   police and firefighter response to, 181,
    185–86, 186n9
World War II, 91n6
   CMHs awarded for service in, 91
   recruitment rates and, 91, 91n7
Wyatt-Brown, Bertram, xii

xenophobia, honor syndrome link
   to, 125–26
Xerxes (king of Persia), 163, 164–65

Yemen
   Ali from, 156–58
   gender-based violence, 157–58
   tribal systems of law, 157
   women few civil rights in, 157

Zidane, Zinedine, 167–68, 167n2
Zimmerman, George, 38–39